AUTOBIOGRAPHY VOLUME 2
(1968 - 1986)

"HELL OR THE GARDEN OF EDEN"

Myron Evans

Published by New Generation Publishing in 2015

First Edition

www.newgeneration-publishing.com

New Generation Publishing

CHAPTER ONE

My decision to go to University College of Wales Aberystwyth was based on the fact that I had been there on holiday once in the fifties - to Sea View Place. I expected it to be the result of enlightenment and a pleasant college for dedicated scholars. I was fiercely determined to try to do well whatever it turned out to be. In the summer of 1968 I had worked in the machine shop of Aladdin factory deafened by noise and surrounded by machines to which human beings were bound like slaves, ashen faced and resigned. I had cycled there in the early morning, often from my grandmother's house after listening to the BBC waking up with Handel's music followed by the shipping forecast on a small transistor radio. One day when walking in to the machine shop I heard that Prague has been invaded by tanks. The machine shop was full of presses for parts of an Aladdin oil lamp. There was a quota for each part, a thousand an hour for the small parts, so the machine drove the human being mercilessly. The quota for bigger parts was less because the press ran slower. I remember an ill tempered aggressive outburst from some manager when the press became jammed. I worked so hard that the regulars were threatened and threatened me in turn - slow down or else. In one of the breaks from this machine enslavement I was told suddenly that Aberystwyth was very corrupt and not worth going to. My most lasting memory was working a double shift and arriving at my grandmother's house very tired long after dark. She had less than a year left to live, and I dug up the whole garden here for potatoes to last her the winter. I was completely unwilling to leave this village of Craig Cefn Parc and sensed the trouble that Aberystwyth would cause me in the years ahead. It would not be a place of enlightenment, I had to learn that myself.

The trouble started, as it often did at Aberystwyth, with

a letter. I was not going to be given a room of my own in a hall of residence. As with many things at Aberystwyth that seemed unfair and arbitrary. I remember thinking to myself: why couldn't they build enough halls of residence? The answer unknown to me is that they had suddenly decided to expand under the Robbins reforms and had flooded the place with students. They had lost their Welsh identity before I even started, apart from a few Welsh medium departments and protesting heroes like Ffred Ffrancis. So my parents reluctantly drove up with me to find what was known as "digs", a metaphor dangerously close to a hole in the ground. I think I drove up and back most of the way, having no idea where to go in Aberystwyth. So I turned off instinctively towards Sea View Place using a list which one way or another must have been sent me. The first place we called at was a grim black terraced house that looked out on a bog full of seagulls, the pungent and incredibly boring Aberystwyth harbour. My mother told the landlady that I had failed to get a place in a hall of residence and she shook her head, no vacancies. My father became suddenly enraged as he often did, I had not failed to get a place, the place had failed him entirely. He was an intelligent man, an overman at that time with lungs 30% filled with the killer dust. He had the coal miner's hatred for middle class existence, which in turn regarded miners as being well below them in altitude.

I was glad to get away and turned the corner into Sea View Place where my great uncle and aunt had hosted us in the fifties in a fascinating stay filled with bacon and gas, the bed and breakfast establishment. There were digs to be found in "Brig y Don", and we were met by Mrs Hayes, a fluent Welsh speaker married to a sad and wholly defeated man called Mr Hayes who suffered some lung problem. She was at least a little like what was expected of Welsh speaking Wales. I was fixed up with half a room in an attic for about three pounds a week, bed and breakfast and full board on Sundays when we were stuffed like turkeys. I saw it again recently, it had been boarded up and looked like a damp and decaying cardboard box. Into this digs would be crammed six or seven students, all living in one small room with no TV or radio. Was this what I had worked for at Grammar School? At the time I did not know that there would be six students, I expected one other student or two at most. I was filled with a sudden revulsion and was very glad to start the drive home to the farm at Pant y Bedw. It became all I could do to drag myself back to Aberystwyth and counted the days to the start of term, looking backwards not forwards. Why leave the peace and beauty of Craig Cefn Parc? The primary reason was the quarrelling between my father and sister and the always present pressures to do well - by then my own self imposed pressures. My mother did have some understanding of life outside and always tried to help, but the other two members of the family often reduced everything to ashes in front of her eyes.

The day of departure finally arrived and very reluctantly, almost paralysed, I got into the car and slowly started to drive. The sheepdog was sitting on the dirt yard in a state of intense misery. As usual my sister had vanished somewhere and was not to be found. There was a large trunk with clothes and books that my mother had carefully packed for me, and I took my Yashica camera that I had bought in the Arcade in Swansea. I cannot remember much about that journey except for a sense of deep foreboding. Somehow the trunk must have been pulled up to the small attic room, which I had to share with a small, mature student with spectacles whose name I have forgotten entirely, doing teacher's training. Slowly the place filled with students, none of whom could speak a word of Welsh. So what was I doing there I wondered. My parents left and were none too happy either. I remember only one name - a student called Tony Atkinson from Bolton. He had one older friend from Bolton. There was one from Cardiff, and one more from the South of England. It was a remote exile that I stepped in to. It was not Athens of Pericles nor was it Florence of the Renaissance. There was no sign of Dafydd ap Gwilym.

I had to get into a routine as quickly as possible so as not to be overcome with intellectual paralysis and the screech of seagulls, the monotonous crashing of very damp waves. There was a first week in which all kinds of weird things were happening, many weird hicks. I even forget what it was called, maybe rag week. There was a lecture with a professor who was bombarded with abuse in King's Hall. This was supposed to be funny but I never saw the joke. Later I became slightly acquainted with him and he turned out to be a gold medallist in geography, a scholar of the age of British and Irish saints. In his old age his back was bent from years of study, his breath was short, and he was abandoned completely. He was looked after by an Indian colleague of mine from Calcutta, Deb Najumdar, who lived in a cell like room crammed with books and newspapers. My only real thought was collecting my cheque for the year, I think it was 282 pounds which had to be used for rent, food and books. It may have been divided into three terms, but I cannot quite recall. This had to be collected from the Old College, waiting in line with students from everywhere but Wales. Having collected that I knew that I could survive, if only in damp digs with one bar of electric fire, and to keep out of the bad smelling pubs.

I do not recall really expecting anything at all, just a desire to do exactly as I was told. I knew that there were three subjects to take: chemistry, physics and mathematics. So after this first and pointless week was over there would be an opportunity to learn something. In that week the weird hicks were jumping off the bridge into the harbour, and at that point I decided to try to do something useful and look at the places where I was supposed to study. I knew Aberystwyth quite well, and was not fascinated by the place in any way at all. I had walked along the tree covered avenue below a grim prison like building in the distance, set on a small hill. At that time in the fifties the crazy golf and train up Constitution Hill were overwhelmingly important, not this pile of stone. I don't think I ever noticed it. The mural on the Old College wall was a lot more fascinating from Aberystwyth Castle. The time came to walk from my damp digs up to this old pile of stone. It turned out to be the Edward Davies Chemical Laboratories (EDCL). I suppose that I had to attend my first lecture there one morning after a breakfast of the usual poisonous stuff, plus toast. Some breakfasts were digestible. One thing that became clear early on was that I couldn't be beaten up by the students. At Pontardawe with its rugby elite one could be thrown into the railings hurled to the ground, tackled from behind and in general massacred in a friendly kind of way. At Aberystwyth we were supposed to be grown up, the weirdest joke of all because none of the lecturers were.

My mother had very kindly bought me a modern looking brief case which I still have here so I thought that this would be useful, and also a pad of paper and a good pen. I was also told to buy a lab coat. I had no idea at all of any of the staff at the EDCL and had never heard of any of them. I knew that a lecture would be given by Dr. Colin Young in what was referred to as the New Lecture Theatre. This was later smashed to pieces by vandals and has long been demolished. The weird College propaganda does not refer to the EDCL at all, it never existed. I had to walk past the station and turn off on a small road that seemed to lead to nowhere. In fact it did lead to nowhere as I found out to my cost much later. I eventually left the EDCL in a small mini car stuffed with my belongings and an interferometer and achieved so much that I was never allowed back. It eventually destroyed itself so completely that no one remembers its existence. So why leave Craig Cefn Parc? I found that I had to turn left at the end of this small road, then right again, and walked into the Post Office building. After thinking for a while I found I had to walk up a path towards the pile of old stone. Only then did I see that a new building had been attached to it. Otherwise

I thought it was a jail or detention centre for seagulls.

There were stone steps in through double doors and a staircase made of wood. The new lecture theatre lay at the end of a long corridor with windows so badly made that the damp and rain drove right through them. The theatre doors were to be found at the foot of stairs leading to a library. I pushed open the doors and entered a very large room with what looked to me like immense boards, in front of which was a demonstration bench. I was careful to arrive early and soon a trickle of nervous students walked in, all trying to look radical, some already drinking heavily. This was supposed to be a lecture. It started at nine in the morning and lasted for fifty minutes. I had come across Dr. Young earlier when he looked at my A level grades and pointed out the D grade with sarcasm, how had I managed to do that? Later he turned out to be quite a shy type of man who was completely ill at ease in Welsh speaking Wales. This first lecture was by Dr Young in inorganic chemistry and I just frantically started to take down notes, carefully noted the course books, and tried not to miss anything. At last it was down to some learning, but in such a chaotic way compared with the Grammar School. I learned straight away that this mass of notes had to be worked into something coherent from which to learn almost by heart for examinations. For me that needed long hours in the library. Others did not seem to do anything. Eventually at the end of fifty minutes I had a pile of scribble and a list of course books.

I was an obedient and intense student, completely unlike my contemporaries. I had a loathing for drinking, and disliked people who wasted their time at College. I bought all the course books, leaving myself with very little for food. Coming out of that first lecture I found that the library was up the stairs to the right of the lecture and through a small corridor. It was a matter of instinctively doing the best I could to make sense of a ragged lecture, delivered with terminal boredom from scraps of paper. The library of the EDCL became my favourite place over the years, but on first site was a formidable array of books and volumes of journals. In a little cubicle sat a tiny and bent figure, a librarian who also served as a town councillor, and carefully monitored each student like a dalek for any borrowed book. This library and others like it was the only place in which I could work, the digs were stuffed with students already showing the first signs of grotesque alcoholism. If they were not alcoholic, they consumed a vast amount of toxic ethanol. It was not easily possible to work in the digs, except in brief intervals where I had the place to myself. In the library it was possible to find a quiet corner and build up the notes. These were filed in folders that I bought from shops in town, and everything learned off by heart with a fortunately good memory.

All these folders were lost or were thrown away by my family, to whom they had been given for safe keeping. There is and was a great gap between my immediate family and myself. My parents wanted me to succeed but did not know why. I suppose that life for them was just too difficult. So I have to reconstruct the undergraduate years from memory, and bad things dominate the memory. There is no doubt that I found those digs repulsive, and looking at them recently after a gap of forty years, they were indeed. I had deposited myself in Aberystwyth by accident, knowing nothing about the people who masqueraded as scholars. In those early weeks of undergraduate time it was matter of being driven all over town and campus, entirely on my own. I made no friends then. In the first few days, Sir Thomas Parry suddenly appeared in what they called a "common room", a cold and beer smelling relic in the decaying student union at Laura Place. He looked like a ghost, an apparition which disappeared as suddenly as it appeared. He shook hands and mumbled a few words. Maybe he was wondering what he had done, in allowing Aberystwyth to be flooded with people who cared nothing about the Welsh language, or maybe he appeared out of habit. Later on I found that he was Thomas Parry the poet and scholar, better to have stayed as a poet and scholar.

Each dismal morning of cloud ridden and damp Sea View Place I walked my way out of hearing of the crashing waves, up past a grim church, down some narrow, damp streets built for their colonists by murderous Norman invadors. The houses each side were almost black with age and repetition of stone and slate. Recently I found that Oliver Cromwell was my ancestral cousin, and one of the big favours he did was to blow the Norman Aberystwyth castle to pieces with canon from Pen Dinas, or so it is said. Probably it is all untrue, almost all of Aberystwyth turned out to be untrue in the end. In those early weeks the cloud glowered over everything continuously: the crazy golf and putting green were closed, and it was almost always raining. On the route out of Sea View Place I had to digest a breakfast out of Monte Python: bacon, eggs, spam and sausage, spam, spam and buttered toast, half cold tea. It made my mouth feel sticky and stale, the proverbial bad taste. Half a dozen students sat around a table consuming this cholesterol filled junk before a one bar electric fire. I was driven out of Sea View Place by the angry sea, the ancient castle, and undefined ambition. I had to cross the small hill towards the railway station while digesting Monte Python. In the very earliest days all I knew was a lecture time table, and that lectures took place in different parts of the grim little town from which my ancestors were banned by a maniac called Edward 1st. In the grey damp October days, it was matter of getting there in time, with paper and pens ready. The dismal performance by Young was the first time I had come across a lecture. The teachers at Pontardawe were much better, and everything there was in the same place. I had just left seven years of familiarity for the eternal dampness.

The time table indicated that some lectures were to take place as far away from Sea View Place as it was possible to get without leaving Aberystwyth completely. That was in a place called a "campus". It had been put up in the early sixties when the Government decided to make education freely available to the dubious working classes. Concrete was arranged in strange shapes called architecture. The most hideous of these is probably the campus of East Anglia, which appears in the last episode of Kenneth Clark's "Civilization" as a sign of grim optimism. All the students are shown seriously looking at books inside concrete cubicles. They were all posed and felt like circus clowns, painted with enthusiasm and a fixed grin. They looked young and spotty. The effect on Aberystwyth of this age of concrete was Penglais campus. It was thrown up behind the classical facade of the National Library of Wales. The only thing that I noticed about it was the route to physics and mathematics, which were housed in a half rounded tower which was supposed to be a symbol of something, perhaps the wave function psi. I thought it was the Communist hammer and sickle. Lectures were to take place inside this pile of concrete. I found it to be a dismal place full of very pale students who all looked as if they had measles. It turned out that they had been scraped up by the College from anywhere it could find and let in with two E's, compared with my A, B, B, and D. So Young was bluffing with his sarcasm. The only sign of hope was that some spoke Welsh and like me had been fooled into thinking that this concrete had been made in Wales. They also tended to have the best grades at A level. Even at that time the College had to import the great majority of its students from places in which the Welsh language had never been heard. This was the second phase of Norman colonization, importing its settlers. A mere forty years later this mad mercenary scene resulted in the sale of courses and grandmothers and the end of the univer ity. So I outlasted the concrete.

This place called physics was so utterly boring that I can recall very little of the lecture material. The reason for that is the complete concentration needed to make sense out of arrogant imports or ego trippers like Sir Granville Beynon. His first lecture was delivered from scraps of yellow paper that looked like "The News of the World" cut up for use as toilet paper. He kept these scraps of paper in a cupboard and took them out each October. The large concrete cubicle called a lecture theatre was fronted by a construction made out of about six boards and a gigantic demonstration bench behind which the lecturer could shelter in case of rebellion. To reach the top one the lecturer had to have arms like an octopus. I suppose the idea was that the boards could be hauled up with string, so if one ran out of one there was always the other. Beynon must have scribbled something in chalk on those areas that he could reach. All I remember now is his scribbled introduction of the Lorentz factor gamma. I am sure that he had no idea of its real meaning. So the ignorant were being lectured to by the knight in a very large cold dungeon. This was the second time I had bumped in to a knight at Aberystwyth. The lectures were so awful that all I had at the end of fifty minutes were a few pages of scribbles, desperately trying to follow what Beynon was saying and writing. At that point most of the students must have given up. Some instinct told me that I had to make sense out of them, and must do all the lecturer's work myself. Beynon epitomized the sordid banality of life as the ancient academic. It was clear to eighteen year olds that he had no interest. Much later I remember him snarling at me in the reception given for my D. Sc. degree, snarling in envy and hostility that I was "too young", meaning that he was too old.

I found that the concrete called architecture housed three departments, piled on top of each other with physics on the bottom. Up a bit was applied mathematics, and at the top was pure mathematics. The lecturers each had a cubicle, and the professors a larger cubicle with secretarial help. There were cubicles or cells called common rooms from which the students were banned like a spotty plague. Physics had laboratories somewhere, but it was a subject that I loathed and dropped at the end of the first year. Beynon was enough to kill off any bright young hope but was advertized as a radio astronomer. As a graduate a few years later I was slightly acquainted with a communist alcoholic called Gareth Kelly who had to work on one of these telescopes. No wonder he was an alcoholic and revolutionary. He is probably by now a respectable member of the middle classes and a professor in his own right for all I know. There is one photograph of that era which appears in volume one in which I blink at a camera with great caution. Physics was methodical and photographed its students in case one became lost. In among the maze of cubicles were undergraduate experiments, and the lurking danger of practical examinations. All the physics lecturers were awful, it would have been much easier to pick up a book and read it out, asking the students to take down by dictation. In fact there was no need for lecturers. This was the first discovery I made at Aberystwyth, there was no need for anything to come between the book and the reader. The mess of notes had to be untangled in the library, which occupied a floor of its own and served physics and mathematics. There may have been another library hidden in the trees somewhere but I never found it.

The library was a place of refuge and sanity. There were books and journals there on two floors. In my first few days at Aberystwyth I had been given lists of course books which I bought, being a completely obedient and earnest, pious student who had no money to waste on drink or drugs. The former was tolerated but the latter was not. The drugs of the era (late sixties) were, I suppose, pot and LSD but I never came across anyone who used them. There were many revolting alcoholics with whom I was forced to live at close quarters. After spending a lot on these books I realized that very little was left over for food and landed up on two meals a day, breakfast and chips and green peas in the student union, with free salad cream and maybe free bread. The idea of the 282 pounds a year grant was that parents should contribute, but I knew that mine could not. My father had had the idea of putting me to work on a farm or in a coal mine and by the time I was eighteen he was glad to get rid of me. If I had done badly at College I suppose he would not have let me return home to the Pant y Bedw of volume one. The library had some of these course books and I noticed that it was possible to borrow them for a few days, but the idea I had in my head was to make sense of those terrible, chaotic, arrogant lectures and to construct good sets of notes. This was of course the Grammar School model. Some of my carefully constructed notes from the Grammar School have survived and are on www.aias.us.

The fact that my parents threw away all my undergraduate notes and almost my entire collection of books left with them means that they had no idea what I was doing at Aberystwyth, and in those early years, neither did I. They were interested in the glittering prizes and first class degree, but not in the work that produced them. They were therefore as parents everywhere, they were good parents, but very early on departed from me in matters of the mind. By the time I was six years old I started to be told that they did not understand my primary school work. It remained like that until they died. This does not mean they were unkind, they were good, kind parents, it was the world outside that they did not understand. Looking back at things I suppose I would ask - why should they? If no one understands what you are doing you develop a great inner strength, until you suddenly find that tens of millions read your work all the time. I was often told by full professors that they did not understand my work, that it was not their speciality, that although they were professors of physics they were lucky to be tenured, knew the right people, and to be honest preferred the salary, committees and pension. So who can blame a coal miner and shop assistant?

I bought some ring binders into which to gather and order my notes, written out after many hours in the library, using several books. This process resulted in some degree of understanding, but after forty five years of study I know

now that it was a shallow understanding. The thing that strikes me now is that no one understands nature at all. If they did they would not destroy it. The lectures in mathematics consisted of ideas and equations written out on a board, but kicked back with problems to be solved in what was known as "home work". That assumed that the students had a home. In my case it was a table crowded with alcohol and half an attic room. In the evening I was too tired to walk up to a library, so the problems must have been solved in day time shortly after the lecture. The mathematics lecture theatres were smaller, with smaller boards, so I suppose that the lecturers had shorter arms. I remember none of the names of the maths lecturers with the exception of a Mr Breen (or similar) who gave a course on Schaum's vector algebra and stopped suddenly as tensors approached. There was no social contact whatsoever between lecturers and students. The mathematics examinations were deadly, there was no room for waffling or wavering.

Chemistry was my main subject but I never understood why. Perhaps because it was a colourful reaction that I had seen in the Grammar School, or a lump of sodium exploding in water. So now I was trapped in the grim prison of the EDCL and had to make the best of it, otherwise my father would not let me back to Pant y Bedw. The lectures in that first year in chemistry must have been organized into physical, inorganic and my least liked subject of all, organic. The physical chemistry course must have been taken by the acting head of department of that year (1968 to 1969). I had never heard of him before my transplant to Aberystwyth. In the time table appeared the name Mansel Davies, the strange first name being Norman in origin, the second name commonplace. The time for that first lecture came around and I climbed out of my shared hole in the ground. It seemed as if I was looking up at the crashing waves, and that Sea View Place was beneath sea level. In fact you cannot see the sea at all and it is a few feet above the sea. I did not notice anything - I was just wondering what this lecture was going to be like. Judging by Young's lecture it was going to be awful. Being intense and obedient I got to every single lecture in time, and was seated and ready, biro drawn. The biro was used for scribbling and a fountain pen for writing up. It was a good luck gift from my parents, and it was a faithful excalibur. As a post doctoral and as I thought his obedient assistant, I got to one of Mansel Davies' lectures late and he blasted away in a crazy hysterical voice as was his custom. The image was not the man.

The other students drifted in and sat all over the large lecture theatre of the EDCL, which again had one of those ridiculous gigantic boards and a large demonstration bench, designed in the same way as physics. At the back was a slide projector and room, on the sides were small windows. The last time I saw this theatre was the summer of 1993. It had been smashed to pieces by vandals and left to rot. It was later demolished and never existed, because the College is always excellent and could never have had any failures. So although no one understood what I was doing, or so I was told quite frequently, I outlasted the theatre. I can now fill a hundred thousand lecture theatres without having to suffer any dampness or stale bacon. While I was sharpening my biro the double doors of the theatre were pushed open and in walked an apparition with a black gown half hanging off its shoulder. It had white wavy hair and a very pale face with lines of age incised deeply upon it. To me it looked mean and threatening. There must have been a green tie to indicate a radical open mind. That was the custom of the thirties, but this was 1968. This was Professor Mansel Davies, who had received a personal chair. At the time I thought it was a bit weird because no one at the Grammar School wore a gown, and no other lecturer. I remember almost nothing of the actual lectures, because of the intense concentration that it took at the time to make any sense out of them. I recall a course book called "Valence" by Coulson. I did not notice that some fingers of his right hand were missing. I noticed only that the writing was terrible. Much later, when I was sitting with him in his office, I realized at last that there were stubs where the fingers had been. They had been blown off in a synthesis. I began to see that he was an intelligent man, but could at any time explode in a rage and was very unstable. He could play the common man, but immediately become the snobby middle class Cambridge don if you became too familiar, o even if you cracked a joke. In fact he was never a don, he was a post doctoral in Peterhouse. He was given a job at the EDCL without open competition in 1947. At Aberystwyth you had to know the right people, which is why it is such a barren failure. I will have a lot more to write about him.

In 1968 however it was again a matter of retiring to the library to write a good set of notes. I did not even know that there would be examinations at the end of that term, I think it was called Christmas term. Luckily I found out in time and memorized my notes. After memorizing they were regurgitated in a frenzy and almost immediately forgotten. By the time I was a graduate under this same Mansel Davies I had forgotten almost all my undergraduate work, and the real learning began. I remember nothing about those first term lectures by Mansel Davies except for his teaching of the Schroedinger equation. This was strangely reticent for a man who boasted of his Cambridge friends and never tired of explaining how superior they were in intellect. He seemed to be in slow motion, wrote down an H followed by a psi, then an equals sign, then an E followed by a psi. There seemed to be nothing deeper in his understanding. When I was a post doc he suddenly dropped the facade one day and told me that of course he did not understand operators. I maintained a straight face by locking my jaw. I knew all along that he did not understand operators. One bright spark of an eighteen year old may have asked why the psi did not cancel out, and then he would be stuck, ossified in time, or probably would have blasted away again. One look at that face was enough to teach me to be perfectly obedient and perfectly silent. Then he could be kindly and erudite, and very helpful. As a fellow Silurian I found him infinitely preferable to some blue nosed genius of string theory.

The other part of physical chemistry may have been taken by Dr Alun Price, who had also attended Pontardawe Grammar school. He was a good lecturer and a diluted version of Mansel Davies. With Alun Price there was a chance of understanding what was going on during a lecture, but I worked on notes with all lecturers. Physical chemistry or chemical physics was much preferable to inorganic or organic chemistry in that first year. It is difficult to know how I survived the course of lectures by Young in inorganic chemistry. The organic chemistry in the first year was given by Dr. Harry Heller, of Austrian extraction. He wore a leather coat and came from Heriot Watt University in Scotland. He openly hated the Welsh language and people, so revenge was taken upon him in the set scrum and he never played again. I have vague recollections of a course book called Morrison and Boyd. Heller was fond of talking about why he was a genius, and how many patents he had. In the throes of Jeremy Jones he suddenly vanished to Cardiff in the early eighties. All the talk of great fortune came to nothing. His lectures were delivered in a way that took no notice of undergraduates, they were monologues from which one had to scribble as much as possible. The only thing I remember is that we were told to buy a set of sticks to make molecular models. Morrison and Boyd was a huge tome from which I chipped away at understanding.

The most awful part of that first year was organic practical in the old EDCL. The most random part of that course was crystallization. At the best of times this could go wrong. I clearly recall Heller as one of the class supervisors. After I had boiled a flask dry trying to crystallize one day I was told that I was never going to get far like that. So I dropped organic chemistry as soon as possible. Unfortunately this was not until first year graduate. I took a deep dislike to Heller and the feeling was mutual. I recall that Mr John Bowen and Mr. A. J. S. Williams took part in organic chemistry to some degree. They had written a short book with a yellow cover which contained many syntheses. Somehow I must have got through this because I was awarded the Mathews Prize for the best first year chemistry results. The experiments in physical and inorganic chemistry were cleaner and easier to deal with, and I seemed to have got through those well. I attended all lectures and practical classes in all subjects and missed only one due to a charity walk to Llanbedr Pont Steffan one Saturday morning. John Bowen was a Welsh speaker and good at his work, but A. J. S. Williams was a poor lecturer and worse tutor. Both were appointed without advertisement and neither had a Ph. D. degree. At some point there were cold, damp tutorials every Saturday morning with A. J. S. Williams and a weird character called Dr. George Morrison, an eternal cigar smoker, a boorish ill tempered man who could be a complete fool. These tutorials took place every tedious Saturday morning in a small side room off the reeking organic chemistry laboratory. They served no discernible purpose because both were organic chemists unable to understand physical chemistry or mathematics. I thought that both were weird or disturbed, having been in the EDCL for many years and in no other place. Morrison had the habit of falling over suddenly in a tutorial or lecture, in order to save his weak ankle. He said he could feel it giving way and ould fall flat on his face, throwing away his cigar. A. J. S. Williams always wore a white coat and observed the collapsing Morrison with total indifference. The undergraduates tried desperately not to convulse in laughter. In the third year Morrison gave a completely incomprehensible course on enzymes in the ancient wooden lecture theatre of the EDCL, and would fall flat on his face with a thump. By that time it had stopped being funny. The class knew that they had to face the outside world and were being subjected to a farce. Morrison was at last thrown out of his lab of by J. M. Thomas and J. O. Williams but hung on endlessly until retirement. Later on I observed A. J. S. Williams falling down the wooden stairs of the EDCL, having tripped over a formula. He nutted the plaque devoted to Soddy, who was disingenuously claimed by the EDCL as its Nobel Laureate. The undergraduates developed a deep dislike of him for his lecturing and his habit of extending the course to twice its length at the last moment, with a set of scribbled notes.

Each day of that first term was very exhausting, especially as I had little to eat and began to lose a lot of weight. I think I lost three stones in weight that first term, forty two pounds, and it was lucky that the landlady gave us three meals each Sunday. I was not yet in athletics training so the whole thing was unhealthy. The memories of that room with six students are laced with hunger to this day. Gradually I realized that I had a talent for debating with my fellow first year undergraduates when they had not been drinking. There was one other from Cardiff. So I developed all kinds of ways of explaining that there was a Welsh language, and that it was a great and ancient language. None of them was a scientist, two or three of them had to buy a course book called Plato's "Republic", with which they struggled. Gradually some trust was built up until one day Tony Atkinson offered to lend me his bike for a road run of about thirty miles around Aberystwyth. I had managed to get away from the lectures and lecturers once or twice on a Saturday afternoon, I remember a walk up the Rheidol taking black and white photographs of the quiet, ancient, salmon laden river. During that walk the elements of sanity prevailed, no falling Morrisons. Another walk took me down to the mouth of the Ystwyth (the river that winds) along the south beach past Pen Dinas. This is a giant Celtic hill fort with rings still easily visible. On another occasion I had a look at Aberystwyth Town playing soccer. Those were the only breaks from the tedium of work.

With the bike I could go further and set out for Devil's

Bridge, out of Aberystwyth and back in to the real Wales, which at that time had not been destroyed by turbines and immigration. The healthy and pure sounds of the Dyfed dialect were still to be heard everywhere and I began to feel human again, not a digit amidst student numbers. After the hard initial struggle up hill the road levelled off a bit and I found myself in the countryside. There were not too many cars in those days, and they were smaller and more carefully driven. On the left hand side I was soon able to look down on the deep valley of the Rheidol, with a newly built dam. Somewhere down there was the narrow gauge railway built from Aberystwyth to Devil's Bridge. On holiday as a seven or eight year old this was a journey from wildest fantasy, and ten years later as an eighteen year old it was none the less exciting. In the distance there were some beautiful hills of the Cambrian Mountain range. It was late autumn so the colours of the leaves were a painting from van Gogh. The air filled my lungs and I exhaled the accumulated pyridine. The farms were populated with Friesians and Herefords and were still human sized. The giant cowsheds and giant black bales had not yet made their ugly appearance. Towards Devil's Bridge the road goes sharply downhill and very suddenly bumps into a railway siding and hotel, built by the Victorians. Devil's Bridge has three bridges built one on top of the other, and there are paths down to the bottom of the Rheidol Valley. I sped past these and over the bridge in an effort to climb the other side - but was forced off to push the bike.

This was a push in to the wilderness for me, I was suddenly enclosed by the primordial land. It was a rare day with no rain, so the colours of autumn dazzled the imagination like the Mabinogion. Although I did not know it I was pushing the bike up the shoulders of Punlumon and towards the main road from the east in to Aberystwyth. The road from Devil's Bridge met the main road a short distance from the George Burrow Hotel, and a short distance from the road up to Punlumon itself. Being out of condition and (without knowing it) weakened from severe loss of weight I could not ride the bike up but walked it up. Suddenly I was on the summit and there followed a long, tremendously exciting descent to the floor of the Rheidol. The black mountains shadowed from the sun flew past either side. It was the longest descent I had ever made on a bike. It ended with the flat long road of the Rheidol valley, a rare flat stretch in Wales along which I could use the top gear and really fly back into Aberystwyth with screaming muscles freezing up and turning to lead. A few years later this became part of my regular ten mile road run. The road came in to Aberystwyth and I cycled slowly back to the hole in the ground in Sea View Place. The oxygen going through my brain meant the digs looked like home for the first time.

Sometimes the students from the digs walked around the Castle like tourists and listened to the boom of the sea on the walls, but I never went drinking with them, so I tended to be alone in the digs on a Saturday night. If not too tired or hungry I would read a book, or as examinations approached revise some notes. There was no TV or radio for the use of the students so we did not know that there was a danger of being conscripted for Vietnam if Britain became embroiled in that. The first thing I knew about it was when Atkinson became frightened one evening and very scared of being conscripted. He was very nervous and highly strung, sometimes difficult to live with. In the second year in another digs in Powell Street (a terrible hole) he broke down a door in a drunken haze and attacked Roger Goodger and myself. That was the only time such a thing happened. The other students were not worried about Vietnam. One other student from Cardiff was also nervous, and had a lot of problems with examinations. He dosed himself with caffeine tablets as they approached and danced like a kangaroo around the digs and streets. After all, caffeine is not much different from quinine and heroin. His intention was to keep awake in the night for last minute revision. The others did not seem to prepare very much for exams., but my method of preparation was strictly methodical, based on revision which began weeks before the examinations. Having memorized the notes there was little chance of running in to an unforeseen problem. The exception was mathematics, where one could be hit with a stinker of a paper no matter how much revision you had made. In this sense chemistry was the safest subject to take. It had continuous assessment for some practical courses. Some poor students were hit really hard with examination nerves and could not finish the course. Others would waffle their way through to a lower second or third.

To get a first class degree the work had to be good for the whole three years. As usual I started slowly and was not fully aware of things until about half way through the Christmas term. As soon as I heard that there were going to be examinations the methods of the Grammar School were used, that meant reading and memorizing a really good set of notes. The atmosphere at the time was that of the late sixties, with student uprisings and general discontent. None of that could be allowed to interfere in my aim of getting a first class degree and doing as well as I could. I was a most sincere student in most cynical world, and so it has remained ever since. None of my immediate family had ever been to university or even a grammar school, so I was completely on my own. I did not ever ask questions of lecturers or tutors, but in a sense took over the material for myself. I quickly realized that there was to be no time for any distraction, with the exception of Saturday afternoons, some walks and that one exhilarating bike ride in a wonderful new country.

Of that first term there are only shards of memory, because all my concentration was focused on getting good marks. I cannot remember whether the assessment of practical classes as continuous or by examination. The practical class in physical and inorganic chemistry took place in the upper level of the new wing of the EDCL, built in 1962, destroyed by 1993. This is appalling maladministration. The new wing was built because money became available, and that seems to be all. There was no thought as to the number of students likely to be available from Wales, so this stupidity was bound to harm the Welsh language very greatly. Each student was assigned some laboratory apparatus in physical, inorganic and organic chemistry, and I recall that there was a mania for making the students wash glassware until their fingers dissolved. The apparatus differed from the school in that it had ground glass stoppers in place of corks. The class was administered by lecturers and demonstrators who used to deliver the occasional sarcasm and little else. There were small rooms off the main laboratory, which was filled with far too many benches for student numbers, but the first years were not allowed in them. There was a furnace for crucibles near the windows, which looked out over a mass of greyness - the damp town of Aberystwyth - then out over the cold black sea. Each experiment came with a set of instructions, often incomprehensible, and there were long stools to perch on like chickens. The heaviest days were those of a lecture at nine followed by a practical class. Then the notes had to be written up the following day or as soon as I could in the library. As the examinations approached there was the additional work of memorizing and revising. It is impossible to know at this distance in time how I managed to memorize those notes in a crowded alcoholic room filled with students who seemed to never to work at all.

I have a vague recollection that the worst experience in practical classes was physics. It was a long walk stuffed with bacon up to physics on the Penglais campus, through Aberystwyth and on to the Machynlleth road, up a hill past the hospital and entrance to the National Library of Wales, past Pant y Celyn Hall and cutting through the campus past the biology building. Physics seemed as dry as dust, the main lecture theatre was used because there should have been a hundred or so students, but there never was. It was an entirely dark theatre with no windows and was filled with irrelevance, spotlights, large boards, projectors, and a vast number of seats for a small number of scraped up students. One lecturer called Kersley used an overhead projector and a roll of transparency on which he scribbled in between loud bouts of sniffing. Maybe he was blowing last night's snuff or heroin out of his long nose. The scribbles were in red, white and blue. He was a permanently irritated Scot loaded with a first year class. I forget entirely what he taught, which is not the greatest of commendations. There was one revolting course in thermodynamics for which a course book by McGraw Hill had to be bought, making me even hungrier. I have never come across anyone who could teach thermodynamics, least of all Morrison of chemistry. There must have been the usual physics courses, but I am sure that they never got as far as the Maxwell Heaviside equations.

The physics practical courses were held in cubicles called laboratories hidden inside the Penglais concrete maze. Again there were set experiments with instructions to get through each as best as I could. The school work was not coordinated with the work at first year undergraduate, so it was matter of following a set of instructions like Mecano. Obviously I learnt nothing, but I must have got through them somehow until I could ditch physics as soon as I could at the end of that first year. In the first few weeks of that term in the autumn of 1968 time stood still, one interminable, ugly, day following the other. There was no common room for undergraduates, and at the end of the first year I still did not know who they were. It must have dawned on me at some point that there going to be examinations at the end of the first term in chemistry, physics and mathematics, but where and when was not made clear. In a very vague way I remember being told in an offhand kind of way that the purpose of these exams was to make sure that all the students were working, or whether some had blown a transistor or valve. I seemed to be working, but my ribs were protruding

The most desiccated subject was mathematics, with

lectures delivered in small rooms with windows. Probably there were very few mathematics students to be found. One course book from 1968 has survived, Stephenson's "Mathematical Methods for Science Students". I still use it now. It was taught by I forget whom by simply reading out the material. We were told that the mathematics may seem to be very boring now, and in fact it was very boring, but would be useful later. I vaguely remember a half bald red headed man whose task it was to make students enthusiastic about mathematics. He seemed to cough out his lectures as if under a great weight of being stuck in this place forever. Later on as a post doctoral I came across A. R. Davies, who told me that all students are morons. Naturally he became a full professor. The subject of mathematics was preferable to physics because it had no practical work but it was impossible to be enthusiastic about limit theorems. In later years I taught myself mathematics, and it is indeed useful and very elegant. One would never have guessed it in 1968. Everything was dominated by looming examinations. In the mathematics papers one pounced on a problem that could be solved and frantically looked for more.

The term dragged itself onwards like a tortoise with pneumoconiosis. October crawled to an end and November was upon us innocents. Greyness became deepening greyness, and it began to get cold as well as damp. The nights drew in and the mornings got darker, so all that was left of Sea View Place were the shadows of ancient violence cast by the blackened castle stones. The flowers withered on the putting green. All that stood between life end hypothermia was a one bar electric fire and a single bulb of light in a small box called "Brig y Don", the crest of the wave. It was really the bottom of a dustbin. In all the pubs of Aberystwyth pseudostudents drank themselves into oblivion, and puked over the promenade. What was renaissance Florence compared to this? I threw this barbarism out of my mind by gulping in fresh air as I emerged from the greyness of the EDCL portico. Sometimes there was the sound of an engine in the distance, shunting around some wagons. Sometimes the sun shone briefly, and for a few minutes life emerged from the shadows.

Only the discipline of scholarship would get me out of this flat and unsalted existence, once or twice I toyed with the idea of joining a club, like the fencing club, but gave up straight away. It was just a nothingness of the middle classes. The amount of work dumped on an earnest young mind meant that there was no time for anything except study. Many must have given up by the end of that first term and concentrated for the rest off their lives on building a big round beer pot. As November dragged into its second week I knew that the examinations could be only three weeks distant, but after them was the trip back home to Pant y Bedw, a respite from prison and toxic ethanol, a return to sanity. In grim reality my parents were already planning to sell Pant y Bedw without breathing a word to me, the loyal farm servant, and luckily that did not come about until I was a graduate. Then Pant y Bedw was gone, to be replaced by a development out of hades. In those grim November days life hung on like a thread to ideas that came from afar.

It was at last made clear that examinations would take place in the Old College adjacent to the booming and angry sea. To an eight year old the mural on the Old College was magnetic in brightness, being painted on an utterly grim greyness, a gothic transplant fronted by a pier whose end seemed always to be falling in to the waves. The sea wall stopped the grim pile from being washed away. Underneath it was the crazy golf course, where I putted the day away. That was the only thing of interest to an eight year old, and the only thing of interest today. Now in that empty November I would enter the gothic world to throw up my notes all over exam papers. I must have made sure that I knew where the door was - it was hidden in a small alley off Pier Street, logically named because it was nearly opposite the pier. I wondered what would become of Pier Street if the pier were washed away one violent night in January. It would probably have become the Street of a Thousand Dust Bins, or the Alley of Five Star Excellence.

Having made sure of the door, it was back up to physics prac again and the underground lecture theatre. In reality it is an artistic bulge coming out of the side of the physical sciences building that may be a wave function or psi. The architect tells us that it is an ineluctable modality of the Joyceian visible, and that we should all know what it is anyway. Having scribbled frantically through a catatonic Beynonic delivery one day I hurried back down the hill and bumped into an angry man. This turned out to be Prince Charles, near him was another angry man with a gun. His equery and body guard. I suppose they thought they would be assassinated by a frenzied Ffred Ffrancis, but they were just ignored. Charles learned a few words of theoretical Welsh in Pant y Celyn and left it at that at the end of a year. With gravity in your favour it was easier to get down the hill and usually I headed for the digs to catch a few hours of learning on my own unless the time table has been designed very badly. That meant a half run down from physics and over Buarth to chemistry. The real places of learning where the chemistry and natural sciences libraries. The place of eating very little was the student union canteen, situated underground in Laura Place. It smelled of frying chips, and rocked to the sound of Led Zepelin. Each chip had to be eaten slowly, draining nurture out of the remains of a stale and blackened and massacred potato. Each chip had to last until the Monte Python breakfast the next day. Accompanying the chips was a scoop of green peas dumped on to a plate by a bored and hostile cook, and the creme de la creme was a cheap bottle of Heinz's salad cream. This was free on the table, along with salt and vinegar. So the chips and peas were loaded with yellow pungent liquid. I must have had a stomach like a Bessemer converter, lined with slag. Each pea had to be rationed, and the chips and peas were mixed with the yellow cream so that they could taste of something.

There were pin ball machines in the student union, and pin ball wizards blasted out of the walls. The tea or coffee tasted exactly the same, the colour of the coffee was darker. Whether I got it from a cup or a melting plastic cup I mercifully cannot recall. Later in the EDCL they installed a coffee machine at the top of the slippery wooden staircase. One of these cups was sent flying when A. J. S Williams tripped over a formula and the machine was replenished with pyridine. I could not yet have graduated to the chippie, a name usually given to a carpenter, but in Aberystwyth reserved for a fish and chip shop. These were dug into the walls of the sombre streets. Among the streets and alleyways of blackened time I searched for the meanings of this little town, dominated by the brutally clashing styles of the National Library of Wales and the Penglais Campus of concrete boxes. There was nothing except flickering shadows, its entire existence was compressed into binders of loose leaves upon which the nonsense of the lectures had been crystallized. Had these notes been stolen or lost there would have ended Aberystwyth. There was no contact with lecturers, none could ever explain what they were trying to say. Although they had an easy life and were lavishly paid, everything was left to the pea eating student who had nothing. This was the unjust world that I was of told of in the roar of the Aladdin machine shop. Those who were trapped there by the pounding machines had wisdom in their lost souls, along with the steel and iron of Jean-Paul Sartre. The greyest of grey Novembers was the back drop to a deadly struggle between nothingness and the always evasive enlightenment, the firefly of the mind. Aberystwyth focused fiercely into a memory trial the likes of which the sun had never contrived: either I memorized those notes or I would be condemned to a mere existence of TV watching and reporting the TV to others who knew of the TV. In the cardboard box digs there was no TV, only a room upon whose faded wallpaper condensed an uneasy burden, the life breath of students. They slowly became aware of the oncoming trial by fire that was to take place in the damp gothic pile by the crazy golf course by the eternally pounding sea.

As the Christmas examinations approached the alcohol bottles began to run dry. Minds must have cleared and books searched for. I do not know how the other students prepared for those examinations, none were taking the same subjects. I have a vague recollection of the Republic of Plato being skimmed through more than two thousand years after Plato wrote it, but if I mentioned that I was a republican the shadows of the middle classes would shy away. One would never get tenure with political views like that. Plato was not welcome in the chippies or circles of small businesses, whose money depended on political correctness, students and tourists. They produced nothing of their own. They would destroy and demolish chapels for their stone and wood, leaving themselves with a wilderness as desolate as that left behind by locusts or barbarians. Slowly the notes were memorized somehow. I have no recollection of how it was done, maybe in the quiet spells when I had a corner of the cardboard box to myself, or when all were studying or more accurately, becoming nervous. With the greatest and most detailed of care I made sure over and over again that the dates and times of the examinations were incised in my mind like Roman letters in marble. The examinations were timed for the convenience of lecturers, some were in the evening in the Old College, some were in the morning in other buildings, some were on the moon for all the administration cared. First year students were there for numbers only, so the admin could boast of how excellent it was. These days all universities describe themselves as excellent. All are superior, yet all are the same indifferent nonentities.

I began to hear stories of how some wretches had been devastated by examination nerves - the shell shock of the academic world. These were put about as the examinations approached, some had jumped off Constitution Hill, some had gassed themselves or hanged themselves from a bannister, some had taken an overdose of rat poison. Probably none of it was true, but I began to see fear in the eyes of the unprepared. Some had already given up and were there just for the pubs. My own method was the same as at Pontardawe, the only difference was that the school teachers were much better than the lecturers, who delivered lectures like man traps on the old aristocratic or church estates. Traps that could amputate the illiterate and starving poacher, or illiterate and starving student. Some were content during lectures to listen to this low quality rubbish without taking notes, with folded arms and yawning jaws. They were doomed to a life of empty materialism. The lecturers were ego tripping their way through tenure, in many cases given to them by accident. No one really knows how the lecturers were tenured. The College still keeps it a close secret, even from the Information Commissioner. I know that they were tenured because they made themselves the friends of the influential. Their low quality is instantly apparent to the young mind, which enters university at its most critical of society and its endless corruption.

My method was to isolate myself from the surrounding noise, or Brownian motion of random student numbers and small shopkeepers. This was not difficult because there was and is nothing to hold the intelligent mind at Aberystwyth. Contemporary roads are designed to by pass it as completely as possible, so motorists can fly from one tescoed town to another, all tescoes being the same, burning as much petrol as they possibly can in a Wales all geared up for tourists. I had no money to buy anything, having expended reserves very dutifully on course books before I became aware that they were to be found in libraries. The one exception was a strange cap that I bought to keep my ears warm from the Army and Navy Stores. Later my ears toughened up and I never wore a cap again. In any case my mother was repelled by it and probably threw it away. She was also repelled and alarmed by how thin I was after that first Aberystwyth term, but my father thought it was proper and that I had kept in training. My ears and mind were insulated, and I focused on those loose sheets of notes. The only thing left of these notes is an address which I wrote on the inside cover of "Mathematical Methods for Science Students", it was neatly written with strong determined tee's with a fountain pain. It says "Myron Wyn Evans, "Brig y Don", Sea View Place, Aberystwyth." It was just a few yards from the bed and breakfast house of the fifties, described in volume one. It may as well have been on the back of the moon. Its language was English with foreign accents, and not Welsh at all. The Aladdin machine shop had been right.

So apart from the loose leaved notes, no doubt written with the same fountain pen in the same blue or black ink, there was nothing at Aberystwyth in a grey November. The shed of the putting green was locked, and down its wooden sides dripped the rain, mixed with condensation of salty water. The castle alleys stank of urine, a by product of materialism and small pet dogs. The markings of ink on paper became existence. Cogito ego sum, I think therefore I am. If I did not think I would go mad with blankness. The thought became attached to neurons and the memorization of these notes flooded out the slot machines as if the pier had collapsed in ruin. There was no alternative to memorization, when on rare occasions I observed the gambling machine slaves endlessly pouring their dole money into oblivion, trapped by the hope of becoming rich, clothed in the habit of mere existence. I glimpsed into pub doors and recoiled from the stink of beer and vomit. Many a lost wretch would waste a life in one of those dives, many of them students. In the second year I remember one such product vomiting rum and black over the bed clothes in his room. The blankets had been dyed purple like a Senator's toga, and all had been awakened by amplified seizures as the body desperately strove to get rid of the poison. Is this excellence? The landlady did not think so but would not get rid of the student. She needed the money because her husband was not working, and stole money from the students.

Suddenly we were told that this was the last lecture of the term and the lecturer disappeared, striding down the corridor towards his own corner of the academic empire, a concrete cubicle or a small room of the old EDCL, a room with curved walls to fit the architecture. Lecturers and senior lecturers were fitted into such corners. A reader may have have had slightly more space, but I doubt it. Only the head of department was allowed a fire place. This room was a sanctum from which all undergraduates were excluded unless they were going to be told that they had been sent down, or had failed first year, or maybe even that was done by letter. The head of department was as remote as a head of state, entered lectures imperiously and bored us brainless as Beynon. If we were not attentive early on a bacon filled morning the brow of the almighty clouded over and the cold wooden seats got colder. His lectures were perfect and we had to appreciate it. Price and Cadman were fitted into curving cornices each side of the main entrance of EDCL, and Cadman suddenly told us in the library that it was all politics. He had thrown up in his own way, a last gasp for freedom before tenure imprisoned him with bored freshmen for the rest of his days. This is one incident of that first term that I remember. I was angered by this because Cadman could speak no Welsh, never learned it, and of course stayed there all his life. Some years later, J. O. Williams told me that Cadman had been awarded a D. Sc. for collecting the tops of corn flakes boxes. This was not the conversation of philosophers, not the School of Athens of Raphael. Even today, M. P.'s are fitted into small cornices of the House of Commons, from which they are hooked out for a vote, and from which several fiddled expenses.

The last lecture and the last practical class disappeared, and there was silence upon the waves as in Genesis, but there was no sign of creation. The remains of the shattered castle were saturated by a cold mist and a colder rain and glowered over Sea View Place. How glad were those lecturers to get rid of the students. I have only the vaguest memories of those Christmas examinations. Having found the door of the Old College off the alley of dustbins (Pier Street), I could at least find the place of trial. The door is situated in a very narrow alleyway of its own, along which putting tourists stray if they hit the golf ball too hard. None of our lectures took place in that grim Gothic pile that used to be the railway hotel. The University of Wales was founded in the late nineteenth century and the hotel became the Old College. This was a great and noble aim that was corrupted quickly into meaninglessness, so by the time I arrived on the scene in 1968 nothing of the ideals remained. There was a small department of Welsh but that was kept carefully hidden in a corner. There were a few friendly Welsh students, and there were courageous people like Ffred Ffrancis, often imprisoned for his efforts on behalf of the Welsh Nation and Welsh language. None of these ideals remained in chemistry, physics and mathematics, departments which should more comfortably have been housed in Surrey, may be Tunbridge Wells in Kent, another spa.

So among the rubbish, dark alleys and dustbins of discarded ideals, I had to make my way to that hidden doorway one howling rain sodden December night, and find the examination room. I must have ordered two scoops of green peas to fortify mind and body. I had to leave my notes behind and make my way directly to the door. The alternative was life down a coal mine, and that would have been the end of me. The second choice was the machine shop of Aladdin, amid the crashing presses and grease removing poison for the rest of my life. I had gone through these trials endless times at the Grammar School, ever since the age of eleven or twelve. This Gothic relic must have a room in it somewhere, a room filled with desks and overseen by a grim prison master, hauled out for exam duty and in no good humour. The route to the hidden doorway of the alley way was through a graveyard flanked by a castle wall. All of this was a Norman idea, the churches were built close to the castles. The Norman thought that all natives should be excluded. I think I went around via Pier Street or down the side of Laura Place, very quickly and straight for the door. It was indeed open and there was a light inside. Come to meet your destiny it beckoned. A piece of cardboard on a stick guided the student towards the examination room. At that point things began to feel familiar. I had gone through the trial by fire many times before. There could have been three written examinations in chemistry: physical, inorganic and organic and these were the ones that took place in the Old College. There could have been just one examination. The examinations in physics and mathematics must have taken place in the campus on Penglais. They were concerned only with a few weeks of lectures, but needed to be attacked and demolished. I recall very vaguely that the questions set by Mansel Davies were hand written with fingers missing, so had to be deciphered. The examination papers must have been stencilled out and placed on rows of desks. The smell o the stencil solvent was the first thing that greeted a student at an examination desk before the age of xerox. No calculators were allowed because there were no calculators in 1968. We did everything by log book. Even these may have been issued to prevent students writing crib notes. Perhaps the nostrils of each student were examined in some universities for hidden crib, but we were spared this.

At an examination there are two pieces of paper, the exam paper and an exam book which stared blankly like the empty eyes of a skull. Very appropriate for a Gothic setting with a graveyard on one side and fifteen foot waves on the other. Only the Victorians would have built a railway hotel in the middle of the sea. The railway actually ends a long way away, near a modern fish and chip shop. It is now upmarket and all poisson and pommes frites. It still tastes like fish and chips, even in French. Welsh as is not allowed in order to please the tourists and prevent indigestion. The feelings engendered in the innocent by these objects of the examination room are ones of extreme panic, but I was well used to dodging the guillotine and looked for a question that could be devoured, a question at which all the ammunition of stored up memory could be expended unmercifully. I kept a clock in my head so as not to overrun the time. There was probably a real clock on the Gothic wall, ticking out its existence like the pit and the pendulum of Edgar Alan Poe. Then all memory poured on to the paper in a frenzied gunfight. Questions with problems could be avoided in chemistry, and to a lesser extent physics, but not in mathematics. The A level papers of volume one show how difficult these could be. In fact no lecturer at Aberystwyth could have passed an A level of the Welsh Joint Education Committee. They were there because they were acquainted with influence and had the cunning to do so at the right time. They remained frozen like that forever.

Sometimes the exam book was replaced by sheets of foolscap paper, so as each sheet ran out the student had to do a bit of running himself, to get a new sheet of foolscap kept close under the eye of the gulag guard, who may have had a machine gun hidden in the lobby. A genius must have been struck by inspiration one day and invented the examination book. The foolscap was replaced by A4. I always carried two six guns, a fountain pen carefully filled with ink, and a biro for back up. Armed with pen and biro I was undefeated in three years of examinations at undergraduate. I had to buy my own ink. At the end of that first Gothic exam I hurried out of dracula's reach before his dental problems got too severe, and starving and cold, may have ran back between the graveyard and castle walls directly into Sea View Place and to the one bar electric fire - my only source of heat. As usual with examinations I had no real idea of how well or how badly things had gone. I went through many hundreds of such examinations spread over ten years, from age eleven to age twenty one. There was very little time before the next set of examinations on the campus. I have no memory of practical examinations in first year chemistry. Perhaps the practical courses in chemistry were assessed by continuous assessment. This was certainly the case in the third year with the exception of one examination in organic chemistry. The only time that I came close to failing an examination or doing badly was one practical examination in physics, in which the teaching was always so appallingly bad. Mathematics examinations consisted of attacking a problem that I could solve, and leaving the most formidable ones to last. Time could be gained by solving one problem quickly at the beginning of the examination. For the mathematics papers I practiced endlessly at set problems or on past papers if I could find any.

The system was therefore fixated by examinations and naturally I learned over ten years to pass examinations. That does not mean that I learned much about the subject matter, and there was almost never a shred of inspiration. The latter is supposed to happen in conventional autobiographies, but to be honest, it does not. I think that the lecturers had sets of notes which were much less well prepared than my own. Sometimes as in the case of professors such as Sir Granville Beynon and Mansel Davies there were just scraps of paper and scribbles on a blackboard. These grand old men had no time for students, who interfered with committee work and egotism. They thought themselves to be gods descending, a strange attitude of mind that sets in by an excess of tenure. From this perspective at the time of writing I know why there was no inspiration. It must come from within and must be accompanied by a perfect freedom of thought. Human society almost never allows such freedom of thought in any era.

Somehow the last examination of that pitch dark December was over, so it was a time of delight because I was free and could plan my journey back to Pant y Bedw. I decided to travel back by bus and ship the trunk back by carrier. I have no idea why I did this, perhaps it was a gesture of independence. The students quickly began to drift away as soon as the examinations were over. I was perhaps thinking it unfair to burden my parents with anything from Aberystwyth, so one cold day I found myself in a laundry not far from the chippie with the now French tasting chips. It was about fifty feet from the bridge from which in a weird week of September those hicks had jumped into the harbour. That September was infinitely distant, and I had only one desire, to see the small farm again. I had a large bag of unwashed clothes that I dumped into a slowly rotating machine, then slotted in the persil powder. There were incredibly boring things to read and there must have been a drier into which the sodden output was dumped like coal. The machine spluttered to a stop and I dumped the clothes into a bag and thence into the trunk, along with books. Before starting the journey home I took a long walk along the seafront at Aberystwyth and up Constitution Hill. In the fifties this had been a place of great adventure, with a funicular to the top and a path to Clarach. I decided to walk up around the funicular and take some photographs, finding myself on what I thought to be a very well kept field. It was a golf course upon which a little ball was sent flying now and again by the middle classes. There was one such course above the school in Pontardawe and I still cannot think of a more pointless activity. Years later Dr. Cecil Monk told me that he had been quite a golfer in his younger days. Cecil Monk was about my only acquaintance among the EDCL staff and was a kindly man. He introduced me to computers in the third year of undergraduate and a few years later saw one of many savage outbursts from Jeremy Jones, listen ng to it with a face like stone, saying nothing. During that walk on the golf course I wore my cap to keep the wind out of my ears.

The carrier must have called in at "Brig y Don" for the trunk, and I was left with what I could carry. It was foolish and dangerous to entrust all my belongings to a carrier, if they had been lost, my undergraduate days would have been over. I hope that I was not as stupid as to ship off my notes, which I took back with me in a bus. I remember this time very well because it was not despoiled by drudgery. The bus stop was at the entrance of the railway station at Aberystwyth. By that time the rail link to Swansea had been destroyed and nearly all traces of the line had disappeared almost completely. The bus ran through Llanbedr Pont Steffan (Lampeter), the town nearest to the unknown birthplace of my great great grandfather Tomos Jones. It took a circuitous route towards Llandeilo, I doubt whether this was the road through Tal y Llychau (Talley), founded by my ancestral cousin the Prince Rhys ap Gruffudd.

The further from Aberystwyth the happier I felt. After Llandeilo the bus skirted the foothills of Mynydd Betws, then a place of great beauty and not ruined by turbines for the convenience of barbarians. It was making its way slowly towards Swansea. I got off in Clydach and appeared suddenly in this house on a cold grey morning. My grandmother was failing rapidly and my mother was here on one of many visits. Both were surprised and as it seemed to me, not altogether pleased, with an unannounced appearance. The trunk was supposed to follow a few days later but I had not realized it was to be picked up from a depot. I did not try this method again and for the rest of the first six terms at Aberystwyth drove back with my parents.

I was very thin but pleased to be back in one piece. The sheepdog that had been my constant friend of many years went wild with delight. Very soon, in a year or so, he too would be gone. For four weeks around Christmas there was no need to think of lectures and ambition that was there for no understood reason. Unknown to me at the time, the real goal of this ambition was original thought, and that was still distant by years. Things were not the same at Pant y Bedw, there was a reticence that had not been there when I left in September. Probably this is because the farm was to be sold and preparations were being made without my knowledge. This secretive sale happened during my first year as a graduate, in about 1972, and was the worst event in my life. This house had been sold off in 1969, another shattering blow. There was no report at the end of that first term, and nothing for my father to exhibit around the village. Very soon I set about the farm work again, cutting up bales on a frozen field. Memories of the cardboard box began to fade very quickly. There are photographs of that time now on www.aias.us, with the black and white dog sharply contrasted against the snow of Gelliwastad, then unspoiled by mindless vandals. There was, though, a gap in existence, a fault line in time of just over two months, but infinite in implication. This was the effect of an outside world that was worse than I could ever have imagined. It took many years to get rid of that world, so I am able to write about it back here in my grandmother's house.

During that break from university I found myself much against my better judgment shaking hands with the headmaster at Pontardawe, the same Silwyn Lewis who had evicted me forcefully from his study a few years earlier. This was not a successful reunion, the school had become remote, I was not at Cambridge and of no interest. So I escaped as early as I could and drove home in the car borrowed from my father. I was learning the lesson that one can be forgotten instantly, that time can schism very suddenly and never be the same. If there was no glittering achievement one was an embarrassment to any over ambitious headmaster. I never saw Silwyn Lewis again or any of my teachers at Pontardawe. They disappeared as if they had never existed, and the school itself has been turned into a hideous development. The only things left are ideas and volume one of this autobiography: ancient Llan Giwg outlasted the school.

The Christmas of 1968 at Pant y Bedw must have been overshadowed by my grandmothers' failing health, but must also have been one of the last true Christmases, with a thirty five pound turkey grown on the farm, so I ate as much as I could to rid myself of lingering memories of chips and peas. I had learnt that there was no need to buy the very expensive course books, and for four weeks I had food and shelter and must have rapidly regained weight. The enormous reserves of cash saved in this way meant that I could buy a pie or pastie as well as chips and peas. A reasonable sherry or two was consumed when my father made his annual visit to my Uncle Raymond. The Grithig children are all gone now, but were a close family. Recently I found that my grandfather William John Evans was a fluent Welsh speaker and hardly drank at all. That stands to reason because I come from four generations in the direct Evans line of hard working labourers: Edward Evans Llanigon, Edward Evans Cleirwy, William John Evans, and Edward Ivor Evans Y Grithig. For those four weeks there was freedom from study and note taking, and the sanity of the small farm compared with the craziness and instability of Aberystwyth. The idea of a University of Wales will work only if the staff and students are all fluent in Welsh, otherwise it will be anglicised very quickly with the familiar colonial mentality. The end result will be the opposite of that desired - hostility towards the language. In older times learning to a high level took place in farm houses, chapels and churches. Families held together for generations.

As the new year arrived, 1969, the last of a turbulent and very dangerous decade, the spectre appeared on the horizon of a return to the cardboard box of “Brig y Don”. This was even more difficult than the first term, but in the end, towards the middle of January, I drove my father up to Aberystwyth with some belongings meticulously prepared by my anxious mother, and the safely guarded notes. The trunk was left safely at home I think. I still have it here now. It was a gloomy mid winter journey and the doorway of “Brig y Don” eventually faced us. I was the first student to arrive, so I had one bar of electric fire all to myself. The landlady in a fit of generosity may even have let me switch on a second bar. My father caught the huddled gloom of the occasion, and mentioned suddenly that it might be better for me just to return home with him, and give up this strange insanity. It was very difficult not to comply with his wishes, but very soon he would be pushing me out again: down a coal mine or into a factory. So he disappeared back down south, and I was on my own. It was not an unpleasant feeling because there was no one to contend with. There was time to order my thoughts, look up the timetable and to find out with some relief that there would be no examinations at the end of the Easter term. At least I cannot remember any. There were problems and homework. The lecturing styles were getting more familiar, and the note taking skills were honed up a little.

The other students dribbled in, looking miserable, and the room settled down to some debate and discussion about all the topics under the moon. The novelty of drinking had worn off after that first term. I can remember virtually nothing about the lectures or practical classes, but recollect that the course of lectures by Mansel Davies lasted half a year, so stopped in the middle of Easter term. They must have been taken over by someone like Cadman, who was very difficult to follow, almost incomprehensible. Cadman had quite a pleasant character sometimes, but Mansel Davies was as remote as the moon. I don't think I asked either any questions at all. Very soon it began to get cold, so gloves and coats were needed to supplement the one bar fire and to sit in the cold lecture theatres. The biro ink was in danger of freezing. The snow came down on Pen Dinas like a curtain of primordial lace, and the ice made patterns on the tiny window allowed us. The snow came down over all of Aberystwyth and over all of Wales, blanketing the pitiful and babbling wisdom of humankind in primordial silence. The sea looked green and black and menacing, and the snow mingled with the sand and pebbles on the beaches. The black castle stones were jigsawed with white.

So the students of "Brig y Don" took the back of an old chair up to Pen Dinas and used it as a bobsleigh. I captured them on camera just as they were beginning to realize that they were out of control. This was a lot more fun than practical classes under the glowering Heller, or exploding solvent bottles hitting the ceiling, or looking for crystals in the blackened remains of a flask. The chair hit a bank of snow at the foot of the iron age hill, and luckily enough, not a stone wall. Then it was back to the drudgery of lectures, practical classes, tutorials and frenzied note taking. The bitter cold howled through the windows of the long EDCL corridor. My very first memory of the EDCL was of trying to say hello to a lecturer as I walked along this corridor for the first time, and of being ignored and almost shoved aside. This may have been the half crazy A. J. S. Williams, who was completely bald, and known as "knobhead". He always wore a white laboratory coat everywhere, even in tutorials. The earliest of these took place under his control in the small lecture theatre of the EDCL as it was called, with wooden seats as hard as iron. Of this first year I have very little memory, so the work must have been very hard and very monotonous. Only the unusual remain in the memory at this distance in time, and one of these events was a walk for charity from Aberystwyth to Llanbedr Pont Steffan.

This walk took place on a Saturday, so I missed my one and only lecture, tutorial, practical class and seminar of my entire undergraduate and post graduate time. It was a summer term lecture in organic chemistry by John Bowen in a wooden lecture theatre stuffed into a corner behind a storeroom. This was the main lecture theatre of the old EDCL building. I was persuaded into doing this walk against my better judgement, and half way through my feet blistered very badly. So I was left at the side of the road and hobbled my way into Llanbedr. It was a distance of about twenty five or thirty miles. It was very difficult to find anyone who would give me a good account of the missed lecture, so I never missed another one. There were examinations again at the end of the first year, I recall one physics examination taking place in the biology building, surrounded by pickled frogs and similar. Such was the chaos that substituted for organization.

At the end of the Easter term there was the usual delight for me of being able to get away from Aberystwyth and back to some decent living. During these Easter holidays I took some colour photographs which are posted as albums on www.aias.us. The aged black and white sheepdog appears in some of these, with greying muzzle and clouded eyes. These photographs record for example the unspoilt Mynydd y Gwair, soon to be obliterated now by monstrous wind turbines that remind everyone all the time of crushed democracy. It was still possible in the first year's vacations to spend the time without study, but in the second year that ceased to be the case. The summer term was a very short one, and again I was almost caught by surprise by the examinations at the end of the first year. Only after some questioning was the examination system made clear to the students. For example were the examinations to cover the entire first year or only the second two terms? In any event the notes assumed great importance, they were the only record available. I was not told to make notes - I did so out of pure instinct. Effectively therefore I rewrote all the lecture courses in a much clearer way than any of the lecturers, doing all their work for them. I always thought that they had a very easy time compared with school teachers, and that it ws all a closed shop. Only in this way could such poor lectures pass as teaching.

Yet through all the hardship there was always the fierce determination to learn and do well, so solve the problems, and even to please the lecturers. I had always wanted to please my parents with good results and to minimize the financial burden on them to almost nothing. Otherwise there was always the danger of my father trying to pull me out of university. Obviously he never read any of my work and understood none of it. Doing very well was the only way to survive. In the vacations from university I was tolerated at Pant y Bedw provided that I kept to myself and did farm work, or found vacation work. After completing that set of summer term examinations in 1969 I found a job at B. P. Baglan Bay as a laboratory technician. That meant a thirteen mile journey by Honda 50 scooter to work and back. The pay was good and so I was able to build up reserves to stop me starving on chips and peas. The analytical laboratory at Baglan Bay was situated next to the chlorine plant, and was well equipped with a range of apparatus for routine analysis of fractions of oil from Llandarcy. Sometimes there was some experimental work. There was infra red, gas chromatography, and specialized equipment. It was tolerable work but in the long term it would become repetitive and tedious. The unusual again stands out, for example a major fire, a leak of chlorine gas, and a bad wound to my finger caused by cutting it with a low temperature thermometer. On the way home one day I crashed the scooter into a roundabout but was unharmed.

My grandmother Martha Jane Jones, born Newlands, died in July 1969, after a long illness. She had been devastated and paralyzed by unhappiness since her husband Thomas Elim Jones died in the early sixties and for her death was a good companion. In her last days she was brought down to the music room of this house and the doctor was called in repeatedly He could do nothing and she slowly departed this world, my anxious mother and other relatives remaining with her all the time. She could not talk at the end but grasped my hand with her remaining strength. There was nothing I could do and in a wooden minded condition drove in to work. She died during the day in this house where she had been born. That evening I went in to see her - a small, ashen grey figure whose agonized breathing had silenced. A coin had been put in her mouth as was the ancient custom. This house became cold and silent, and I retreated to Pant y Bedw. There was nothing for it but to prepare for the second year at Aberystwyth, my early life at Craig Cefn Parc was drawing quickly to its end.

Almost as an irrelevance, I remember the letter informing me that I had won something called a Mathews Prize. I opened it outside the small whitewashed shed at Pant y Bedw and showed it to my parents. It did not have much effect - it did not solve the mystery of why a good life is followed by a painful death. Many years later I found that the Mathews Prize is for the best first year results in chemistry. How I managed to do that is unknown. It must have been those notes. So the lecturers were not so remote after all, they could recognize merit and reward it. There was no time to reflect on the Mathews Prize because a violent quarrel broke out between my uncle and mother resulting in this house being sold for divided cash and divided belongings. Even at the age of nineteen I had the sense to realize that they could have done anything rather than sell it. The last I saw of this house in 1969 it was cold and empty. Many years later I found that someone had stolen all the fine oak doors. I stood for a few minutes before the empty cold hearth, and left. It was many years before I could buy it back again and put it in Trust. I think that all houses of historical value should be put in Trust. This house, Bryn Awel House, was sliced into two and a wall put between. My uncle and mother never talked to each other again.

Even these disasters did not make me want to go back to Aberystwyth to begin the second part of the physical sciences tripos. On another dismal day filled with grey mist my parents and I arrived at 8 Powell Street, a new digs found by accident and for no reason. Atkinson, one other student and myself moved there from “Brig y Don”. The house was run by a small, defeated woman and her husband, whom I later caught stealing money from the students. They asked me to talk over the matter with him. We did not do anything about it so as not to upset his wife. These digs were opposite a finely built chapel, which has been demolished now by people interested in selling its stone and fine oak, in selling civilization to the highest bidder. Recently I saw a levelled weed ridden square where the chapel had been. There was no sermon, no singing, no congregation, only the ghosts of culture and language. I wonder what they did with the Bible, it could have had little second hand value to the illiterate. Perhaps like the Vikings they threw it into the sea.

CHAPTER TWO

In early October 1969 I began the second year of my undergraduate days. The course was split into part one, the first year, and part two, the second and third years. In the second year I took chemistry and mathematics, majoring in chemistry. So physics had been dropped. The classes in the second year were smaller and I even began to recognize a few faces. There was a greater range of courses in chemistry and a very intense year in mathematics, with homework problems and work set for vacation time. The same note taking method was used in both subjects and chemistry was divided once more into physical , inorganic and organic with about twenty hours a week of practical classes. Having got through part one of the tripos I sensed that there was a chance of getting a good degree, and getting rid of physics made life easier. I worked with great intensity during that second year, which was the most difficult of the three years. I must have taken care to eat enough, either from a fish and chip shop or from the student union in Laura Place. The usual breakfast and meals on Sunday were provided by the landlady. There was almost no interaction with the other students of the digs because of the intense work schedule. There were about six students again in 8 Powell Street, one of whom, Roger Goodger, came from Kent and was a first year student. Another called Henrik was from Yorkshire and originally from Poland, and a third came from Crewe, I forget his name. There was also Atkinson and one other from "Brig y Don".

The chemistry courses were a little more technically advanced and diverse than in the first year, and one or two of the lecturers sparked some interest. The practical courses were a matter of following written instructions and by this time I had realized that writing up the experiment was of basic importance. Some of the mathematics reached quite a high standard and there were examinations and set problems in both subjects. I do not remember practical examinations, which to me were the worst kind of all. This second year was tiring because of the combination of lecture and practical class. For me, time always had to be found for writing up the lecture, and making sense out of it with books from the library. If an experiment went well I took great care to present it accurately, using logarithms. The problem was that I could afford only two meals a day, a breakfast and an evening meal, so a day lasting from 9.00 a. m. to 6.00 p.m. in the laboratory would leave me very hungry and tired. The laboratory work had to be finished promptly and lectures written up on days free from the laboratory. There was no point in asking any lecturer or tutor for help, it was not forthcoming.

I have a vague memory of lectures by Dr. Graham Williams and Dr. Alun Price which were quite clearly presented, and there may have been a course by Dr. Sam Graham in organic chemistry and by Dr. Cecil Monk. In that year a new head of department was appointed, Prof. J. M. Thomas, along with Dr. J. O. Williams and Dr. Eurwyn Evans, but there were no lectures from them in the second year. It was a matter of rewriting the lectures via my notes. Mathematics could get difficult, and the department had a habit of giving examinations after vacations, thus ruining the vacation with study. I cannot remember whether chemistry adopted the same method. The worst thing about the second year was the fact that there was no clear idea of when and if examinations would occur, and over what time span. For example, would they be confined to term by term examinations or one examination at the end of the second year, and how much would the second year count towards the final class of degree? By that time nothing less than a first class degree would do for me. Mathematics was the support subject, and I had no clear idea of how much it would count towards the class of the final degree, and no clear idea of the percentage needed for a first class degree, whether one had to attain that percentage only in the final examinations, or throughout the whole three years.

In view of this intense ambition of mine to get a first class degree, I hoped that my fellow lodgers at 8 Powell Street would turn out to be likeable or failing that, would not drink too much and lose control over themselves. If they lived on their own it would have been fine for them to drink any amount, but if they lived in close proximity with others there could be trouble. I also had to share a room again, this time with Roger Goodger, who turned out to be stable, intelligent, witty and likeable, and remained a life long friend. Henryk (I think his last name was spelled Kolodzie or similar) died some years ago of alcoholism, and was probably alcoholic already in 8 Powell Street. He was a brilliant chess player and apparently a good student. I lost touch with all of them at the end of 1969, when I moved to another digs in which I had a room of my own. This was another attic room in which I studied very intensely and in the needed solitude in my third year. It is again difficult for me to understand at this distance in time how I coped with the digs at 8 Powell Street, because my method of preparation required long and careful memorization. Perhaps the onset of examinations made them concentrate on work. The digs system at Aberystwyth was in general a disaster, by now they may have had the sense to build accommodation with individual rooms for serious minded students. That is the least they could do in return for the very large student fees. There might be treatment centres for alcoholism now. Roger wrote to me some years ago that Henryk had died after years of neglect and self neglect, and that it was profoundly depressing. Someone had stolen his money and he died in destitution. I think that his family were refugees from the old Russian Polish border, and he had a broad Yorkshire accent, probably Halifax.

Unfortunately there was a cult of alcohol at Aberystwyth and many pubs into which the unwary could find themselves embroiled. There was one just a few yards from Powell Street overlooking the harbour. I suppose that it sold the traditional rum of sailors. One evening the student from Crewe must have drunk rum and black (maybe blackcurrent) in this awful dive and staggered his way back. In the middle of the night he vomited vast quantities of purple and violet and in this way probably saved himself from ethanol poisoning or asphyxiation. The noise woke up the whole establishment. He had no respect for the landlady or for responsible students, often myself in a minority of one, or myself and Roger. The landlady might have kicked him out but she needed the money. This was the worst aspect of these digs, being trapped with people with whom one would never associate voluntarily. There could be some very weird goings on in the digs, like a seance organized by Atkinson. He was prone to such rubbishy beliefs and was easily frightened. I think his friend was called Tony McGuinness, also from Bolton. I had to be very careful to keep away from these two when they had drink inside them, they were hypersensitive to any perceived criticism and could take offence at the drop of a hat. One evening, in a drunken frenzy, they smashed open the lock on the door leading in to the room occupied by Goodger and myself, and were with difficulty led back to their rooms to sleep it off. I could have done without all of that in that very tough second year.

On other occasions the digs could be a lot of fun, I remember climbing up a lampost and taking out its massive thousand watt bulb or similar and putting it into the lamp socket in a drunken student's room. He switched it on and was enveloped with profound enlightenment that must have sobered him up permanently and could have led to an effortless first class degree. The whole digs became one gigantic spark of wisdom. The bulb was then carefully put back in its lampost. This is the kind of innocent fun expected in student days, not a vomit trip around the pier, or drug induced swim in the dangerous sea. During the whole of my undergraduate days there was not a single student in the digs who could speak Welsh. This was the disaster of the sixties, when University College of Wales Aberystwyth was flooded with students from outside Wales. They did not know the Welsh language and would not learn it. The alcoholic haze of their lives was to me immoral, and showed that they were not there for learning. Some were there on a permanent seaside holiday. This influx of low grade people greatly damaged the Welsh language. My own life at that time was in complete contrast, I aimed to do well. I continued to hope that Aberystwyth would one day become the home of a true university for Wales, one in which all staff and students were fluent in the Welsh language.

The things I liked about Aberystwyth were Pant y Celyn, which had been made into a Hall of Residence for Welsh speakers, and the elements of life in Welsh speaking Wales such as Siop y Pethe, the book shop in the centre of the town. I liked Cymdeithas yr Iaith, the Welsh language society. The Thesis by Phyllis Timmons on www.aias.us is a vivid description of the struggle of those times for the language. The foreign tongued influx regarded these natural things of Welsh speaking Wales as some kind of sinister plot to overthrow London as the world's imperial capital. I disliked the remoteness of the staff, their unwillingness to teach properly, and their pointless arrogance. Surely a learned philosopher must be able to teach, but very few could. I profoundly disliked the town of Aberystwyth, permanently geared up for tourists, it had no existence of its own. It was a parking place for nomads and on a rainy day enveloped the imagination in deep and sombre greyness, the pint potted dregs of existence. It seemed and seems beyond belief that students were expected to live in such squalor. Recently I had occasion to see such digs in Swansea, and they are worse than ever. I suspect that this squalor still exists today in Aberystwyth, and that students are eagle eyed by landladies as a necessary evil that brings in cash. This is not Periclean Athens or Florence in the high renaissance. It was a small, damp little town that described itself as "sun, sea and scenery", a commonplace alliteration, not Dafydd a Gwilym at all.

I was beginning to think for myself in the very few hours left over from a week stuffed with chemistry and mathematics. The most profound irritation was directed at those teachers who delivered their lectures in such an offhand manner, bored and defeated by years of comfortable tenure. I wondered how they had been given their comfortable tenure, and why. I wondered why they never learned the language, why they had flooded the place with people who never learned the Welsh language, and why they and I were there. The answer in every case was and is - money. Everything was done for money and not for learning. Everything was done in Aberystwyth as if it were a resort in western England. The situation has worsened since 2000, when the Welsh Assembly made its loudly trumpeted entrance. Aberystwyth caters for all languages except one - its own Welsh language, the sow turns on her piglets and devours them. Everything is in Welsh and English, but no one speaks Welsh, they just quote the TV.

I also wondered why the lectures were delivered in such an awful way, by scribbling and mumbling, back turned to the lecture theatre. When I became a full professor at University of North Carolina Charlotte I used an overhead projector and slides prepared clearly with the help of my first wife, Laura, who was always a generous human being. They were printed and not hand written. The students could read the notes and I could face the class all the time. In that second year at Aberystwyth the mathematics lectures were excruciating, the students were expected to learn very quickly, lectures were followed very quickly by tests or homework, but there was no clear idea if these tests were meant to contribute towards the final grading in mathematics, or whether the final grading in mathematics counted towards the class of final degree. All was perfect chaos, and often the only thing I could think to do was to do as well as I could all the time. That meant missing no lecture or seminar, doing all the homework, and trying my best in tests. The element of individual tutoring was entirely missing. So all the learning was self learning. If so, is there any need for universities and lecturers? Many of the best artists think that there is no need at all.

I have a memory during that second year in College of starting my regime of athletics training in order to blow the cobwebs out of my lungs. The first attempts were a run around Gelliwastad, which took all my will power and effort. I was not a natural distance runner at all. I felt that I was in a very weakened condition after that first year and instinct told me to start training. Getting to the top over rough roads felt almost impossible, gasping for air with limbs refusing to move. This must have been in the late summer of 1969. It was not possible to train regularly with that heavy work load of the second year. This spilled over into the vacations, which were taken up by mathematics problems to be marked after returning from vacation. The training regime around Gelliwastad became a regular daily experience during the vacations, and in all weathers. During these runs my mind wandered over many topics, in a vague kind of way due to oxygen debt. Strangely enough I began to think of general relativity, although I had had no lectures in that subject. Was it a great achievement or just a maze of mathematical symbols? The teaching of mathematics had stopped short of tensor analysis, which had to be learned much later.

The summer of 1969 had been a harsh and bitter experience, not only was this house sold, but there was also a danger of Pant y Bedw being sold. Although I was the eldest son there seemed to be no thought given to inheritance. The effect on me was to make me determined to lead my own life as soon as I could. I had been made to work on the farm since the age of seven, while still recovering from major surgery. I could see that there was going to be no reward for that all that farm work. There was also no understanding of my university work. The only thing I could think to do was to apply myself with all my will and strength to getting a good degree, a first class degree, in the hope that this would lead to independence. There would be no further danger of my home suddenly disappearing under an auctioneer's hammer or by a casual sale by word of mouth to anyone at all. So I studied with great dedication in the same room as I had studied for the examinations at the Grammar School. This was as far away as I could get from the violent quarrels caused by my sister, who dropped out of school at an early age. Almost all the family resources went to her throughout the entire lifetime of my parents. I was told that I could look after myself and gradually lost contact with that early family. Relations with my parents remained good, but very much at a distance. The utterly dreary existence in that second year means that I have lost all memory of events that could have alleviated the underlying boredom. I can remember only the bad things, as is often the case. Strangely enough I was regarded as a kind of student leader in 8 Powell Street, and years later Roger Goodger told me that I was always expected to get a first class degree. I had no sense of this at the time. I felt completely out of it in Aberystwyth and still have no knowledge of its dark and reeking pubs. One of the worst incidents was theft by the landlord. He was a strange man who kept to himself in a small room at the back of the tiny house, so was as a prisoner in a permanent cell, surrounded by squalor and decay. He had been stealing money from the pockets of the raincoats, very petty theft. For some obscure reason the others asked me to deal with it, so I just asked him to stop, risking getting thrown out of the digs. His wife was very distressed so we all left it at that. We all decided not to return and this meant that I had to find new digs for the third year. I forget entirely how I found them, but they were with Mrs Gill (I think that this was her name) in a house on Alexandra Road opposite the park called Plascrug Avenue below the EDCL, just adjacent to a large library. I must have found these digs in the summer term of 1970, towards the end of that second year. They had the one great advantage of a room to myself in an attic. This was a very small, stuffy room under the slate roof, with a small window, but I could study there in privacy.

In that summer term of the second year I have memories of Lagrangian methods of analysis and of endlessly going through problems. The very strange looking Euler Lagrange equations gradually began to take on meaning, but always required insight that could not be taught - one always had to find the Lagrangian variables. So problems on Lagrangian dynamics in examinations were really dangerous. One bad examination result could destroy the entire degree, or so I thought. I still do not know to what extent mathematics contributed to my degree in chemistry. Not only had I to get a degree but a first class degree. I did not know why, it was a deep innate desire to do my very best. At school it was to please my parents and teachers, now it was an overwhelming necessity. So there must have been summer term examinations in mathematics. These were got through and I could drop the subject to concentrate entirely on chemistry, which had begun to show some small signs of interest. By this I mean that some lectures actually interested me a little. It was no longer a matter of frenzied writing to random dictation and then the inevitable hours in the library trying to make sense of it all. It would have been much easier if we had just been given books from which to compile sets of notes. Having written that though even the poorest of lecturers injects some element of understanding in a mysterious way. The entire scene was always under the threat of the guillotine - of examinations. In that second year it was not even clear if and when examinations were to be upon us. I could only suspect that I had to excel all the time, and that became my everyday existence. There was no element of intense competition with other students, I hardly knew any of them towards the end of that second year. I wished to do well for myself alone. By that time my friend of many years, the black and white sheepdog, had been "destroyed" as they say. I was told this suddenly when I returned from the Spring term. He had been dead for a long time before I was told. So I was truly alone as the third year of the undergraduate degree approached.

The second year ended as had the first, with a sudden evaporation and a fault in time. The students at 8 Powell Street went their own way and I never saw any of them again. Many years later I corresponded with Roger Goodger for a while but the others disappeared as suddenly as they had arrived. I do not recall clearly whether or not I worked at B. P. Baglan Bay during that summer of 1970 as well as the summer of 1969. At the time it was a giant petrochemical refinery adjacent to the vast steel works at Margam. I have some vague recollections of using a lecture bottle to collect ethyl chloride from a pipeline. My father was working there as a labourer at the time, having left the coal mine at Bryn Lliw with the rank of overman, or underground manager. I saw him in the distance pulling a trolley one day and he looked profoundly unhappy. The coal miner was the aristocrat of the working world in South Wales. I was never told much, and I still do not know why he was not given a job as an above ground manager. My mother told me just before she died that he had been diagnosed with 30% dust in the lungs. I remember that the chlorine plant was next to the laboratory at Baglan Bay, chlorine was made by electrolysis of sea water. One day there was an accident in the chlorine plant, and an evacuation of the laboratory. Another day there was a fire in a tower, maybe making propylene before being converted into polypropylene. The petrochemical plant always smelled very badly, and on a rainy day the distant mountains looked very bleak. The B. P. Plant was stuck out on a flat plain near the sea, alongside the dreary Sandfields estate and the angular shadows of awkward giants in the distance, the steel making towers. The hillside behind the steel works had been blasted into a primitive ochre colour by the sickly fumes, the rotten eggs of carbon disulphide and the acidic sulphur dioxide. Fumes poured out of the steelworks and out of the cooling towers at Baglan Bay. I can see no sign of these towers now, they must ave been levelled and destroyed.

It was beginning to get very uncomfortable at Pant y Bedw, but I still had very little desire to return to Aberystwyth at the end of that summer of 1970. Eventually I made my way back to the new digs at Alexandra Road. Mrs Gill was a small lady married to Mr Gill, who worked in the Post Office building opposite the EDCL. He had captured a Japanese sword which was placed in the corner of the student room. There were about four other students but I cannot remember their names, and we had the great luxury of a T. V. Fortunately the students were good natured and stable and the food was good, the usual bed and breakfast and full board on Sunday. My parents came up with me in September 1970 and seemed to get along well enough with Mrs. Gill. This was the most intense year of my time at Aberystwyth as undergraduate and graduate. The entire year was devoted to chemistry, in a class consisting of eighteen students. So it was possible to get to know them and put names to faces, although there was still very little communication. I was on good terms with students and lecturers, although I often disliked their methods I never disliked them as people at that time. The third year consisted of six lectures a week at nine a.m., two and half days of practical classes and a seminar on Wednesday afternoons in the small lecture theatre with very hard seats. The entire staff delivered courses, about twelve or thirteen in all. These were more specialized than physical, organic and inorganic and reflected the research interests of the lecturers, if they had any.

I began to feel better in that third year, and at home in the EDCL. If it had not been for Howard Purnell I would have been happy at the EDCL my entire career - or maybe not. Even Heller seemed to be more amiable and began to realize that I had some talent after all. It helped that he did not take practical classes in that third year, these were taken by Sam Graham helped by A. J. S. Williams, and taken in the relatively new custom built organic chemistry laboratory. I have a better memory of that third year and its various courses. My method was to produce the best set of notes that I could and memorize word by word the entire set, about two hundred pages in all, kept in one folder. I recall that I still had those notes in that folder in Ithaca New York, in 1992, and they may still be here. If I find them one day I will post them on www.aias.us. In that third year it was at last made clear to us that the final examinations would be based only on that final year, and that large parts of the practical courses would be by continuous assessment of notebooks. This was much better than that hazy second year. There were lecture courses in the third year from Prof. J. M. Thomas, Prof. Mansel Davies, Dr Cecil Monk, Dr Graham Williams, Dr Alun Price, Dr. Sam Graham, Dr Harry Heller, Dr. Phil Cadman, Dr. Colin Young, Dr. George Morrison, Mr. A. J. S. Williams, and probably Mr John Bowen. There were practical classes given by Dr. Graham Williams, Dr. Cecil Monk, Dr. Sam Graham and Mr. A. J. S. Williams, and perhaps one or two others.

By that time I had also developed my athletics routine so that whenever I could I trained about two or three times a week on Plascrug Avenue. I forget where I got my evening meals, probably a fish and chip shop on Alexandra Road. So all was tightly organized to devote my entire being to that first class degree. The lecture each morning was followed on two or three days by a practical class, held on the second floor of the New Wing of the EDCL. The first half of the third year was devoted to physical and inorganic chemistry (although I cannot remember the latter). I completed all the experiments, about twenty three of them in all, and my experimental notebooks were considered exemplary. I know this because they were "commandered" by Graham Williams and never returned to me. The second half of the third year was devoted to practical organic classes, backed up by NMR and similar techniques of analysis. Organic synthesis was still the most unpredictable type of experiment. The morning lectures were held in the small lecture theatre on the ground floor of the Old Building of the EDCL. This was a very dreary and ancient place, and looked out on a blackened pile of stone with smoky windows. I remember that it looked like Swansea Prison from the Vetch on Saturday afternoons and was the corner of the EDCL's chemical stores. Below it in a kind of pungent smelling cellar was Grendel's Cave, Heller's organic chemistry laboratory and a mess of poisonous distillations in and out of fume cupboards, poison everywhere. As undergraduates we were not allowed in either the stores or the Heller cellar, and never knew any of the technicians as they were called. I just noticed now and again that there were people walking around in white coats who were not lecturers. These must have been the technicians of the mechanical and electronic workshops and the glassblowers, and the storekeeper. Later I found that these were Mr "Griff" Griffiths, glassblower, Mr John Poley, Mr Bob Meredith and Mr Harold Jolley (mechanical works op), Mr Dyson Jones and Mr Irfon Williams (electronic workshop) and Mr Colin Thwaites (storekeeper). Later on they were joined by Mr Jim Jenkins (electron microscope and photography dark room) and one or two others. There were also porters and assistants who wore green coats. The technicians were second class citizens and the porters third class citizens. The undergraduates were not allowed to use a common room and there was no café or restaurant anywhere near the EDCL. By that time (1970 / 1971) the coffee machine may have been installed on the landing of the main staircase, and perhaps a chocolate machine. The coffee and tea were truly revolting but were the only things to drink.

This arrangement of lectures and practical classes meant that I had to find the time to write up the usual scribbled notes of a morning lecture delivered sometimes in a semi catatonic condition by a lecturer who often seemed bored out of his skull. On one occasion, Dr. Cecil Monk forgot to turn up completely, and was ushered into the class only at the very last minute, by an irritated and balding J. M. Thomas. On another occasion I was told that Monk had driven into a hole in the ground made by some workmen on the very obscure approaches to the EDCL through a back road. Later on I found that Cecil Monk was one of the most innovative of the teachers, and introduced us to the College computer , the Elliot Brothers 4130 with about 48 kilobytes of memory for the entire College. The other staff had no idea of what to do with a computer. At this time in the third year of my undergraduate course I was under the impression that the teachers were there on merit. Much later it was found that almost none had been appointed in open competition. A few had served one or two post doctorals but some did not have a doctoral degree, notably Mr. A. J. S. Williams and Mr Bowen. I think that the set of notes I wrote would have made better lectures than the original. There were no student assessments so the lecturer once tenured could do anything, especially if they had done no research for some years. Recently I tried to find out how the appointments took place, but the College refused to answer, even to the Information Commissioner. This is a sure sign that the process was not one of appointment of the best candidates. My interest has always been in research, and not in teaching, but the student assessments at UNCC show that I would have been a good teacher if I had chosen to be. Eventually the EDCL collapsed in a heap in 1988 and was closed without trace. Recently an attempt has been made to replace the Charter of the University of Wales and to destroy its Federal structure.

In the autumn of 1970 however it was back to the dutiful routine of taking down lectures almost word for word, deciphering scribbled formulae and making sense of the result in a library. The most interesting and fluent lecturer was Sam Graham, I recall some lectures on sugars and steroids, carotene and similar. Dr. Graham was so fluent and seemingly likeable that one was almost lulled into forgetting to note what he said. I am sure that many students fell in to this trap so at the end of the lecture they went home, or to another class, and at the end of the term or year had nothing. Suddenly the examinations would be upon them. Mansel Davies lectured on dielectrics and the theory of hydrogen bonding, but his lack of mathematical ability was all too evident to some of us. I remember that he set a problem one day, either in class or for home work, and I solved it in my own, original way. He presented a different solution to the class and went through that. He was not critical of my solution, but his own solution had obviously been given for many years. Some members of the class became irritated at this, seeing it as an example of blinkered thought. I was not particularly bothered. I could see that behind the facade, Mansel Davies was rather a vulnerable man, he had a seemingly kindly nature when he chose to be in the mood. His strength was the generous recognition of talent, and the nurturing of talent, so overall I remember him with respect. The bouts of almost uncontrollable anger that made him difficult to live with for some. I was on the receiving end of that random anger and acidic contempt a few times. The next day he would behave as if nothing had happened. It was the archetypical child of nature, but still, one could have done without it.

Graham Williams was an over ambitious and wholly unlikeable product of the Mansel Davies group but at that point had quite a good lecturing technique. Again, Graham Williams was way short of the mathematical technique needed and as far as I know, never worked with a computer himself. His students and post doctorals may have done the computing work for him. It was never clear why he was promoted so rapidly while others such as Alun Price were not. I thought that Alun Price was more solid, capable and reliable, but was never promoted beyond senior lecturer. In 1970 however it was again a matter of taking down what Graham Williams had to say with such forced enthusiasm, and unravelling the content after hours in the library. Cecil Monk was a painfully shy lecturer who only half looked at the class, but he was competent and kept up with the times. I remember that he gave some lectures on nuclear physics and isotopes, his own speciality, and designed an isotope titration in the practical class. The radio active iodide sample was kept heavily shielded with lead. He also designed an experiment with polarimeter to measure the optical rotation of sugars and similar compounds. These were well built experiments. Much later he became a friend as well as a colleague, and sometimes would give me some apples from his garden, being a fine gardener. He came from quite a distinguished family that had fallen upon hard times, and freely admitted how tenure was given in his case, suddenly one day he was tenured and that was that. In Monk's case he deserved tenure. His most important contribution as far as I was concerned was output from the Elliot Brothers 4130 computer. I had never seen computer output before and it appeared in large sheets of perforated paper. In introducing us to computers Monk was well ahead of all of his colleagues. He was promoted to reader but never further, despite being the founder of the Soddy Laboratory of the EDCL. He was a gardener to begin with, then a mature student at Birkbeck Colleg London during the bombing or blitz and did some important secret work during the war. He disliked Mansel Davies very much and the feeling was mutual. With Monk one could always get an honest and razor sharp analysis of humbug, and evidently he regarded a phoney like George Morrison with ill concealed contempt. Monk thought that someone like J. M. Thomas was a vaguely necessary cog in a machine. I would just ask why the machine is there. When Morrison was sick all over me one day in the corridor, having lost his violent temper over some triviality, Monk burnt him alive with a glare like sulphuric acid. This showed to me that I was not alone in the assessment of these weird and unstable characters one had to live with, and who never seemed to have any idea of the social graces. The last time I saw Monk was in the summer of 1993, on an ill fated visit to the EDCL and then up to the Campus with Gareth Evans and my first wife Laura to see the remains of the chemistry department. It had been shoved out of sight as a chemistry unit, and the EDCL had been smashed to pieces, literally. Everything had been taken away from him, even his office space, and he was sitting in the middle of a biology lab. He did not seem to be at all pleased that I had turned up unannounced, or that I was a full professor. Probably he no longer saw any meaning to such things and he was feeling humiliated. He had a right to feel humiliated after fifty years of service, and there is no meaning to those things.

The hyperambitious J. M. Thomas (who pounced around with springs in his heels) gave us some lectures on heterogeneous catalysis, using his own textbook as a course book. He lectured like a Minister giving a sermon, with an excess of zeal considering the rather mundane subject matter. A technician at B. P. Baglan Bay could have lectured on the same subject in a more interesting way, or so it seemed to the class of 1971. I vividly remember an incident one morning when he seemed to be tired and irritated with having to deal with a class of pale faced, bacon stuffed and very bored undergraduates, and suddenly lost his cool. He fired a hostile question at the class and received total silence as an answer. In order to break the tension I thought of trying to say something intelligent, but I did not know what he was talking about. As usual my understanding developed much later. In this case I wrote up the notes feeling very tired at the end of a long day in the library adjacent to the digs in Alexandra Road, ploughing through the book on heterogeneous catalysis week after week. He was also a newcomer to the EDCL, so was regarded with some caution by the class, now the senior third year class in chemistry. I was not interested in heterogeneous catalysis because the course lacked precision. This was the unacceptable side of academic existence, the false authority of uninteresting ideas being put across in an authoritative way, and blaming the students for being bored. J. M. Thomas and myself are the very opposite of scientists, he is a manager, I am an artist. So we never communicated and never worked together. I am never interested in merely organizing the work of other people. No artist can ever be interested in that.

I forget almost entirely what Heller lectured on, it could have been something to do with Woodward Hoffmann rules, but it became apparent that Heller was capable in his own field or so it was said. He founded a company called Aberchromics, which is a ridiculous name. It means the mouth of the chromics, and summed him up perfectly. I remember the very envious Mansel Davies almost blasting at me one day that Heller was going to make his fortune, meaning that he, Mansel Davies, was not. These were mercenary waters for a humanist. In the event there has been no sign to date of Heller making a fortune and if still alive he has been long retired. He left very suddenly for Cardiff in the time of Jeremy Jones. I remember this happening in about 1983, just after I had been worked over by Jeremy Jones and Graham Williams for three hours. After I had been well and truly beaten up verbally, Heller appeared and announced he was leaving. As for me, I was publishing too much, would never be given tenure, and not even a cold piece of cod from the chippie. This is because I had refused to do what Howard Purnell had told me to do in 1977 - go to Swansea or have my career destroyed. So much for the School of Athens. With the Human Rights laws now in existence both could have been sued or even prosecuted as they should have been. Later on the nineties I met Hoffmann at Cornell, and he gave me a book of bad poetry. I mentioned Woodward to him as a memory of the long lost Heller, but only got a glare in reply.

The practical classes in the autumn of 1970 went well. The true and deeply hypocritical Graham Williams had not become fully apparent, although there was general unease among the class of 1971 with his false American accent disguise kit, complete with a forties "gee wizz". We wondered why he was still at a dump such as the EDCL and had not freaked out, the slang of the sixties, not the forties. I wrote up each experiment with great care, and completed all twenty three. My notebooks were taken by Graham Williams and I never saw them again. I would have expected that they be returned. They never were and were exhibited as model notebooks, or so I was told much later. This same man participated in the verbal harassment with Jeremy Jones. So unknown to me in 1970 the whole facade was a crumbling relic full of petty intrigue and malice. For me it was business as usual and very hard work. The digs were occupied by about four students whose names I entirely forget. They were good natured except for one loud mouthed Yorkshireman. The land lady gave us a vast amount of food on Sundays. She was a small lady and a fluent Welsh speaker. A little bit of relaxation was possible with a T. V. and if things got too obnoxious at the EDCL, there was always that Japanese Samurai sword in the corner. It had a very sharp edge, and apparently Mr Gill had captured it in the war. I sincerely hope that he was not captured himself. He seemed to be in good health but suffered a heart attack in the autumn of 1971 or winter of 1971 / 1972.

There was supposed to be some good research work going on at the EDCL, and on the whole this claim may be quite accurate. This work did not filter through, however, to the senior undergraduate class. Research was going on in the basement of the New Wing of the EDCL, but during my entire three years as an undergraduate I did not see any of it. The undergraduates were not allowed in to the research laboratories. In the entire three years of undergraduate life I never got past the new Lecture Theatre of the EDCL, so did not see the room in which I later worked as a graduate, room 262. I do not think that any of the class of 1971 knew what was going on in that room, far infra red spectroscopy. We were not allowed into the Soddy Laboratory or any other research laboratory. In that final year of 1970 / 1971 Mansel Davies's group was doing some research in the far infra red with an interferometer borrowed from the National Physical Laboratory, but as an undergraduate I knew nothing of its existence. There are some claims that J. M. Thomas and his group were the first to observe atoms on the ground floor of the New Wing of the EDCL. This looked like a submarine full of pipes, but undergraduates were not allowed near it. Recently I have come across many papers that reported the observation of atoms prior to the J. M. Thomas group.

As the end approached of the Christmas term of 1970 I think that I was still happy to go back to Pant y Bedw, but with nothing of the exhilaration of Christmas 1968. Unknown to me it was one of the last Christmases at Pant y Bedw, and not very much of a Christmas at that. I also had to study throughout the vacation. Around that time (December 1971) my father had to stop working as an underground manager or overman at Lliw colliery, which was a deep pit. For some time he was redundant and must have been feeling that the world had passed him by, leaving him with 30% pneumoconiosis. He was more irritable than ever, and blasted out at me very suddenly as I was studying one day, more or less asking what was the point of all that rubbish. The harsh hostility in his tone was a clear signal that I was no longer really welcome, which was no surprise. At that point the pressures were made much worse, pressure at home and pressure at the EDCL. The only small island of escape was the digs at Alexandra Road, and my attic room. The latter was the only place free of sudden verbal assault or overwhelmingly false authority. For the first time I began to feel that it may be better to leave for Aberystwyth early, but in the end stuck it out until about mid January 1971. By that time the final examinations were only about six months distant, so the atmosphere among the class of 1971 was one of nervous anticipation. The class was particularly anxious that they be lectured to clearly, but a vain hope. There is a lot wrong with the lecturing system itself if not tightly disciplined and clearly delivered. This is what I tried to do a few years later at UNCC.

The change over to practical organic chemistry took place in the middle of the Spring term of 1971. This meant classes in the new organic laboratory built behind the main EDCL Building. I had a look at the place on google maps while I am writing this, there seems to be a stub left of that organic chemistry laboratory but little else. It has a ludicrous existence now as some kind of pottery shop for something described as "Aberystwyth University". In the Spring Term of 1971 the eighteen students of the final year chemistry class were guided up the staircase past the stores, around an obscure corner, and sideways into the new organic teaching laboratory. It was an improvement over the reeking atmosphere of the old laboratory, full of ancient fumes. Each student had a cupboard of apparatus and I still have distinct memories of that new organic laboratory. For example I spent a short half term break in a synthesis on my own. On another occasion Sam Graham talked in quite an interesting way on analysis of compounds using NMR, interpreting chemical shift patterns in the manner of an organic and analytical chemist. There were interesting side rooms with ultra violet apparatus, and perhaps gas chromatography and infra red. All of that was totally destroyed in 1988 when the EDCL closed. Practical organic chemistry was my weakest subject so caused me the greatest amount of anxiety. This level of anxiety was increased by a practical examination. The course was not assessed entirely on that one practical examination, but it contributed quite a percentage.

The practical organic examination took place towards the end of that Easter term of 1971, but before that happened the EDCL was evacuated one day by a fire alarm. The class of 1971 huddled together in a white coated heap on the grass outside the old lecture theatre and started chanting: "burn, burn, please burn down, burn,

burn please burn down" in a scene from "The Lord of the Flies". Just before the final practical examination I was interviewed in Welsh by the BBC in that laboratory. I was the only one who could speak Welsh and was singled out by J. M. Thomas for the task. I improvised desperately as the other students watched and at one point let slip a remark that chemistry was not as important to me as cynghanedd. For this I was scowled at by JMT, who was already trying to use the BBC to get himself an FRS. He managed this at last in 1978 and vanished never to return. I believe he went to a place called Cambridge where no Welsh was spoken. During his tenure as head of department the EDCL greatly declined as a teaching laboratory, it graduated eighteen students in 1971 but only five in 1978. The entire sixties expansion had been pointless.

The practical examination itself consisted of an unseen synthesis ambushing the unsuspecting students. Russell Drury was next to me and set off at a furious pace. He had been a technician and thought that the examination was a race. There were crucibles, flasks, retorts and electric heaters flying everywhere until someone put him out of his misery and told him that it was an examination. At the end of the synthesis there were supposed to be blue crystals to be handed in to the supervisors, Sam Graham and the completely bald Knobhead (A. J. S. Williams) who had come so close to being roasted in effigy on the day of that fateful fire alarm. I was never so glad in all my life as when practical organic chemistry ended. It was time once again to move back home to Pant y Bedw for the Spring break of 1971. I carefully gathered the accumulated notes, which now consisted of notes from an almost incomprehensible series of lectures by Cadman, Young and Morrison whose details I forget completely and utterly. The latter's efforts were really awful, and gave me the greatest amount of trouble in the last paper of the finals. In the summer term there would be just two weeks or so of teaching followed by a break for revision, then the chop - the final examinations.

The entire vacation before my final term as undergraduate became one of the most intense few weeks of my life, day after day was spent in the little stone room of Pant y Bedw where I had studied for my Ordinary and Advanced level examinations at Pontardawe Grammar School. The day was broken only by a run around Gelliwastad, which in 1971 was still in its pristine condition, undespoiled by savages and monstrous wind turbines in the distance, flailing at and mocking democracy. This method of memorization worked well for hundreds of examinations between 1961 and 1971, and in the Spring of 1971 the class knew clearly that they finals would be on the third year only. The entire undergraduate class was aware by now of the fact that the three years would be wasted if they did badly in the finals. Some had already given up long ago and were just going through the motions. Others asked me for help with notes or problems and I tried to do my best. For me there was only one way out of that little stone cell. The method I used was to go through that set of notes many times over. They were all contained in one binder, so if I had lost that, or if it had been stolen, my entire there years and the rest of my life would have been lost and badly damaged. There was no easy way in 1971 of copying the notes. Gradually the whole binder was absorbed into my memory, and the time came around once more for the drive back to Aberystwyth and the Alexandra Road attic. As the summer drew on this became very warm and airless, but had the advantage of being quiet and undisturbed. My entire being was focused on the final examinations as never before.

There were two or more weeks of lectures and seminars to contend with, but no longer any practical work in the Summer term of 1971. My fellow students of the class of 1971 were tense and in some cases sombre and depressed. Not only had they to contend with appalling lectures, but also with job hunting and examinations which seemed like an assault into a machine gun. Some lecturers seemed to show a glimmer of understanding but the class was infuriated by A. J. S. Williams, who handed out a thick wad of notes in the very last lecture, doubling the course load only a couple of weeks before the examinations. He was not even going to bother lecturing on half of his course material. There were no student assessments and he could do what he liked. From this distance in time it is beyond belief. He was deeply disliked but due to the blatant freemasonry at Aberystwyth was allowed to go on working in the College well into his eighties, even without a Ph. D. degree. The disgust and anger of the class of 1971 knew no bounds. That was the worst incident I can remember, but Young was also dragging himself in a stupor into the class every week and giving catatonic lectures. A few years later he resigned or left for somewhere else. The whole degree system had come down to one big pointless drag, as the slang of the sixties and seventies would have it. The final two weeks of lectures sputtered to a halt and there was silence. Most of the class would have walked home to wherever they came from were it not for the finals themselves. Most never saw the lecturers again.

In June 2013 the discovery was made of my final year notes from Sept. 1970 to May 1971 and they have been posted on www.aias.us. There are almost five hundred pages which I memorized entirely. These notes were constructed after hours of effort in the library. The lectures themselves were often entirely incomprehensible, and sometimes it was a desperate effort to follow all the ramblings with the lecturer's back turned to the class, talking to the blackboard and scribbling on it. The lecturers were all tenured and there were no student assessments so they could do anything they wanted as long as they turned up and said something. In the following a brief description is given of each course and who gave it. These are historical source documents that accompany this autobiography on www.aias.us and its blog. The site and blog are archived every quarter at the British Library on www.webarchive.org.uk in its section on Science and Technology, AIAS.

The first course in my notes is "Molecular Properties" by Mansel Davies, later my Ph. D. supervisor, and was based almost entirely on his own books. So the class was seen as an opportunity to sell his books. The course dealt with the elements of spectroscopy of various kinds with the minimum of mathematical detail. Its archive is to be found in all detail on www.aias.us by clicking on "Myron Evans" then "Genealogy / Family History", then "Autobiography Part Two, College Notes". My notes are meticulously constructed with a fountain pen in writing that is much smaller than I use now, with diagrams carefully drawn in pencil. This course is 74 pages long and so must have covered one and a half or two terms. It does not go into sufficient mathematical detail for any deep knowledge of the subject, so in later years I found that my knowledge of quantum mechanics was lacking and I learned it all myself, making many original contributions to the subject. Mansel Davies finally admitted to me in private that he had no knowledge of quantum mechanical operators, so that explains the vagueness. I was not aware of the vagueness at the time, my whole mind was concentrated on making as good a set of notes as I could, memorizing them and in doing as well as I possibly could at examinations. Mansel Davies was difficult to follow, his injured hand meant that his handwriting was nearly unreadable, and these notes are therefore my own to all intents and purposes. He was also dogmatic, on one occasion I devised an answer to one of his set problems that was different from his own, and to the disgust of the class refused to accept my version. In graduate years however he did allow me some freedom, described in later chapters.

The second course was "Nuclear and Radiochemistry" by Cecil Monk, who was a terrible lecturer of quite good material. He advised the use of two course books that can be seen in the archives. This course amounts to 42 pages so probably covered one term only. Monk tried to keep up with developments and was the only staff member who ever learned to use the computer, amazing as this may seem these days. Again there is not much mathematical detail, not enough to go really deeply into the subject. Monk was a very good experimentalist and in the second war worked on a classified project, having started life as a gardener. He came from a good family that had fallen on bad times. He founded the Soddy Laboratory at the EDCL and was treated very badly when he retired. During the blitz in London he worked at Birkbeck College but again was appointed at the EDCL without competition. He was the only one of the lecturers who actually admitted this to me, and I was told that tenure is a matter of pure luck. On one occasion he was late arriving and was treated very roughly by J. M. Thomas, even after many years of service. So that put me off JMT for life.

The third course was "Chemical Bonding" by Mr Gee Wizz, Graham Williams the interrogator and career destroyer and hypocrite. He suggested a few course books which can be seen in the archive on www.aias.us. Obviously he had just constructed some brief notes from these books. He was a fairly good lecturer but I had to work hard in constructing my notes, so I produced something a lot better in quality, notes that were clear and which could be used in that deadly examination system which killed off so much talent. His group theory was taken almost entirely from a course book, so he may as well just have given us a list of books without delivering any lectures. The lecturers put in very little of themselves. This was covered up by a few words to the effect that the student at a university must work at learning. Too bloody true. My notes are meticulous and could be used today for any course with some updating.

The fourth course was "Enzyme Chemistry" by George Morrison, an arrogant and probably senile individual whose courses were incomprehensible. There were no student assessments so he got away with giving the same old rubbish for many years, par for the course. There were no course books and it was all I could do to make any sense of what he was saying. As far as I know he produced no research by that time, and very little in his entire career. There are a few elementary equations and reactions but the whole lot was a terrible jumble. His question or questions on enzyme chemistry gave me the most trouble in the final examinations, in the fifth paper on the last day, when I was nearing complete exhaustion.

The fifth course was "Heterogeneous Catalysis" by John Thomas. There are thirty seven pages of notes so he lectured only for one term. As for all the courses, the notes are meticulously prepared in very tiny handwriting. If they were typeset they would run to almost a thousand pages of print which I memorized completely. Again the lecturer used his own book, which either had to be bought or borrowed from the library if copies were available. I had to spend many hours in the library making sense of these lectures, which were delivered as sermons in an over loud voice. At the end most students were none the wiser. On occasion the nastiness of Thomas' temper became apparent once more as most of the students dozed. I suppose he expected us to see him as the great professor on the make, but we were either frantic with trying to understand him, or stone bored. Half the class did not bother to turn up at the degree ceremony, including the two other first class degrees, second and third to myself as the top first. There is almost a complete lack of mathematics, betraying his lifelong lack of knowledge of mathematics and computing. He was very good at getting others to work for him, but not me.

The sixth course was "Reaction Kinetics" by Phil Cadman, a very scruffy course needing a lot of work. There are forty three pages of notes, so again this must have been a one term lecture course. Very probably, Cadman was appointed to tenure without competition by Trotman-Dickinson, and would often not turn up for work. A vivid memory of my first few very uncomfortable weeks at the EDCL was his pronouncement that it was all politics. He was a poor lecturer of routing material taken from course books or journals and hastily written on some sheets of paper. Most of the lecturers just repeated their courses form year to year. Cadman also had a bad temper and a revolting attitude towards work people, for example road workers whom he castigated insanely one day within each of my hearing. My later co author Graham Davies of British Telecom, who later became a Dean of Engineering, described Cadman as the worst appointment ever made at the EDCL, which is really scraping the barrel. When the EDCL closed he somehow managed to get a job in physics, again with tenure intact.

The seventh course was "Organometallic Compounds" by Colin Young, who resigned his job about five or six years later. This course edged towards organic chemistry but Young was basically a lecturer in inorganic chemistry, who gave a long first year course on that subject. He was probably appointed by Trotman-Dickinson without advertisement, and it showed, because he was demoralized and unhappy at the EDCL, and what decent human being would not be? Young delivered his lectures in a heavy voice as if short of breath, and may not have been in the best of health. This had the effect of boring the class toothless, so it was a constant effort to take down the notes. All the formulae are written out meticulously as in the archives, but there were no recommended course books. Sometimes I felt sorry for Dr. Young, who was not a bad man at all.

The eighth course was on electron spin resonance and nuclear magnetic resonance by Alun Price, who was the best lecturer at the EDCL and a product of Pontardawe Grammar School. Again there is not much depth of mathematical detail, but the lecturer did make an effort to keep up with developments. He disliked Graham Williams intensely as did almost all at the EDCL and was overlooked for promotion. Only much later did I realize that these courses left out a lot of mathematics that I had to learn for myself. There are only thirty two pages of notes with suggested course books, so this was again a one term lecture course.

The ninth course was by Harry Heller on "The Conservation of Orbital Symmetry", which is based on quantum mechanics and the Woodward Hoffmann rules. Heller had next to no in depth knowledge of mathematical quantum mechanics but had a certain superficial skill at lecturing. He was quite a good practical organic chemist educated at a private university in Edinburgh called Heriot-Watt. He had the shattered remains of a refined Edinburgh accent and was an Austrian Jew by extraction. He wore a shining leather jacket as often as he could. On other occasions he was encased in a white lab coat. All the formulae are written out meticulously in my notes for this course, which is thirty six pages long, again a one term course. It was very difficult to know what Heller was talking about, so many hours were spent again in the library. He was an impatient demonstrator in the practical classes, and taught next to nothing. He made promises of fortunes to be made, but these never materialized, and as soon as Jeremy Jones arrived he made plans to leave. He was probably appointed without advertisement by Trotman-Dickinson. At Cornell much later I met Hoffmann and mentioned the Woodward-Hoffmann rules to him. He seemed to be unwilling to be associated with Woodward, and as usual at Cornell thought highly of himself. In his case this self opinion was probably justified, but in Heller's case it was second hand regurgitation to bored students.

The tenth course was "Carbohydrates" by Sam Graham, again without course books. Sam Graham could instill some enthusiasm to a class made catatonic by random verbal bombardment in a small, old lecture theatre with super hard benches. Despite my profound dislike for organic chemistry he did make me interested in the optical activity of such molecules as the sugars, and I made many original contributions to this subject with molecular dynamics simulation. This course has thirty four pages of notes and some tutorial problems and is again an ideal set of notes even now. Sam Graham was also in charge of some NMR tutorials in practical organic chemistry. He was an able organic chemist who had been severely injured in an explosion and died at work shortly after I left the EDCL, maybe of a stroke caused by the after effects of this accident. He was a Scot and was interested in my trip to Mull and Iona. He surprised and offended me greatly however when he tried to pressurize me into going to Swansea, showing a bad temper and an ability to cover up corruption for careerism. This was the problem with nearly all of those cats appointed from afar without competition and imported into Wales for no reason other than careerism. There are some loose pages on the alkaloids which may also have been part of this course.

The eleventh course was on "Metal Complexes" by John Bowen, perhaps in cooperation with A. J. S. Williams. It is quite a good course but on material which could never spark my interest. As mentioned already, Williams infuriated the class by handing out a large wad of formulae in the very last lecture, showing complete contempt for the students. The course is 41 pages long and again meticulously prepared. I attended all lectures, practical classes, seminars and tutorials, the most excruciatingly boring being the ones on Saturday mornings with George Morrison and A. J. Williams. Both of whom being disliked intensely by the students of the class of 1971.

The finals were due to start about 31st May 1971 and to last five days, consisting of five three hour examinations each morning in the Old College, the Gothic cave by the sunny sea and crazy golf course, full of sun and scenery and pointless tourists doing pointless things. As usual for Aberystwyth the weather became blazingly warm as the examinations approached, and I slowly cooked in my attic room, mind detached from physiology. Some of the time was spent in the library of the EDCL, which was looted in the late eighties and reduced to a ragged smashed up box by the time I saw it last in 1993. It was then demolished completely, and of course, has never existed. The discarded students of the class of 1971 huddled together towards the back of the library as if in some fetid trench. There was nothing to do with the appalling conduct of A. J. S. Williams but to try to sink his notes into the mind. These were of far poorer quality than my own and had just been hurriedly scribbled together. My binder of completed notes was very carefully taken backwards and forwards between Alexander Road and Buarth, on which perched the EDCL like a prison with an extension that looked like a big prefab or a failed sixties high rise that got so far and threatened to do a leaning tower of Pisa. I suppose that the staff were scribbling out some questions or were looking forward to their long summer break on full pay. Some of the questions must have been repeated for forty years. Even the students in the digs were actually studying.

I cannot recall how the schedule of the final examinations was given to us, I suppose we had to find out for ourselves and that would be healthy for us. By that time I knew how to get to the door of the Old College, off Tom Cat Alley towards the graveyard. By now even the graves have been torn up and laid down flat, systematic desecration. None of it was remotely reminiscent of the crude propaganda put out eternally by the College to scrape up students from anywhere (except Wales). As the end of May approached we were at the low point of existence, no longer students, and completely uninspired. I had no time even to be angry, my mind had been focused on the tip of an atom sized needle, and all else was blotted out. On 26th May 1971 it was my 21st birthday and my parents paid a surprise visit. I was very tense but tried my best to indulge in conversation. They chatted a while with the landlady, Mrs Gill, and very kindly gave me a birthday gift of a new fountain pen. Having taken no examination themselves they could not have known what it was like. I did use the fountain pen in the finals and attacked the papers with it, as with the sword Excalibur. They did not tell me that my grandfather William John Evans was seriously ill. He died on June 8th 1971 and I was later told of the funeral. This was considerate of my parents at that critical time.

The schedule of papers was known and I implemented my method of concentrating on each examination the night before it was due. Every detail of the relevant section of the notes was meticulously packed into my mind. This meant that I knew a lot of facts, and developed techniques to solve problems, but the imaginative and creative process of self learning was missing. The actor knows a lot of script but does not write it. The day of the first examination should have been a Monday logically, but perversely it could have been a Friday. Whatever day it was I made my way quickly from Alexander Road to the Gothic pile. I remember that it was a warm sunny day, but saw nothing at all, and heard nothing at all. The class of 1971 were gathered together as if in a trench, awaiting the order to walk into a machine gun, but not too quickly, on a nice sunny day. They were completely silent, looking ghost pale and intensely frightened, very Gothic indeed. They were about to walk into destiny. If the ink marks they left behind them were suitable, the class of degree would determine their lives. If not they would fail miserably. There were stone walls and a closed door. It opened as if by a spell cast from within, and on shaky legs the class walked in. There were rows of desks, looking like rows of guillotines, and on each desk was placed the examination paper. A transplanted lecturer sat at the head of the silent scene.

At that point of an examination I looked for the easiest question to devour, not taking too long about it, and attacked it ferociously, emptying my mind like a ready mixed concrete lorry all over the desk. There was no time to look up, except at the clock whose ticks I could not hear. The paper had been printed, and not scribbled upon as in earlier examinations, so at least it could be read easily. Some questions were easy - a matter of pouring out my mind, others were awkward. Mansel Davies for example had written something like “Entropy - discuss”, and had scribbled down the first thing that had come into his mind in the middle of a committee meeting. That kind of question is dangerously vague. There was the accumulated mind-junk of a year to get rid of, about twelve course in all. I aimed as usual at getting through the easiest questions quickly, to build time for the later ones, or to have time to spare if there was any difficulty. I dodged past any problems that I did not know how to solve with ease. The easiest questions were from lecturers who had put some real effort into the course. I have a vague memory of logarithms being allowed, or logarithmic books placed on the desk to stop any cribbing. The worst part of the examination evaporated into hard work, the sound of a nib racing across a paper, which is the sound of silence. As the room warmed up the heat became as a glass house, and if I ran out of an examination answer book I had to get another one as quickly as I could. Sometimes as the end of the three hours approached my writing became frenzied in an attempt to pack in as much as I could. This routine was much the same from 1961 to 1971.

The time ran out and the captive lecturer must have told us to stop writing or similar. I cannot recall whether were had to hand in the answer books or leave them on the desk. I walked out of the intensely stuffy room and quickly home to Alexandra Road to start the work for the next examination the following day. My mind emptied itself almost immediately of the course work that has had just been examined, about two or three courses per examination. I worked up to about eleven p.m or midnight on the next examination, and the routine was followed the next day, and the next and the next. That left just one three hour paper where the junk by Morrison had to be gone through. I remember clearly that that paper, the last one, gave me the most difficulty because Morrison’s lecturing was non existent, and full of the most abstract rubbish imaginable. I think that he was already senile at the age of fifty from smoking endless cigars in a laboratory full of enzymes. The class of 1971 loathed his attitude and mannerisms. They loathed being in the hands of such a relic. I forced my way through that last three hour paper and with a sense of great relief, walked back again to Alexandra Road, this time at a much slower pace. I finally noticed that all around me there were people walking through a town called Aberystwyth. Some had been playing crazy golf by the sunny sea. It was indeed a sunny day - about June 5th 1971.

It was then a matter of waiting a long time for the results. My binder was carefully shelved. For the first time in a decade there were no more examinations, or so I thought. It had not been made clear that there was to be one more examination on the same day as the results were announced. This was a verbal question and answer examination. Not knowing of this I did not prepare for it. I did not want to go anywhere near the EDCL, so walked around with my camera taking photographs. The class had to remain in Aberystwyth until the results were announced. I was curious what the interior of a pub looked like after three years of echoing and vomiting alcoholic abstraction, so went in for some cider. We used to drink this at the end of the hay harvest, (cywain gwair). It tasted like bitter toxic ethanol in a dark cave, without the sun and the smell of hay. That was the first and last time I took a look at the interior of a pub, unless asked in by colleagues whom I did not want to offend. I recall walking down the park towards the railway line and narrow gauge railway line to Devil's Bridge, and gradually my exhausted mind began to recover from an massive overload of facts. I walked across to the River Rheidol and took some photographs of the river against the light of the sky - the ancient sea soaked light of western Britain. This was much better than some poisonous fume cupboard or some eccentric fool of a lecturer holding me in thrall like La Belle Dame Sans Merci. Unknown to me my grandfather died on 8th June, perhaps during one of my walks by the banks of the Rheidol. He had crossed over to the other side of the river to find his wife Gwenllian, who had died in 1944. They now lie in an unmarked grave in Callwen, and deserve the finest of destinies.

After a while I became bored with Aberystwyth and its pointless tourists, but did not know what lay ahead of me. Now I know that I was completely vulnerable to corruption in the system. I was saved from this because the undergraduate degree is externally balanced and kept up to a given national standard, and a department would do itself good by producing good degrees. I had no idea of whether I had done well or not. I knew that there were graduate students and that I wanted to be one of them at Aberystwyth, but did not know that I had to win a studentship - the Dr. Samuel Williams Studentship. I had a vague idea that there was a quota of studentships. There was in fact only one, and I had to win it. I had a vague idea that a first class degree would be something that I could keep for life, and indeed I am very proud of it now. I began to feel that the time for going back to Pant y Bedw was coming around again, but it was difficult to live there too. All depended on the degree results and I could still land up in a coal mine or factory. I walked slowly up to the EDCL and into the large lecture theatre for the last time as an undergraduate. The class of 1971 was assembled in the front two or three rows, and to my horror J. M. Thomas announced that there was going to be another examination. The class looked as if it would throw up. He gradually made his point - only a few students would be subjected to the torture of a verbal examination to take place that same day. These were borderline cases between classes of degree. The rest of us had to wait and assemble in the afternoon in the small library and common room of the old building of the EDCL to hear the results being intoned by Mr John Bowen. I think I went home to the digs for a while, or took a walk.

Guillotine time came around and we were ushered into

the small library. John Bowen began to read out the results from the bottom up. Any failures first, followed by pass degree, third class, lower second and so on. My heart was pounding like road hammer, I remember these minutes the most vividly of almost my whole undergraduate time. Upper second and my name had still not been called out, so I threw up my arms as if I had scored a goal, and a startled John Bowen looked out of the corner of his eye. There were three firsts, two ladies from the South Wales Valleys and myself. Even at that point I could have still landed up in a coal mine, because a first class degree meant nothing to my father if he could not see me earning money or becoming independent. I was told to go to the office of the head of department, J. M. Thomas and innocently walked in. This was the first time I had been talked to by the two professors as if they wanted something. In fact the College had told them that I had won one of its studentships, which were shared out among departments. Chemistry had managed to get itself a Dr. Samuel Williams Studentship via yours truly. Unknown to me I had just earned the best undergraduate degree in the history of the chemistry department. I was not told that at the time, but was just asked with whom I wanted to work. I chose Mansel Davies because I had seen some of his research apparatus, and had been put on guard by that outburst from J. M. Thomas earlier in the year. Thomas did not look at all pleased, in fact he looked rather evil and I stood carefully between him and the door. I suppose I was silage that refused to be eaten. They had hogged me at the first opportunity but they were supposed to let me have the time to talk with other staff members. In reality I was feeling elated and wanted to get out of there as soon as I could. I knew very well the type of people they were, unthinkingly ambitious, letting no student get in their way. So I got out of their way. I had earned my degree despit them.

It was decided that I would work with Mansel Davies and I walked out of the room. I was given a Thesis by G.

W. F. Pardoe to study over the vacations and this must have been handed over to me by Mansel Davies. So I must have been summoned in to his office at some point. This was opposite room 262 in the New Building. There did not seem to be any time for goodbyes, and the class of 1971 melted away into the dark rain. I remember one distressed student being shocked at a third class degree, and being brushed off impatiently in the corridor by his tutor. I emerged from the EDCL into a cold shower of summer rain, and half ran back to the digs. Mrs Gill was happy at the first class degree, and I must have been allowed to phone through the results to my parents, who greeted it in a mildly pleased but subdued manner. There was no way for them to understand what it meant, and in fact, neither did I. The other students in the digs congratulated me generously, and I asked for digs from Mrs. Gill for the first year graduate. The ordeal by ink and fire was over at last and I took another few walks around. On one of these I bumped into Pete Strydom, who for the first time told me he was from South Africa. Then the binder with notes was carefully packed and taken back to Pant y Bedw.

This was the first time that anyone from Craig Cefn Parc had earned a first class degree, and one or two articles were published about it in the newspapers. I tried to explain that I was going to do a Ph. D. in far infra red spectroscopy but obviously that had no effect at all. I had walked home from Pontardawe Grammar School with my friend Huw Griffiths, and he told me that he did not think I would so as well as a first class degree. I remember those well meant gestures of congratulation. The farm of Pant y Bedw was still intact, and there are photographs of that era on www.aias.us. One is of my father looking sallow eyed and none too friendly, another of the sunset on an unspoiled Mynydd Betws, now hideously destroyed by turbines. There would be a degree ceremony in July 1971 and for the sake of my parents I decided to attend that. My attempt at pleasing them with a first class degree had barely worked, showing indeed that it meant next to nothing to them sometimes. At other times they seemed very proud of it. The problem was that they were planning to sell Pant y Bedw without telling me anything at all. For many years it remained a gaunt ruin, and then was finished off with development. Garish ticky tacky replacing the homely farm. The degree ceremony meant ordering a graduate gown and a cap from Ede and Ravenscroft and going to a photographer in Swansea to have my picture taken in a suit. I looked like a self satisfied cat emerging from a dustbin, the street of a thousand dustbins near the pier. All of that dampness was forgotten at Pant y Bedw.

The first thing I did on getting home was to turn all the hay for my father, the whole farm in a day by hand. I was thinking of showing him that I could be a labourer, as he wanted. He looked a bit happy for a short while, but how can anyone be happy with dust in the lungs? Then the fields were baled and put into the hayshed, the harvest was over for another year. I could help him as the prodigal son returned, but that was the last hay harvest, Pant y Bedw would soon be gone forever. That was the last summer at Pant y Bedw, and I spent a lot of it in my tiny room there looking out over the field, trees and hedges towards Gelliwastad, reading and rereading a book I had bought for myself in Swansea - Kenneth Clark's "Civilization". This book is a classic and based on the BBC2 series of the same name, the first series to be produced in colour. I have been reading it and watching it ever since. One of the many things that sticks in the mind from that book is that one cannot define civilization but one can recognize barbarism instantly. It was with difficulty that I could tear myself away from the book back to the rather boring Thesis by Pardoe that I had been given to read. I suppose it was the only thing that Mansel Davies could think of. He was totally unprepared for my Ph .D. Thesis and soon let me go my own way, hardly knowing or understanding anything of what I was doing as long as I did not do anything to affect his own reputation. He always assumed that he had one. He did of a kind, but not the type of reputation that interested me, being based on image but not science. Lord Clark was opinionated but had a knowledge of his subject, and the programme series was put together brilliantly by the producers. Its choice of music is particularly memorable. The book had an instant effect on me because it brought together concepts and ideas in a way that always make me think and which I had never seen before. So the summer was spent for a few weeks only with two books, "Civilization" and G. W. F. Pardoe on the Debye plateau. I thought that this was a place in Antarctica that I was going to explore. It turned out to be the end point of the Debye relaxation theory, the point at which the theory went bananas. I have been interested in such things ever since.

Pardoe had been a Ph. D. Student of Mansel Davies and had worked at the National Physical Laboratory (NPL) with Gebbie, Chantry and Chamberlain. The NPL had developed Fourier transform spectroscopy in the far infra red and had given Mansel Davies a spectrometer on permanent loan. I may have been allowed a glance at this spectrometer on that day in June 1971. I studied the Thesis very closely and many times, but making little sense out of it. I was also very tired after three years as undergraduate so increasingly turned to"Civilization". The book opens with a Viking raid on Paris, the Viking art being contrasted with that of the classical world, a world which fell apart because it was paradoxically barbaric. Its art became stylized to the point of catatonia, one marble column looking exactly like the other. The Vikings (my ancestors in some branches) carved vigorously in wood and built ships, and could navigate brilliantly. They could be a little cutting on occasions, but so could the Romans and Greeks. The high point of Celtic art, the Book of Kells, seemed to outshine them all. This was the insular style that started under my distant ancestor, St. David, and spread to Ireland. Kenneth Clark mentioned that he had a home near Iona off Mull as a young man, and I was fascinated by this mysterious island that had produced such brilliance, a manuscript of the type that the world had never seen before, and scribed among the pounding waves and rocks.

In contrast Pardoe's Thesis read like the dead, it was produced with the best that science could provide, but the result of that work needed something much more. It needed the input that my own mind could provide, new ideas that the world had not seen before. It needed the imagination of the scribes who produced the Book of Kells. I began to feel that this was my way in life, to produce something new like an artist within the rigours of science. I had to learn, master then add to the learning and I could never let anything get in my way. This is what happened in Europe from late mediaeval times onwards, the great flowering of architecture known as the perpendicular and Gothic styles, the eternal questioning of someone like Peter Abelard, and the manuscript work of the great scribes. I began to realize that undergraduate work had been drudgery, a blotting paper existence. Things were not fully formed in my mind at that point in time as the degree ceremony approached, but for the first time I felt that I wanted to get back to Aberystwyth. In 1968 I had not wanted to go there at all. The return was helped a good deal by the fact that my father had bought a new car and let me have the use of his old one. This meant that I could drive up to the computer unit from the EDCL to process data - contained in a pack of cards and a roll of paper tape. So perhaps he was pleased after all.

The degree ceremony was at the Great Hall in Aberystwyth, a place that I had never been to before. Less than half of the class of 1971 attended and I did not meet any of them, but it was a way of thanking my parents for their efforts on my behalf. I was dressed up in the gown and cap when it arrived and sent to Swansea for a portrait in a suit and tie. This mediaeval intrusion was photographed in the field, as I held a rake and pretended to turn the already harvested hay. Those blistering days of the fifties had resulted in this meeting of mind and time. The programme for the degree ceremony indicated that it would be in the Great Hall at Aberystwyth, a place that I had never seen. The area was populated with parents and students walking around like owls in broad daylight. When my name was announced I walked up to get the certificate and gave it to my parents. They seemed proud this time of the certificate scribed with Summa Cum Laude, with highest distinction. Not anywhere as magnificent as the Book of Kells, but distinctly civilized. They framed and kept the certificate through many years of further hardship. A photograph of the three of us that day was taken by Mrs Gill in the infinitesimal back garden of her house, and I drove them back to Pant y Bedw.

I did not work in industry that summer, I was too tired and needed a rest. In order to keep my father as content as possible, I stayed a lot in my room studying. The book "Civilization" is lavishly illustrated in colour, and one of the first things I saw was the famous chi rho iota page of the Book of Kells, Christi autem generatio, with the page dominated by the Greek letter chi, denoting Christi. The incredible detail can be studied for a lifetime, and much later I saw the original in Trinity College Dublin. The inks have lasted almost a thousand years and a half. It was scribed in a small cell about the size of my own small room at Pant y Bedw, a room just larger than a single bed. At the end of each term or some exhausting set of examinations I would read a lot in this room, all kinds of things from Sherlock Holmes to Silas Marner, and often studied in it until the early hours. The time after examinations was always the golden time, when I could read anything I liked and could take a walk in working clothes with the perennially faithful sheepdog. This page is the masterpiece of the insular style, and based on geometry, with the infinitely beautiful triskelion interwoven magically. Sometimes little cats and mice appear beneath the letters, as if the scribe was getting bored or asking for divine intervention to get rid of mice. I am not sure whether any self respecting mouse would be found on a place as wild as Iona, which I visited during my Ph. D. If there is any civilization this must be it I thought, and if it could be produced in a small stone cell, I could use my mind in the same way and justify my existence. I do not think that any scribe, sheltering from the savage Atlantic, would be too much interested in promotion or a pay rise. His motivation would have been much different, and he would have known it as the glorification of the Deity. The Baconian scientist works for the glorification of nature, not for committee work or tenure.

There is a tremendous condensation of energy in the Book of Kells, albeit abstract and reminiscent of an age long past but always present. This energy can be found in the David of Bernini, whose sculpture I found to be finished to perfection. Bernini also designed St Peter's and carved and cast the reredos out of bronze. This is of a much later age than the Book of Kells - the former scribed in the simple Celtic scriptorium and relying on the individual, the latter in the high renaissance and relying on organization. I found that such things could be achieved by the human mind, and hoped immediately that I could make my contribution, and would be allowed to make my contribution. In this spirit of hope and enlightenment I gradually decided to move back early to Aberystwyth, where I expected to be given the respect due to a Graduate Scholar and Top First. My father and mother reluctantly accepted my decision, none of us were ever happy at any departure. None of us was ever happy at the intrusion of the outside world into our little corner of civilization.

CHAPTER THREE

The last I saw of Pant y Bedw in that August of 1971 were two grey haired people waving goodbye in the driving mirror. I drove towards the future on the dirt road towards Rhyddwen Road, then up to Mynydd y Gwair and Mynydd Betws, then in the pristine beauty of late summer, unchanged for ten thousand years, now desecrated by turbines, pylons and gas pipelines as humanity rushes headlong to destruction. Down the steep mountain side to Rhyd Amman and across the flat fat land to Llandeilo, the land of Deheubarth. The road ran close to Tal y Llychau as it had done in the fifties, past the lakes and Abbey founded by Rhys ap Gruffudd, and after many tortuous bends reached the main road to Llanbedr Pont Steffan, across a range of hills to the Aeron. I was suddenly confronted by the sea and drove up the coast to Aberystwyth. The same attic room was awaiting me and for a while I had the place to myself before the other students arrived. The car was parked on Mrs Gill's doorstep. Later I was given a ticket for parking a car on this doorstep, on the wrong side of a road, as if a road had a right and wrong side. This was a made up offence by some lurking copper looking for promotion. I paid it in vomiting disgust and he probably became chief constable. I turned the car around in the same parking space and doorstep and was never bothered again.

After breakfast I walked up to the EDCL in an infinitely cautious state of mind because most of the class of 71 had evaporated in anger and never looked back. After reading Kenneth Clark all summer I knew that there was civilization and that it originated in the mind, but after reading Pardoe all summer I was not so sure where it could be found in the EDCL. The undergraduate experience had made me very cautious of Mansel Davies, he was unstable and pretentious. I recall being given an audience in the imperial office opposite room 262, which had strange doors leading in to it. There was a set of double doors. Much later I found that these had been designed by Orville-Thomas for a custom made infra red laboratory. Mansel Davies had forgotten all about me and the Thesis by Pardoe, which I handed back dutifully. I have vague recollections of a note being scribbled out and handed over. Only then did I notice the missing fingers. I thought he had shaken hands with too many politicians, but they were blown off during a synthesis in Cambridge. A synthesis should have warned me that I was going to be put through the same dangerous process, as if Mansel Davies was reliving his younger days. He was a post doctoral for a while at Peterhouse, and gave the impression that he had met a lot of famous people there. At some point I must have been told to go to room 262, which was a quiet room looking out on the green bank of the Buarth. I was soon dissuaded of great expectations. I may have been a Graduate Scholar, but all I was going to get was part of a long laboratory side bench and a chair. Alongside were spaces for other graduate fodder.

I was also dissuaded of any detailed supervision, because Mansel Davies left to answer a phone or go to a committee and never returned that day. There was blankness and I wondered what I was doing there, not for the first or last time. I thought that a supervisor should supervise. By pure luck there were two students there who helped me get started: Arnold Ivan Baise of the University of Witwatersrand South Arica, who was finishing a Masters course, and Graham J. Davies of Swansea who was finishing a Ph. D. course. Arnold Baise taught me the use of the instrument at the back of me on the old rough bench. It was a Grubb Parsons / NPL far infra red interferometer. This instrument had been drawn out in Pardoe's Thesis and in reality it was a box of electronics attached to optics, two mirrors at right angles to each other. It was quite easy to operate and Arnold Baise was a good teacher. When operating, a beam of light from a high pressure lamp was cut by a rotating blade before passing through a cell containing a sample, and finally into a detector that worked by heat, called a Golay detector. One mirror was stepped forward by a motor and at each step a paper tape machine punched out a code. A mountain of tape slowly accumulated on the floor, and the noise of the paper tape punch reverberated behind double closed doors. Inside this cave of Grendel I worked to produce my Ph. D. I was told many years later by Mansel Davies that it was one of the best two he had produced. In fact, I had produced it using my own imagination. The truth is that Mansel Davies did not contribute anything directly, but signed post doctoral applications as the supervisor. I won these three post doctorals on my own merit. The critically important thing is that he allowed me to publish my own scientific papers as a student. That had never been done before at the EDCL.

A circular hole had been cut in the rough old wooden bench to make room for what what was called a pot. This was a steel chamber made in the EDCL workshop by three ascerbic and anti heroic technicians: John Poley, Bob Meredith and Harold Jolley, who were second class citizens but allowed to wear white coats. Fortunately for me it took a long while before I had any occasion to ask them to do something, that took great persuasion and discussion of politics, but once they started they did their best and were all good people. It was very difficult to get anything done because J. M. Thomas would use the workshop facilities to build models for his London lectures and his assault on F. R. S. Mountain and generally hog everything for his own group. Arnold Baise explained that this pot was attached to a high pressure cell made with thick quartz windows and designed with hope to withstand several hundred atmospheres of pressure with bolts and O rings. They could have burst at any time, the cell was not designed in any scientific way. I used a wrench to bolt them down as much as I could, gouging the metal as I tightened up the bolts. The pressure of gas was built up by heating the pot with electric tape, and a Budenberg gauge slowly began to show the pressure, sometimes well over a hundred atmospheres. This process was the reverse of a submarine diving to deep waters until its structure would begin to implode. All I could do was hope that the cell would not explode and finish me off early, as so many late rivals would have wished. Mansel Davies never came anywhere near the apparatus, and other members of staff were somewhat reluctant too. The paper tape punch recorded what was known as an interferometer in the terrible jargon of physics. This was a pattern made by one beam of light mixing with the other. A piece of black polymer filtered out the region known in utter obscurity as the far infra red, a kind of Beardmore Glacier at the ends of the earth, wild, unknown and inaccessible, leading on to the Debye P ateau. The far infra red lay between the infra red and the microwave, in room 262.

I was also taught by Arnold Baise that the paper tape output had to be processed by the Elliott 4130 computer of the College. It had about 48 kilobytes of memory, microscopic by today's standards, and this memory had to be shared out among the entire College. The paper tape had to be attached to a pack of cards with a rubber band, and taken up to the Computer Unit on Penglais Campus, a mile away up a hill. I had not been told of this before I started as a student, and having an old third or fourth hand car was pure luck. Otherwise I would have had to do a lot of walking in the rain, and would have had to dry out the paper tape and cards on a borrowed cooker or Bunsen burner. My fuel costs were never reimbursed of course. There was no internet and there were no personal computers. These did not arrive until about 1985 / 1986 with the IBM Systems 1 and 2. My first wife and I had the first IBM System 2 near Kingston, New York. The processing procedure was known as a Fourier transform, a long program written at the National Physical Laboratory and loaded on to magnetic tape in the air conditioned room where the Elliott 4130 was kept. The pack of cards and paper tape was handed in to be processed through a little hatch in an office. Then came the best part of the journey, a plastic cup of machine made coffee below the geography tower as it was called, a hideous box of concrete. This coffee tasted anonymous, but it was liquid and contained caffeine. It could have been tea or even chocolate, or if the porter was careless, a mixture.

My entire being was focused into obtaining far infra red spectra, a strange kind of civilization but with imagination waking from the fog in which Aberystwyth was often enveloped. Minds also seemed to be enveloped in fog, the clarity of mathematical analysis was missing. I had tremendous energy and a burning desire to get those spectra, curiosity unbound like Prometheus. When told to synthesize the deadly cyanogen gas, I did so with the enthusiasm of kamikaze. Mansel Davies had chosen this molecule as a matter of theory only, it had a large quadrupole moment. That means nothing to balanced people, it is simply that the molecule has a particular shape to it. The fact that it was toxic, inflammable and so on was an irrelevance, student silage was at hand. The fixation with hyper dangerous synthesis was a left over from those fingerless days in Cambridge, the difference being that the student could be used as spare fingers, and if blown up, everything else too. It would merely be a matter of cleaning up strawberry jam from the floor, and that could be left to a porter. For over forty years I have wondered intensely why Mansel Davies did not buy a lecture bottle of this deadly poison, now at last I have the answer. There was nothing for it but to drip sulphuric acid on to a mountain of potassium cyanide and trap the gas in a solvent. This would have finished off the entire town of Aberystwyth had it not been for a fume cupboard, a device in which dangerous chemical reactions bubble away.

The only problem was that Room 262 did not have a fume cupboard, and even Mansel Davies realized that it could fill with cyanogen which might leave behind dead post doctorals, graduate students, technicians and porters, and even worse, leak in to his office. So for a long and pointless time this synthesis was attempted in a fume cupboard adjoining the grand main staircase of the EDCL in a tiny room. I had to stand out almost in the corridor and consumed all the potassium cyanide in the stores, bottle after bottle. The fume cupboard must have been working, otherwise none of the EDCL would have survived, and neither would the Principal in the Old College or wherever he was. Having trapped the gas I had to take it the entire length of the EDCL back to room 262 and take a spectrum. It was meticulously plotted and revealed nothing but solvent, the gas had not dissolved. I did accumulate some high quality solvent spectra which came in useful later. After many solvents were attempted and with a worldwide shortage of potassium cyanide looming, I saw Mansel Davies approaching rapidly in the long narrow corridor one day, and I said "No luck". He snarled "No luck in what context?" and kept on walking. I have often seen people walking away from a problem, or an injustice, or a crime, or questions about tenure.

This was a slippery slope and a stupid waste of my Ph. D. Somehow or another I managed to get Mansel Davies to expend a small amount of money and buy a lecture bottle of cyanogen, a small cylinder with a valve easily available commercially. I was also switched for a while to work on a liquid crystal called MBBA, which is an acronym for para methoxy benzylidene para n butyl aniline. This was much safer, needing only an ordinary infra red cell. These liquid crystals later became computer displays and so on, and Arnold Baise had left to research on them in the States, Temple University. There are a few patents by him on Google Scholar. I was also doing a great amount of study on the theory behind the experimental work, the Wyllie and Brot itinerant librator and collision induced spectra. The itinerant librator is not a drunk man looking at the thistle, it just means a small modification of the theory of Brownian motion. Without this modification the Debye theory plateaus out and never returns to sanity.

It goes bananas in the far infra red. The theory of collision induced absorption was needed for the work on cyanogen, if it was going to be properly interpreted. Both types of theory were well beyond Mansel Davies and I was well and truly on my own. The full blown theory of collision induced absorption requires the horrendous Clebsch Gordan coefficients. The electronics of the interferometer developed faults quite often, and each time this happened there was a long delay before the electronics workshop could get around to the problem. These were Dyson Jones and Irfon Williams, who were worked into the ground because they were very good at their work. Both were fluent Welsh speakers. Dyson Jones drove up from Aberaeron every day. I do not think that either was wildly delighted to be at the EDCL, leading a basement existence sandwiched between hysteria as apparatus needed to be fixed before than instantly, a little known phenomenon of relativity.

So for weeks I would be left waiting for apparatus to be fixed, and used the time to develop theory, which meant learning the programming language called Algol. This was much better designed than the later FORTRAN. After a while I realized that to write a code the cards had to be punched out on a machine, and all that was needed after that was a data card. I began to spend more and more time on this, and discovered that there was a library of programs by the Numerical Algorithms Group (N. A. G.). Among these were curve fitting programs that could be used to fit a theory to data, so I could describe the liquid crystal spectra with the Wyllie itinerant oscillator and with the related theory of Brot. I worked like this with manic ferocity, curiously observed by the pipe smoking Alun Price, who guarded a Honeywell hand calculator and would be extremely reluctant to let anyone else use it. He looked at me pounding the keys with my eyes blazing, and the forgotten smoking pipe almost caught fire, it threatened a solvent explosion in the stores next door. Scientific papers had not yet entered my mind, so I could not be told just yet that I was publishing too much. Later, Price would peer over my shoulder in the library and whisper close to my left ear: "Not another paper". No doubt he meant well, and came from Pontardawe Grammar School as I did. He was a very careful careerist who had been appointed to tenure without competition. In fact everyone at the EDCL was appointed this way with very few exceptions, so it was a tightly closed shop. My work day gradually extended from about nine in the morning, stuffed with bacon, to about five almost continuously, then a dive into a fish and chip shop followed by more hours at the EDCL up to about ten or eleven at night, complete with keys to digs and EDCL. I had to sign the working late book at the EDCL entrance and that gradually filled up with my signatures. There was a cult of students and post doctorals working late at the EDCL, one student called Dylan Mo re used to play a twelve string guitar while boiling benzene at midnight in a baked bean tin the Heller cellar. Some like rum, some like benzene. So anyone walking in from the street would have found the powers of darkness exalted, with Dylan Moore chanting Bob Dylan. At the other end of the EDCL it was cyanogen bubbling from the pot or cauldron: bubble, toil and poisonous trouble, and the rhythmic, drum like pounding of the paper tape punch. Any visitor expecting sun, sea and scenery would not have stayed long, especially on a moonless night.

As the autumn of 1971 drew on this delightful manner I felt the need to get the poison out of my lungs by athletics on the Olympic standard track at Penglais. As with all good things it has now been torn apart. In those days it had about six lanes and a 200 metre straight, and was fully equipped with long jump, triple jump, high jump, pole vault, hammer, javelin shot and discus, and steeplechase barriers, water jump and hurdles. I ran 25 laps or about six miles every Saturday, so at the end I felt like corrugated iron, a crippled cat on a hot tin roof with two legs missing. This was far too long a distance and it took a long time to learn to cut it down to 200 metre intervals. My best distance was the 60 metres short sprint, and best time was 6.92 seconds for 60 metres at Zurich in 1990, when I was forty years old. The world record is about 6.40 seconds. Gradually the 200 metre intervals were supplemented by an eight mile road run on Saturdays and a five thousand metres on the track on Sundays. I was never a natural athlete so all of this was always the hardest work imaginable. Without it though I would have been done in by formulae and chemicals. The fairly good living at the digs had been clouded by the fact that Mr Gill had a heart attack that autumn, and by a troublesome student. I felt it was time to look for a room in Cwrt Mawr, the graduate student accommodation, and got a room there in about May or June of 1972.

The Christmas break was spent again at Pant y Bedw but by that time my father had been forced by dust to retire from his job as Overman or Underground Manager and it was a subdued time, and now Aberystwyth meant the opportunity to use my own mind. I was not quite free of examinations, in the first year or so of the Ph. D. there was as desperately dreary course by Cadman and it was back to the old routine of scribbling away then up to the library. There was also a course by Mansel Davies on dielectrics. There were still examinations to contend with. There was also a course in scientific German in which I learned das wasser kocht nicht, the water does not boil. This is not quite Goethe, but I passed the examination in half the time allotted. I was sick to the skin of examinations, and I think that that was really the last written one of my life apart from citizenship examinations in Florida and New York. For the unwary there was a lecture examination half way through the Ph. D. and a verbal examination at the end. In my case with John Rowlinson, Mansel Davies and Graham Williams. The work on MBBA and cyanogen developed during 1972, the year in which I submitted my first two papers for publication in Journal of the Chemical Society, Faraday Transactions II, Chemical Physics. The first was submitted with Ian Larkin and (in part) Mansel Davies on 30th August 1972, and the second under my own name on 4th Dec. 1972. The entire texts of all my papers are available in the Omnia Opera Section of www.aias.us, so these first two papers can be read in all detail by anyone interested. The "in part" was the idea of Mansel Davies, who recognized that his contribution had been minimal.

My first deeply negative impressions of Mansel Davies were beginning to moderate as he loosened up a bit and began to talk to me as if I were human. One day I surprised him by my knowledge of Latin. As he began to lose the Cambridge airs and graces he became more and more like Aberda^r, but if I got too familiar he was back in his shell again instantly. For example he got annoyed when I used his first name, Mansel, in a note to him. He began to talk about art history and that was mildly interesting, but I had just swallowed the whole of Kenneth Clark. He was not supervising his graduate students but neither were any of the grand old men of the day. I doubt whether the situation is any better now. Some graduate students are summoned in once a week on Fridays at 6.00 p.m.,and in the hyper large groups do not have an existence at all. I was told in that winter or spring of 1972 to go to the National Physical Laboratory to extend the spectrum of MBBA to make it overlap with the microwave. This meant a long trip in the car to Teddington near London. I had never been to London before and had never driven on the M4 motorway. The only detail I remember is taking a break after crossing the Severn Bridge, and taking photographs of the great suspension bridge near the restaurant there. The destination was Teddington in Middlesex, near Bushy Park and Hampton Court, and I was to stay at the Clarence Hotel Teddington, opposite the main gates of the laboratory. At the time it was a complex of low buildings and was known to me only through the work of Barnes Wallis.

I was to work with the Gebbie group of Chantry, Chamberlain and later, Birch. The hotel was a relic of earlier times and offered the usual bed and breakfast. I cannot recall an evening meal, so I may have got some food from a supermarket. The idea was to run a spectrum of MBBA on a different type of interferometer which was hastily explained to me by a member of the staff while I frantically took notes. I managed to get it working and obtained a perfect overlap with the interferometer at Aberystwyth. To my great surprise, Chantry seemed delighted by this and became a kind of patron of mine. Gebbie had left to work at the National Bureau of Standards, now NIST, in Colorado. I remember looking out of the window and noticing that the land was so flat compared with the South Wales valleys. There were also deer in Bushy Park. I took the tube in to London one weekend and took photographs of the London Parks. Then it was back to the M4 through heavy traffic at Clapham Junction, where the M4 entrance is so narrow and easily missed. Once on the motorway it was speed all the way back and across the Severn Bridge, up the Wye Valley of my ancestors and across the wild mountains to Devil's Bridge. This spectrum match appeared in the final paper.

One day I decided to write the 30th August scientific paper on my part of the laboratory bench in room 262. At first it was difficult going, but I knew how it should be written with an introduction, experimental part, results and discussion. The paper gradually came together and I placed it on Mansel Davies' desk. After some hesitation he agreed to it being submitted. That meant that it was given to the secretary to type. Often it would be weeks before the typing was finished, even without formulae. It also meant using stencil and other instruments to draw by hand the diagrams that can be seen today in the Omnia Opera. They had to be prepared on semi transparent paper, and of course I was given no technical support. That drawing to be done among the pungent smell of enzymes in Morrison's unused laboratory. So it took months to prepare a paper. Finally it had to be approved by Mansel Davies. The 30th August paper was the first one ever to be submitted by a graduate student at the EDCL. There had to be three copies and finally it was mailed off. I received my first acknowledgment letter from the Faraday Society, later to become the Royal Society of Chemistry. This was my creativity beginning to awaken. Every graduate student before me had to wait until Ph. D. Graduation and then had to submit a paper with the supervisor. I was deeply uncertain about Mansel Davies and what he would do at the end of my Ph. D. Would I slip back down in to the coal mine again? He seemed to be completely indifferent to what I was doing, so the paper obliged him to take some notice. By luck, George Chantry and the rest of the National Physical Laboratory group had taken a liking to my work, and became strong supporters. They must have put in a good word for me with Mansel Davies, who slowly began to be supportive too. So the paper also brought out the good side of his character, the Aberda^r side. He could be as intellectually enthusiastic and honest as any lapsed Baptist when he wanted, but at another time, much later, he gave Maggie Thatcher his statue of Michael Faraday. She probably threw it in the bin as being of no commercial value. He used to describe himself as a lapsed Baptist, and to his credit, learned the Welsh language.

From this perspective years later I can see that I was amazingly lucky to have been allowed to prepare and submit that paper, which was the turning point in my life. Most of Mansel Davies' students did not go on to a post doctoral fellowship, and at that point I did not even know that there was such as a thing as a post doctoral. Writing the paper was something I had to do, and that is a familiar feeling to all artists who suddenly want to paint, or all poets who suddenly want to write, or all composers. There is no difference between that and the scientific paper. The latter had to be based on a new discovery, and the strange name "paper" was given to the document that recorded a scientific advance or discovery. Usually the student would just be tagged on to the supervisor's name and by the time the paper was published had already graduated Ph. D. and left university life. That first paper on MBBA is on the Omnia Opera of www.aias.us and reads like a mature paper that could have been written by an experienced full professor. Indeed I was told this by Professor Jozef Moscicki of Krakow years later. It is a Baconian paper, data being interpreted by analytical theory because computer simulation was not on the scene in 1972. Testing of theory against data was an obvious thing to do for me, and at that time I had never heard of Francis Bacon. All the Ph. D. papers were rigorously Baconian. It also seemed natural to Mansel Davies to test a theory against data, and that was also the method I had learned at Pontardawe Grammar School.

At that time I had sufficient depth of knowledge of the modified theory of the Brownian motion known as the itinerant oscillator to apply it using the primitive Elliott 4130 to data that I had collected myself. The role of the post doctoral Ian Larkin was to give some advice, but little else, and the role of Mansel Davies was to give some criticism. He was too impatient to give real advice, but could be encouraging. On the other hand he could be brutally dismissive of one of his students. This happened shortly later to Peter Deft of Liverpool, who sadly took to drink. Pete transferred from Bangor could not get any results in non linear dielectrics, another dangerous experiment with high voltages, and eventually I had to take him back to Liverpool by car. I hope that he recovered and did well in life. The use of the computer was something new to Mansel Davies, who never used one in his entire life. I wrote my curve fitting programs using N. A.G. routines in Algol. These are now on www.aias.us. I had to learn Algol myself after Arnold Baise had left for Temple University in Philadelphia. I took a graduate course in computing which helped a little, but the work was really all mine from the word go. Luckily, Mansel Davies recognized this and the creative side of his mind also began to awaken - at least I like to think so. I think that my work reminded him of his own student days, and it was a relief from committees. He frequently complained of having to attend over a hundred committees a year or similar. The Principal Sir Goronwy Daniel refused to have the heat on so all the professors froze. Goronwy Daniel turned up at Whitehall in a land rover and duffle coat of the fifties, maybe he wore wellingtons in committee. He was a permanent under secretary and a product of Pontardawe Grammar School, where everything happened in wellingtons. Numerical curve fitting was a key part of the paper. I knew what I was doing without being taught. I never cold shouldered Mansel Davies, and was never in any way offensive to him or anyone else, but sadly my courtesy was always one sided and I had to deal often with boorish fools. He was intensely suspicious of curve fitting and stated the obvious by protesting far too much. Parameters must be kept to a minimum. None of the CERN junk with twenty five loose canons. He was always afraid that I would do something that might affect his reputation, original thought in a student was dangerous to a careerist.

In that first year of my Ph. D. I was somehow lassooed into being the secretary of the graduate society and editor of the university graduate journal in chemistry, then called “Tetracol”. This was a blisteringly original name which came from the fact that there were four colleges: Aberystwyth, Bangor, Cardiff and Swansea. Using a flash of genius, I changed the name to “Pentacol”, when some UWIST opened in far off Cardiff. I cannot remember much about “Pentacol” except that I had to go to the printers of “The Cambrian News” to collect copies. Being secretary of the graduate society meant inviting lecturers and so on. One of these was Buckingham of Cambridge, who gave a terminally boring lecture which opened with the question “Do you like maths?” The answer was stunned silence. All the staff and students turned up to these lectures and I also had to host the lecturer to dinner. This was a complete waste of time, and I should not have allowed myself to be lassooed. It was always a relief to get back to the laboratory bench in room 262, now lined with decks of cards for the Elliott 4130. These decks of cards were prepared at the computer unit, which was stuck in a corridor between the geography / geology or earth sciences complex and the physical sciences complex on Penglais, two piles of hideous concrete now blackening with age. Special paper was handed out upon which to write the Algol code, and the deck of cards was then handed back after some time. I was allowed to mend minor errors myself on a public card machine.

The digs in Alexandria Road were being spoiled by one unruly student so I decided to try one more time to get in to a Hall of Residence. By this time I was eligible for the graduate Cwrt Mawr, which was newly built at the time and of which I knew nothing. So hopefully I would get a taste of the good life high above the Campus and dark, damp slums of Aberystwyth. One evening in the early winter of 1972, the landlady Mrs Gill was deeply shocked and distressed when her husband suffered a heart attack, so may have had to give up the role of landlady shortly after I left. It was time to go and fortunately I was accepted in Cwrt Mawr. I did not spend very much time in the digs except on Sundays, when we were served generous amounts of food by Mrs. Gill. My athletics routine developed into a dedicated ten thousand metres every Saturday on the Penglais cinder track, whose only disadvantages were caused by frost and high wind. I was very dedicated but no athlete - having been born with limbs too weak for a sprinter and a heart lung system inadequate for the true and effortless distance runner. So the training was to strengthen limbs, heart and lungs - instinctively, not scientifically. In about June 1972 I moved in to Cwrt Mawr, to a room on the ground floor near to the central area which had a TV room and so on. The graduate students prepared their own food, eaten in a shared kitchen, but laundry was done for them. So I had to experiment with making food, and I had to extend my culinary knowledge to the stage where I could prepare more than a boiled egg, or boiled cyanogen. The products were mysterious, but I had to eat them. There were some interesting and mature students in my block of Cwrt Mawr, and fortunately no drunkards. Heavy drinking took place in the bar of the central building and I never went there. There is nothing more repulsive to me than a drunk, because of those experiences in Sea View Place and Powell Street. The problem of drink was ever present, as if students could not cope with reality. Now it is far worse, even though students have only a fraction of the work load and can waffle their way through to any kind of degree. The number of examinations have been reduced and the contemporary education system is a disaster that produces illiterate people when they leave years of school.

I began to buy paperbacks from Galloway on Pier Street and the shelf in my room filled with novels and books of poetry. These were given to my family for safe keeping but were "thrown away" or lost. They included the collected poems of Dylan Thomas, anthologies of poetry, and many novels. I liked the twentieth century poetry of Yeats and Auden and contemporaries, and short stories and novels by Steinbeck, Hemingway, Koestler, James Joyce, George Orwell, Alexander Solzhenitsyn, Jean-Paul Sartre, Albert Camus and many others, poetry in translation from Akhmatova, Machado, Jimenez and many others. I read Vernon Watkins and many others from Wales in both languages. Later I gradually became a poet myself. Later at Bangor I bought the classic "Gwaith Dafydd ap Gwilym" by Prof. Sir Thomas Parry and his classic "The Oxford Book of Welsh Verse". One day I must buy the whole collection again, and that is easily done. I came across Huw Macdiarmaid and Patrick Kavanagh, and W. S. Graham in an anthology. Several are antecedents of mine on the Civil List: including Yeats, Joyce, MacDiarmaid, W. S. Graham and Vernon Watkins. I thought instantly that Kavanagh is a great poet, the son of a small farmer from the rural poor of Ireland. From Cwrt Mawr I started training every day instead of at weekends. I could just run straight out of Cwrt Mawr down the almost vertical road past Cefn Llan and back up again and around. Later on Saturdays I decided to do an eight or ten mile run down to the Plant Breeding Station and back along the main road, dodging the speeding cars.

In about 1972 my parents sold the farm “Pant y Bedw” and moved to an infinitely drearyand anonymous location in the small town of Clydach, at 91 Lone Road. The first thing I knew about it was a short telephone call to say that they had already moved, and that was the point at which I lost touch with my parents to all intents and purposes. I was always polite with them, and visited them quite often, but have always felt angry and betrayed. No doubt this feeling is irrational and maybe unfair to hard working people, but this is the fact of the matter. As usual there had been no attempt to consult me or to hand the farm over to me as the eldest son. So I was suddenly disinherited after years of work on the wholly uneconomical farm from an early age, often very hard work, on top of school work. The whole farm was thrown away in great haste for about five hundred pounds or similar, and all the buildings were allowed to fall in to ruin, including the house. That more or less invited in people with no knowledge of Welsh or even of Anglo Welsh culture. For years I tried to buy it back, but some vulture of an estate agent had already pushed up the price out of my reach. Sales such as this have almost killed the language in small villages such as Craig Cefn Parc and should be prohibited by law as in many other areas of Europe. Their legality should be challenged now in the European Court of Justice because there are European laws to protect indigenous small languages and cultures. I saw the house in a completely and deliberately ruined condition, it was a devilish experience as if time had hit a geological fault and was playing a sadistic trick, laughing in my face in the driving rain. There was nothing to go back to now in Craig Cefn Parc, both houses had been suddenly sold and I was definitely not consulted, my opinion not wanted: this house, 50 Rhyddwen Road, and “Pant y Bedw”. This experience alienated me from my family and made me very cautious of commercialized humankind. The lives of people are dom nated mindlessly by one thing, money, not by things like ideas and literature which have no commercial value. So my friends became intellectual friends.

I was very lucky once more to find the little library in the computer unit which housed the manuals of the Numerical Algorithms Group (NAG) in Algol and FORTRAN. From this manual I learnt how to incorporate NAG routines into my own code. There was also help available from the irascible and overworked computer unit staff, and in through the windows I could see the Elliott 4130 computer itself, in its air conditioned room with racks of magnetic tape. No magnets allowed and no shuffling or card playing. When the code was complete the pack of cards was put between two cardboard supports with a label, and then it had to be submitted through a window in to a tray. There were priorities of turnaround, zero priority took up to a month or so. There was one Elliott 4130 for the whole college. In order to Fourier transform the paper tape output, the tape was tied to the pack with a rubber band. That program worked well because it was standardized, but my first attempts at writing Algol produced floating point overflow and algol errors. These were the twin pillars of devilry with which I had to contend many times, each time they appeared meant a trip in the car up to the computer unit and back down again, and a long walk through the damp and cold EDCL corridor carrying computer output and pack of cards. If I met Mansel Davies in the corridor he would look suspiciously at the output, wondering how much it was costing. In fact they were small programs that cost very little, sometimes they were just failed output from algol errors, but he did not appear to know that some programs consumed more computer time than others. So how I fought for that first paper. A large pile of output began to accumulate in room 262.

I remember my wild delight when I got my first program working, having consumed gallons of petrol and coffee. Once it worked all that had to be done was to change its input parameters. Now I could compute output from the itinerant oscillator models of Wyllie and Brot. I plotted the output by hand on graph paper and varied the input parameters to produce different curves. The problem was how to compare these with the spectra from the interferometer sitting on its table right at the back of me. I realized that the theory had to be fitted to the data, and found that the n parameter least mean squares NAG routine was the solution. This meant that the spectral output had to be fed in to a fitting program and I gradually learnt how to do this automatically. This meant many car journeys and miles of corridor walking and plotting by hand. The far infra red became a fascinating place of discovery, and when combined with the microwave and lower frequencies was a test of theories that few could pass. The rapid development of this work can be seen in the early Omnia Opera papers on www.aias.us in complete detail. It was work different from any other that was going on in the world of chemical physics at that time, and is as valid today as it was then. Its originality was recognized immediately and internationally as the reprint requests began to arrive from mysterious far off places. The big powerful computers of today would not better its quality of thought. Each paper was finished and entire of itself and they are all read now off www.aias.us. The methodology behind them originated in that year of 1972, when it seemed always to be raining, and so I had to find something to do.

I expected a reply to arrive from the Chemical Society but unknown to me at the time I had run into the inertia of the refereeing system, where a paper would be sat upon for a very long time. I was not even aware of the anonymous refereeing system. So week after week passed by, and once more I had to find something to do. This was a continuation of the very dangerous work on cyanogen, at long last a lecture bottle of the deadly poison had arrived from Matheson, marked with a skull and crossbones. That was most encouraging. The high pressure cell had to be used to compress the gas to over fifty atmospheres in order to obtain a spectrum caused by the collision of cyanogen molecules. This was known as quadrupole induced dipole absorption in the far infra red and the purpose of this suicidal experiment was to measure the quadrupole moment. Was my life worth so much? The cell had been built in the mechanical workshop of the EDCL with very thick quartz windows. There was no safety screen or fume cupboard, just a bomb on an old bench with a hole carved out of it. The double doors meant that no one would have heard an accident and I worked late at night. It proved difficult to get the gas into the pot because of a basic design fault that prevented the gas from reaching the pot through the narrow opening between the cell windows. So I had to devise a new method of unbolting the pot and attaching it directly to the lecture bottle with a Budenberg gauge. The pot was kept in very cold liquid nitrogen, so the gas condensed into liquid over a substance called zeolite used to dry it. The pot had to be unbolted and quickly attached to the cell before the liquid turned to gas and wiped out the whole EDCL.

One of my most vivid and ghastly memories of that year is of the safety office Sam Graham walking in to the laboratory just at the moment when the liquid cyanogen was exposed to the atmosphere, before I had had time to bolt it the cell. He walked around room 262, looking for safety flaws, such as a dropped pencil, and peered into the pot. I hoped that he would not sniff what was inside, or if he did, how I was going to dispose of the body. After a minute inspection of all the wrong parts of the interferometer he gradually became very bored and prepared to leave the room. During the whole visit I tried not to breathe and as soon as he left bolted the pot to the cell in a world record time. The gas evaporated and filled the area between the quartz windows. To increase the pressure the pot was heated with electric tape and gradually the Budenberg needle began its ominous journey across the scale. I was told to stop at fifty atmospheres, not for my sake, but to prevent three molecule collisions. There was no way of knowing whether the windows would stand the pressure, or be blown out like bullets. In order to get liquid cyanogen into the cell it had to be tilted over so I could see the liquid running in, peering closely at the windows. That was probably the most dangerous part of a dangerous experiment. No worse experiment could have been devised for a beginning graduate student. It was insanely dangerous and not particularly accurate, and I also had to learn the entire theory and code it up in Algol, without help from my supervisor. At the time he was on the Faraday Committee and was very rarely seen. That suited me because of his character. I could not talk to him so it made no difference that he was absent.

The theory of that cyanogen experiment was way beyond Mansel Davies, and much more difficult than anything we had been taught at undergraduate. It is recorded for history in the first paper of the Omnia Opera on www.aias.us and the intricately complicated equation (2) of the paper gives an idea of what it was like to code it up. With a sense of escaping from a coal mining accident I found one day that Mansel Davies was satisfied with the data and would allow me to write up the paper. It was submitted on 4th December 1972. I may have been waiting still for a reply from the Chemical Society about the MBBA paper. This was a dangerous time for me in more than one way, because I knew by that time that Mansel Davies and the system would take credit for any good work I did, but would instantly dump blame on me for any failure. There was no supervision at all, so it was living under a patronizing guillotine that worked anonymously in far off places. An envelope must have arrived from the Faraday Society some time in late 1972. It returned the paper with some loose copy leaves marked as "referees' reports". I thought that it had been sent from the Football Association to the wrong address, but there two or three reports that had to be contended with. I recall that one started with the words: "I have heard of this young man". This is always a prelude to something ominous. It turned out that only minor changes were needed and the paper was published in 1973, number two on the Omnia Opera of www.aias.us. These things had to be shown to Mansel Daives who grasped the arms of his chair until his knuckles turned white with condensed and compressed anger. For an instant I thought that my Ph. D. had run down a drain but the anger was being expressed at the referee. I had escaped another trial by poison and anonymity. These tedious delays and hurried, almost meaningless reports, had to be contended with throughout my academic life as one of the most productive and well read scientist in history, and not a single one helped me in any way.

In that early winter of 1972 I was further burdened by a sudden announcement that I was to be sent to France to work with Brot in Nice and Rivail in Nancy. So I was told to apply for a French Government scholarship and bursary, which had to be won in open competition. This I was terminally reluctant to do, because I was only just starting my Ph. D. This idea spoiled my Christmas entirely back at "Pant y Bedw" for a short while. I told my parents nothing about the dangerous mess under which I had been obliged to work. I also had to attend a French language course in the Old College, which annoyed me greatly. In early 1973 I chose another gas to work with in the far infra red, the much safer gas propyne. I carried out this study myself while waiting to go to France and the paper was submitted on 26th March 1973. I obtained high quality far infra red spectra by averaging results from many runs, necessitating a very large expenditure of fuel backwards and forwards to the computer unit. The output piled up on the floor or desk of room 262, together with rolls of paper tape and packs of cards. Propyne spectra were more complicated to analyze than cyanogen spectra because propyne is not quite symmetrical. It has what is known as a dipole moment as well as a quadrupole moment. One day a small envelope arrived from the Chemical Society and inside it was an acceptance note, offering free offprints. Once more I threw up my arms as if I had scored a goal and was as wildly delighted as when I got my top first. To me it was like having a painting accepted in the Louvre or a poem in the best poetry magazine. No doubt I was naive, but that can be expected in a twenty two year old, when the age of innocence had not quite burnt away. In fact I am still just as delighted at the overwhelmingly enthusiastic international reception given today to my various papers, which are published in a much more efficient way. They are all read around the world all the time. That is what any scholar wants, that is what any artist desires, that is what any poet wishes for.

The only negative thing about that first acceptance is that Mansel Davies refused to order offprints, pleading poverty. In my innocence I had filled out an order for a hundred, a random number, but he just got angry. The system has pleaded poverty ever since. That was only a minor irritation because of the free offprints. As I developed a strong international reputation those offprints began to fill up large areas of bench space in room 262 and postcards began to arrive requesting them. They started with "Honoured Colleague" and similar, and came in from all the world. However in that Spring of 1973 everything was dampened by the thought of having to go to France to work with someone whom I did not know on something that was not defined. That is how I felt at the time. It seemed that a three month gap was about to be blown in my Ph. D., which I had to finish in three years or it was down the coal mine again. I was worried how I was going to cope with the French language and how I was going to survive. As time went on I received no communication of any kind from Brot, and no arrangements for accommodation or office space. I did not even know where I was supposed to work in Nice. I tried to put all that in the back of my mind and to think that Brot would have made some arrangements. Apparently he was someone that Mansel Davies had met at a conference and with whose work he had become impressed. On top of that I was given the proofs to read of a huge long article by Kielich, full of work that Mansel Davies did not understand. He did no have the mathematical technique to understand it. So I was beginning to feel irritated about being given unpaid work that my nominal supervisor should be doing. Later on Gareth Evans would be asked to walk his dog while Mansel Davies was at Criccieth on his summer break from Aberystwyth.

The only thing I knew was that I had to arrive at Nice International Airport on a given date. I stayed with my parents for a couple of days and my father accompanied me by train to Gatwick Airport. This was the first time that either of us had seen one of these hallmarks of a fuel hungry world populated with nomads. My father was a brave man, a gold, silver and bronze medallist of the Mines Rescue Service and was present at Aberfan, but he never flew in his life, and was instinctively repelled by those gigantic aircraft landing and taking off from Gatwick. For the first time I saw that he did have respect for me. We shook hands at the gateway down to the aircraft. Then I was on my own. I had to board a Comet, which in its early years crashed from window design faults. It was the first time I had been in an aircraft, and it was a narrow tube with seats. The acceleration pushed me back as it gathered speed and gradually climbed into the skies. There was a pattern of fields and suddenly the sea. Everything was obscured by cloud cover so I tried to settle down in my seat, carefully looking for cracks in the windows. None appeared and suddenly we were going to land. I thought “What am I doing here”. Luckily for me Madame Brot was waiting for me. She was Danish and walking out of the Airport we saw Patrick Campbell consuming whisky, or it may have been liquid cyanogen of which I have thought ever since Sam Graham peered into the pot. Campbell was a TV celebrity at the time. Madame Brot pointed him out to me, he was wearing a blue blazer and cravat, all ponsed up.

Brot was away in Paris, probably arranging for his group to move to Nice in Provence, which was as foreign to them as it was to me. My first impressions of Nice were clouded by concrete all the way down the Promenade des Anglais. Madame Brot drove a small car as I seem to remember, entirely on the wrong side of the road. It was a cloudy, rainy day and I was tired from the trip. There were no arrangements at all, I stayed in Brot's flat and slept on the couch with Madame Brot next door. I wondered uneasily what Brot would think of that, having heard of the French temperament, crimes of passion and assassinations. In the morning there was a bowl of chocolate and a croissant I think, and Madame Brot had to go off to fetch Monsieur Brot at the airport. He arrived and looked at me suspiciously with dark, darting eyes. He was a French Jew whose family had somehow survived and his wife was a Dane with blue eyes and sandy hair. She spoke French with a heavy accent, and spoke English well. Fortunately Brot also spoke English, with great reluctance. It was immediately obvious that Claude Brot did not know what to do, there had been no communication with Mansel Davies. I was shifted out into a hotel and taken up to Parc Valrose. This had been the winter house of a Russian aristocrat but was now a campus of the University of Nice. I found that Brot was the Director of the CNRS Laboratoire de Physique de la Matiere Condensee, the Consensed Matter Physics Laboratory of the French National Centre for Scientific Research, with laboratories distributed all over France, an excellent research system that I later tried to establish in Britain.

The drive up to the CNRS laboratory gave me some opportunity to talk with Brot, and to try to find out what I was doing there, but he seemed entirely uninterested. I was deposited in a room with a shade against the Provencal sun of van Gogh, which was strong even in Spring. I was fortunate in having a bright and friendly group to work with: Pierre Sixou, the deputy director, Pierre Bezot, Francoise Freed and Bernadette Lassier. They were setting up equipment which included a far infra red spectrometer and laser system and were capable workers. They invited me to restaurants around Nice. There was another member of the group, a Breton called Bernard Quentrec, in charge of computer simulation, but he visited only once or twice and later committed suicide very suddenly. He seemed to be the most confident and able member of the group, and apparently came from a fishing family. I managed to get my bursary after a lot of trouble from a very angry assistant who spoke no English and who could not understand my French. Brot smoked constantly, and was very nervous. Later he died of cancer, but not before I found out that he was a generous and highly intelligent man. I had just been dumped on him at the wrong time. I was given meal tickets at the Restaurant Universitaire, free food for the students. The food was good, Provencal salads, olives, fish and vin ordinaire which I did not consume. I watched the other students drink it down like water. I was surrounded by a sea of French language. Outside Nice in villages like la Turbie overlooking Monaco the language is no longer French, it is or was Provencal, of which I could not understand a word. I could pick up the French if they slowed down to bottom gear. The Parisians of the Brot group had no idea of Provencal, or seemed not to. Nice was as new and exotic to them as it was to me.

To pass the time in the hotel (a concrete box affair) I read Solzhenitsyn's "Cancer Ward", which had just appeared in print. Its main character was Kostoglotov, or Bone Chewer, caught in an ugly world. None uglier than Solzhenitsyn's time in the Gulag. Later he was awarded the Nobel Prize in literature. I walked to work from the hotel and for the first time noticed the orange trees. There was a booth where I could get a small cup of coffee. I drank it down much too quickly, and danced around in a caffeine induced frenzy. It was as thick as porridge. Near the entrance to Parc Valrose was a memorial to people cornered and shot by the Vichy Police, and its large driveway was populated by basking lizzards. In the distance were hills of parched land above the commercialized concrete grey of Nice. Unknown to me there was an ancient Nice, the Cimiez with its triumphal arch of Augustus, and the old Italian town of Nice transferred to France in a treaty. I arrived in the laboratory and there was literally nothing to do. So I had to improvise, just as at Aberystwyth. I decided to translate a Thesis from the French. There were two types: Troisieme Cycle and d'Etat. Completely by accident this led to an understanding of correlation functions, which could be obtained from a far infra red / microwave spectrum by Fourier transform. Theory was often expressed in terms of the correlation function. I found that they could be evaluated by one sided Laplace transforms that I could code up in Algol. Eventually this led to an entirely new understanding of the far infra red in terms of memory functions.

I was transferred out of the hotel to live with friends of Brot for a while, and there I passed away the time reading Racine and Moliere. One day I found myself in Brot's office and he suddenly asked with ill concealed hostility: "What do you want from me?". I thought of replying "nothing", but waffled something. This was an obvious disaster coming from total lack of communication between Mansel Davies and Claude Brot and I just had to fish myself out of it. There were only six weeks in Nice but it seemed interminable with occasional sparks of interest. The Thesis translation was interesting but tedious work, so I decided to perfect the method of computing correlation functions by Laplace transform. This was another turning point in my research. Brot's group invited me to their dinners in restaurants on the Mediterranean, which had no tides, the fish came straight off the boats on to the quay and into the restaurant, where there were different menus for the same price, thirteen francs, about pound in the money of 1973. There was always a bottle of vin ordinaire on the table. They talked away in French and I tried to grasp some meaning. There was a piano recital in an elegant setting. One day I discovered the Cimiez and the Musee Matisse, where drawings with one line came vividly alive, and attended an out door occasion in the Roman amphitheatre near the triumphal arch of Augustus and perfectly preserved Roman town and baths. To pass the time at weekends I decided to walk first to Cap d'Antibes and then to La Turbie overlooking Monaco. The Musee Picasso at Cap d'Antibes was full of the younger era Picasso and suddenly I walked around a corner to directly above the sea. There was a warm breeze, and not a cold Atlantic blast. The Impressionists spent a lot of time here as did novelists such as Graham Greene.

In late May there was the Monaco Grand Prix and I walked along the Haute Corniche in the hope of seeing something from the vantage point of La Turbie. Earlier, Brot had introduced me to a colleague of his living in this ancient Provencal village with its own microclimate and stone and timbered houses. Monaco lay beneath me and in the distance the Italian border town of Ventimiglia, but I could see nothing of the Grand Prix, only rugged, rocky coastline. So I walked back on the Moyenne Corniche above the very blue sea, dodging manic drivers, and arriving in a heap back in Nice. The driving in France was something that had to be survived. One day on the way to the Nice Observatory, Bernadette Lassier said something to Brot that infuriated him instantly, and he swung the car around viciously in a 180 degree turn, driving like a fool back to the laboratory. At that point I felt that I had had fully enough of Nice despite its attractions. There was a visit to St. Paul de Vance and the Maeght Foundation of Modern Art where another side of Brot's character emerged, more relaxed and cultured as one would expect. The kindly and reserved Francoise Freed invited me for a drive in her tiny car, which looked as if it had been pressed out of one sheet of metal. The rugged mountains of Provence dominated that drive and I have always wondered what happened to Francoise, another highly intelligent French Jew whose family may or may not have survived. She had the infinitely sad, almost black, eyes of an internal refugee like Sakharov.

The time approached for me to transfer to Nancy in the north east of France to the CNRS group run by Prof. Jean-Louis Rivail in one of the Universities of Nancy, Universite de Nancy 1 in the CNRS Laboratoire de Chimie Theorique (Theoretical Chemistry Laboratory). I packed the various Thesis volumes and my translations and notes, and waited in the laboratory, because the train was an overnight one through Marseilles, Avignon and Dijon. I waited and waited, and with a nearly fatal shock realized that I had misread the time and that the train was due to go in half an hour. Very luckily Pierre Sixou offered to rush me through Nice to the train station, driving like a laser, shovelling gendarmes aside with the demonic determination of a condensed matter theorist, or Inspector Clouseau. We arrived in one piece and shook hands outside the station, then I ran to the train and a compartment. It was not a sleeper so I had to sit up all night. At first the rugged country between Nice and Marseilles sped past the window, but it soon grew dark and the train drew in to Marseilles in darkness. At that point I thought of gangsters, drugs and the French connection, and pressed myself into my seat. The train sped off towards Avignon in the south east of France and I hoped it would not take a wrong turning. I got a few hours of half sleep before it pulled in to Dijon and made its way towards Lorraine, of which Nancy is the capital. In the morning I could see flat agricultural land with no hedges, no mad king had been around to enclose the ancient land with stone wall as in Wales. Finally after an infinite journey the train pulled in to the station at Nancy, where I met organization in the shape of Jose Goulon.

Jose Goulon had been sent from Prof. Jean-Louis Rivail's group and had just finished an outstanding These d'Etat, more accurately two Thesis volumes. He was a very capable theoretician and experimentalist, as one glance at the Thesis volumes showed. As usual in France they were published in many copies in paperback, not just two or three copies as in Wales. Rivail himself though was nowhere to be found and again there was nothing prepared for my visit, so Mansel Davies had not talked to Jean-Louis Rivail either. At that point there was only one thing for it - to complete my Ph. D. myself after getting back from France, and work independently thereafter. There were six weeks to go in Nancy, and again the students turned out to be friendly and sociable, some in a highly cultured kind of way. Jose Goulon drove me to my room in a Hall of Residence, so the organization at Nancy was better. The CNRS labo or laboratory was to be found in a kind of doughnut made of concrete that perplexed the French themselves until they were told that it was architecture. The nation of Chartres and the Abbey Church of Vezelay were allergic to doughnuts and had to work in a joke. The laboratory in Nancy had a microwave interferometer and I eventually wrote a paper on my work there which was submitted on 19th December 1974 from Oxford and published in "Molecular Physics" as Omnia Opera number twelve on www.aias.us. This was another advance for me because it was the first time that I used different experimental techniques on the same problem, a method that was later developed in to the Delta Project of the European Molecular Liquids Group (EMLG). The latter was founded at the National Physical Laboratory in 1980 and I was its first European Coordinator. I worked with Jose Goulon on the microwave interferometer and the results are in that 19th December 1974 paper together with results from the far infra red and NMR relaxation. My co authors were Jose Goulon, Daniel Canet and Graham J. Davies, with whom I had obtained data at the Post Office Research Centre in Dollis Hill in North London.

That submission date was more than a year in the future from my time at Nancy in about May and June of 1973. Nancy was a much different France from Nice, the people were taller, many fair haired and blue eyed. The food was entirely different, seemingly dominated by sausage, ham and cheese. One supermarket had a wall covered entirely in cheese, after all this was the land of Charles de Gaulle, who had to govern a nation with as many varieties of cheese as varieties of attempted assassination. Nancy is on the Meurthe and Moselle rivers, and its most famous mathematical product is Henri Poincare. It boasts the Place Stanislaw after a deposed Polish Lithuanian King who was given the Duchy of Lorraine by his son in law Louis XV in 1737. It has some very fine real architecture in the classical style and the Son et Lumiere of Place Stanislaw is memorable. The concrete doughnut though was to be my workplace. There was a violently volatile scientist called Roussy who exploded one day when told something by Goulon, returning a volley across the empty centre of the doughnut. The architect's idea was to place offices and laboratories around this centre. Later the same Roussy invited me to dinner at his home, where Madame Roussy made a delicate and wonderful and genuine Quiche Lorraine. Goulon reacted to Roussy by normal conversation, but I had taken cover under the interferometer. The long midday breaks were spent playing chess and cards with the students, sometimes in an elegant apartment filled with cigar smoke and Beaujolais. The latter was forced upon me as a classic wine, but it tasted like cyanogen. As a joke I was told to drink down a Mirabelle one evening in one go, and fire emerged from my nostrils like a dragon. Cyanogen could not have been more effective. How do the French survive such liquids? At other times I was attacked by fake and playful hand grenades as an Anglais. I explained to them that I was the long lost cousin of Asterix, related to Vercingetorix and Eddy Merckx (Eduard Louis Joseph, Baron Merckx of the Tour de France) and that did the trix. We were all Gauls or

Celts here.

Eventually I bumped in to Rivail when he was trying theoretically to park his car and painting the atmosphere a shade of post impressionist blue with elaborate swearing in French of which I had picked up a few pungent words. He was a small, nervous but kindly man in glasses. He never did park that car, but later took us on an outing to the Vosges Mountains. I think it was with Goulon and his wife Chantal and myself in his powerful Renault car, always driving again on the wrong side of the road. The Vosges is the area to the west of the Rhine, opposite the Black Forest. It has high mountains and forest of its own. The land was completely different from Provence, it was northern European with unfenced farmland, many small churches filled with art, some small towns and villages consisting of farm houses clustered together. By now it is probably all plastered by wind turbines unless the spirit of Vercingetorix, Charlemagne or Charles Martel is still alive in France. We took a walk up in to the high mountains along a forested path where all was silent and full of ancient nature. The oxygen reverberated with vibration and rotation but we did not have infra red eyes. Both Brot and Rivail actually talked to and walked with their students, the only walk I took with Mansel Davies was in to his study and never took a walk with J. M. Thomas anywhere. The French were not so comically self important and pompous and did not pretend to democracy. Rivail took us in the car to a village in Alsace from which it was possible to look down on a flat plain stretching to the horizon. The city of Strasbourg must have been somewhere on that plain. In that Alsace village Rivail treated us to dinner and we were asked by a waitress: "Drei assiettes de chauffer io?", using two languages and a dialect. There was some Rhine wine which was tolerable and sweeter than Beaujolais but still toxic. The others drank it down. Goulon could also drive like a maniac and we headed off to Belfort along straight roads at superluminal vel city. The idea was to see his grandmother ahead of the speed of light. She must have been nearing a hundred years old and thought that I was a Tommie from the first war. This was a region that had been turned into carnage many times over and there were ghosts of Tommies everywhere.

We were due in Paris for a conference and drove down there across the paved roads of northern France turned into modern highways. These are the tree lined roads of many famous artists. The unfenced land again contained small villages made up of clusters of farms, and the occasional small town designed exclusively for the Tour de France. I think that Goulon was driving and Brot had kindly lent me his apartment high above the Arc du Triomphe in the middle distance. Every morning there was the smell of baguettes and coffee, with Parisians drifting in and out of the patisserie just beneath me armed with lances made out of fresh bread. There was little time for all that and Brot suddenly turned up in a hypersized car, probably a Mercedes, and drove me in to the conference in Universite de Paris Sud. I bumped in to Mansel Davies there and was told to walk up to the board in the middle of his lecture to draw out a very large MBBA formula before a bemused conference. Was I going to assassinate my supervisor? Much as I would have liked to, I drew out the formula as he kept talking about my MBBA work in the far infra red, and some work on dielectric relaxation on the same liquid crystal. The purpose of this eludes me even now. Why not use an overhead projector? I suppose it was meant to convey that he was a grand old baron with serfs and squires. I felt like a fool and retreated to the giggling French group from Nancy. My drawing was not van Gogh or Monet. The incredibly ambitious Graham Williams was also there and complained about Mansel Davies disappearing in the middle of the conference. “Where has Mansel gone?” asked Graham with authority, and nobody cared or answered. Mansel had probably gone off to see the Louvre. He thought Paris the best designed city in the world.

Graham Davies was also there and we drifted around the Cartier Latin in Paris for a while, looking at nothing in particular, with one more scientist from Dollis Hill I think, or it may have been someone else from South Wales. There were the usual tourist traps like the Moulin Rouge but it was not Toulouse - Lautrec. There were some dubious ladies in war paint looking at us very strangely from doorways. They may have been early string theorists. Later I took the metro back from the conference and walked along the whole length of the dark wall of the Louvre, there were pavement drawings in chalk all along the Seine. Graham Davies came from a poor area of Swansea and had been a demonstrator during my final year undergraduate in the EDCL. He left one dark evening for Dollis Hill, where he was in charge of an interferometer with a liquid helium Rollin detector. He thought that the EDCL was a holiday resort for people who had never been in the real world, and presumably Dollis Hill was real. To me it looked as dreary, anonymous and car choked as the rest of north London. He later moved to Martlesham Heath and then became an administrator in Birmingham and finally Australia. He could be generous and tried to donate apparatus when I was in Swansea. His donation was refused by the money obsessed and perverse Swansea administration. Back in 1972 he visited Nancy and the Place Stanislaw. He stayed some time and Jose Goulon took him to see the battlefield at Vaux, which he wanted to see and I did not. I tagged along out of my usual politeness.

Fort Vaux was one of the most savage battles around Verdun, and even in 1972 it was pockmarked with shell craters. Why would anyone wish to see a place like that? There was a military cemetery and idle tourists such as ourselves were led through what remained of the fort, a pile of rain swept stone. I had not come to Nancy to see a graveyard, and Goulon had no desire to be reminded of all that. I said something to the effect that it was a waste of life and was glad to leave. Much to the calm natured

Goulon's puzzlement and slight annoyance, Graham lost his cool. There were no dead British soldiers there, only two million dead French and German. That is enough for anyone. These days such carnage is no longer possible because of mutual assured destruction. Although I was slightly acquainted with Graham Davies, I was secretly glad when he left because I had got used to Nancy and he reminded me of enveloping and purposeless and small minded ambition and the provincial EDCL administration. For the time being the administration did not bother me but later they caused science great damage. Mansel Davies' best side was his pacifism, and in this, he stuck to his Baptist principles. He would never have gone anywhere near a golgotha of utter slaughter. I always think of places like that as if I were in them at the time of real danger, and not walking around in safety many years later. A photograph of Vaux from the air shows a pentagonal type military fort looking like smallpox, plastered by thousands of shells. I was glad when Jose Goulon drove us back across a large river that must have been the Moselle or Meurthe or similar, through Metz and back to Nancy. My six weeks at Nancy were almost over and I had a big pile of books to carry back. So I bought a large mountain pack in the town of Nancy and stuffed it with Troisieme Cycle and d'Etat, many volumes in all, along with notes, calculations and diagrams.

I said my goodbyes to my colleagues and friends of Nancy and started back towards Calais on the early morning train. This ran along the ghastly Western Front of which nothing was visible out of the window. It eventually reached Amiens and made its way towards Calais.

My parents were waiting in Dover so I embarked looking like a mountaineer with a heavy pack of books. This was the first time I had ever been on a sea going vessel, and the motion of the ship had not begun to disturb my physiology. After many violently rough crossings of the Irish Sea to Trinity College Dublin I began to suffer later from sea sickness, so I can no longer travel on a ship.

With the internet there is no need to travel anywhere, and after years of being forced to run around strange places that suits me fine. The ship made its way towards Dover in a calm sea and for the first time I saw the approaches to Britain, there was little sign of white cliffs, but what seemed to be a low shoreline. The ship slowed down to a crawl and ropes were thrown across. The passengers disembarked down the side and I joined them. My parents were waiting there and I was very glad to see them, despite "Pant y Bedw". It was a long train journey home through London, and started off badly when my father quarreled with the ticket collector. I was very tired, and had hoped that his character had changed and that he had developed some respect for me but he blasted away as usual in front of everyone. The effect on me was to make me want to return to Cwrt Mawr as soon as I could, there being no "Pant y Bedw", only a small semi detached stone house suffering from decay, chosen at random. After the sophistication of the work at Nancy it was difficult to return to a country where no one understood it, least of all my Ph. D. supervisor. My mother was bewildered and very unhappy that I wanted to leave so early for Aberystwyth but much later I found put that she had been pressurizing my father to sell for a long time. By that time I had no choice but to move on.

So I packed the car and headed off to Cwrt Mawr, where my room was still available. I think I had to pay for it even though I was also asked to work in France. These petty injustices had alienated me from the system at Aberystwyth but I was about to produce the best work of my Ph. D., work that was entirely original and immediately recognized internationally but not with tenure. This obvious injustice was also recognized internationally, not least by the National Physical Laboratory, so in historical terms it means that the system at Aberystwyth entirely defeated its own purpose and I produced research despite of it, not because of it. Neither Mansel Davies nor John Thomas should be given any credit for my work. They were talking about me all over Britain, but refused to give basic support when they could easily have done so, and were trying to promote themselves. One way to defeat such a perverse system is to work wholly away from it, another way is to reform it from within. Nevertheless I did my duty as usual and handed over the French Thesis volumes to Mansel Davies as I had been asked to. I walked in to the EDCL with a heavy pack of books, and the first I saw was Alun Price. I was on quite good terms with him and have remained on quite good terms. He looked over the pack with curiosity and said in Welsh, "You're back are you?". Evidently I was. He asked how things had gone and I was very glad to be back at the EDCL. Things had gone, which is about the best face I can put on the French Scholarship. It had been unplanned chaos, and I improvised myself out of it. I learned how to produce correlation functions and I learned the value of the multi technical approach.

I think that the porters (with whom I was always on excellent terms) had put my mail on my bench top, because at that time I had to share the mail box allocated to Mansel Davies. My correspondence was the largest of the post room quite frequently, one visible sign that the envious did not take to. Mansel Davies was never envious, but had already decided to send me on a needless post doctoral, and to all places back to Claude Brot's laboratory. This was a disaster which finally alienated me completely from my Ph. D. supervisor, and I decided to go to Oxford as the best that I could do. I did not want to go to Oxford at all, but I could see that the system was going to destroy my work if I did not take matters in to my own hands. It is blazingly obvious that I should have been given a job at Aberystwyth as a tenured research associate. Several others had already been given such a post. I was a poet in the hands of the illiterate, a composer in the hands of the tone deaf, and that is academia in reality. There is no need to be anyone's intellectual slave if one can devise a method of surviving. I made my way back to room 262 and at the earliest opportunity gave the books to Mansel Davies in his office. He seemed to take no notice of them, just put them to one side. However I was free to start coding up the Elliott 4130 to produce rotational velocity correlation functions and to finish off a conventional paper with Ian Larkin. The latter was submitted on 29th August 1973 and the paper on the rotational velocity correlation functions on 21st January 1974 and they are now in the Omnia Opera section of www.aias.us. All the papers I submitted as the Dr Samuel Williams Graduate Scholar were refereed and accepted for publication before I wrote up the Ph. D., which is also in the Omnia Opera. This set a precedent for the whole of Britain in modern times.

Some time towards the Spring of 1973 I was due for my half term verbal examination on my Thesis but as this coincided with the French Scholarship it may have been postponed until I returned from France. I recall that it was a lecture on my research work in the small lecture theatre of the old EDCL Building. Having got that out of the way I embarked on the happiest time of my academic years, from summer 1973 to late summer 1974, when life was badly shadowed by the need for another pointless move, this time to Oxford. In the summer of 1973 however I worked out and coded up the Laplace transform method for producing the rotational velocity correlation function from far infra red spectra, a method which led immediately to international recognition. The far infra red combined with the microwave provides correlation functions which are very difficult for any analytical theory or computer simulation to describe completely. They still cannot do so satisfactorily. The region provides the rotational velocity correlation function, which is the second time derivative of the orientational correlation function. With accurate enough data, higher derivatives can also be obtained. I began work on the coding in the now peaceful room 262, because I decided to concentrate on theory. There was no longer any pounding from the paper tape punch and no more gas attacks. I also had good accommodation with mature and responsible people at Cwrt Mawr. For a very short time, things were good at Aberystwyth. Fortunately all this work has been archived in the National Archives of Britain (www.webarchive.org.uk) and the United States, and in the Omnia Opera section of www.aias.us. It is a huge amount of work for one scholar, but it never seems like work. It is obviously poetry, music and art.

By the time I got back from France, Pete Deft had been moved in to Room 262 from Bangor with nonlinear dielectric apparatus. This operated with high voltages and was dangerous and difficult work. Pete worked himself in to the ground but found it very difficult to get results that Mansel Davies liked, and I will always remember with profound disgust how Mansel Davies treated him, particularly one vicious outburst in his office in the presence of Alun Price and myself, where Mansel Davies appeared to be insane. I really thought he was mad, and this was obviously not the public side of obituaries, careerist claptrap and so on. I saw this more than once, on another occasion he pounded his desk like an infant when he could not find a paper, on another he screamed for a porter when he found that his office had been locked one Saturday morning. Pete was destroyed by the time he left that office. I controlled my blazing anger and left as soon as I could. Later I found Peter drinking heavily in Cwrt Mawr, and suddenly he gave up. I drove him back to Liverpool 5 to his mother's house. This was a poor quarter of Liverpool with long rows of brown and grey houses. I think that Pete's father had died or deserted them and there was only his mother. I hope that he recovered and made something of his life. The next day Mansel Davies would talk as if nothing had happened, but it did not work for me. The only thing worse are the dogs who hide behind anonymity or famous people who pretend to truth.

With Pete gone so sadly I was left with Room 262 all to myself for more than a year, an ideal room for thought because it looked out on a verdant bank and was shaded in the afternoons. It also had an air conditioner, because it was designed originally as an infra red laboratory. The production of rotational velocity correlation functions meant that the data had to be fed in to the Elliott 4130, integrated numerically, and transformed into a function of time with a program that I wrote myself. I think that this Algol code is all on www.aias.us. I remember my great delight when the program first worked, and thereafter the rotational velocity correlation function became a central feature of the work that led up to my record breaking D. Sc. Degree in 1977 / 1978, the Harrison Memorial Prize, and Meldola Medal and a record breaking number of distinguished Fellowships. The fact that I was not given tenure has been dismissed repeatedly and out of hand in a historical context as the most sordid corruption. It caused a lot of trouble and kept me in poverty, but makes no dent at all in the delight I felt at this new product of research. I had emerged at last from the Mucker Fog, and the god of imagination was fully awake. When that first program worked, I knew that I was at a turning point of my life. It would not seem to be a spectacular discovery like that of penicillin to the outsider, but it remains highly significant to this day.

Also that summer I began mountaineering. The French Scholarship had been an organizational disaster but I had seen the high mountains of Provence and the Vosges. I had moved to Cwrt Mawr in about June 1972, and began a routine of road and track running that kept me fit and after arriving at Cwrt Mawr again from France I was in need of a run down past Cefn Llan. In the distance from Aberystwyth the mountains of Meirionydd could be seen on a sunny day, and I had cycled down the shoulders of Pumlumon in the first year undergraduate. At Cwrt Mawr I met new friends, and we decided one day to walk up the path from Eisteddfa Gurig up to Pumlumon. I have vague memories only of that first walk, it was fortunately a fine day and the primaeval landscape welcomed us kindly. Later on I would find out with Graham Hall what it was like on Pumlumon in a blizzard. I felt an overwhelming sense of freedom, as if my true role in life should have been a nomad. I sprang out in front of the others and left them a long way behind along a track that led to the summit of Pumlumon. This word means that there are five sources of rivers near the summit, one of which was of the Gwy or Wye, another of the Hafren or Severn. The air was made up of dancing oxygen molecules and there was complete silence except for the singing of larks. There were no revolting wind turbines. Soon the others were tiny figures half a mile or more away in the distance. The summit of Pumlumon is flat and easy to get to on a fine day. When I reached it there was an infinitely memorable view over to the Irish Sea and almost to the English border. Towards the north and south it was all wild mountain. This is the only place in which I could feel human. The only sign of pollution by our messy little species was Nant y Moch Reservoir, with a road winding up to it in the distance. Much later I found that the Battle of Hyddgen had taken place just to the north of the reservoir. My ancestor Owain Glyndw^r has defeated a force ten times his size in the most heroic ising.

With such beauty perpetually in mind, and with a stable existence in Cwrt Mawr, the first truly original work of my scientific life began to take shape back in room 262. I began to realize that the far infra red spectra that I had so carefully accumulated could be transformed to rotational velocity correlation functions that were a stern test of any theory. I had learnt the essence of this in Nice by hours of study and translation of the volumes of Ph. D. material that I read there. I was given nothing else to do by Brot, who did not seem to know what I was doing there. I think I must have decided there and then to go my own way in scientific life. The critically important thing to realize is that the far infra red spectrum can be integrated with a numerical integration routine from NAG. I used Simpson's rule. The integration became part of a Laplace transform, whose output was the correlation function. The latter is an object of statistical mechanics and dynamics, so the far infra red spectrum is a fingerprint of the dynamics of molecules. Early in the twentieth century Paul Langevin had worked out a theory of the dynamics known as the Brownian motion, This theory used a friction coefficient and a random force and was based on the Newton equation. It was later developed by Peter Debye to produce a theory of molecular dynamics called the Debye relaxation theory. I realized gradually that the type of correlation function I was now able to compute could test the Debye theory and all other theories based on it. At that time in 1973, the techniques of molecular dynamics and Monte Carlo computer simulation were also beginning to be developed.

So I gradually worked out the Algol code and wrote it up on the special pads of paper that were handed in to prepare the deck of cards. The work was helped by the fact that Mansel Davies had gone for his three month summer holiday to Criccieth. He did not know how to code computers and was suspicious of what I was doing and how much departmental money I was using. He did not understand correlation functions, so I had to work on my own to make any progress. My intention was to make sure of my Ph. D. as quickly as I could so all my efforts could be focused on this fascinating new world of molecular dynamics. I was aware that I had only a year and a half left for my Ph. D. The academic world was already an impediment, some ancient authoritarian system in which I had found myself embroiled by accident. The coal mine was always around the corner and that had the authority of sudden death about it. With delight one day the program worked, and I rushed back through the dreary Trinity Road to the EDCL to plot it by hand. I think that the department may have been generous enough to give me a pad of graph paper, but I may even have had to buy those. The correlation function gradually took shape, starting at the origin of time (t = 0) and adjusted to unity at t =0. It evolved over picoseconds (a picosecond is ten to the power minus twelve seconds, or one million millionth of a second). With a sense of amazement, I realized that the far infra red spectrum was giving me information on dynamics on this time scale, a motion of molecules so fast that no human could ever detect it by eye. This motion takes place in all liquids all the time. It was first detected by Robert Brown, a predecessor of mine on the Civil List, and named the Brownian motion.

Robert Brown was a botanist from Scotland whose main discoveries were of plant species in Western Australia, but under a microscope could see that pollen particles moved around in a perpetual zig zag. Seemingly there was nothing to cause this motion. The atomic theory of John Dalton, another predecessor of mine on the Civil List, had not yet been accepted and was not widely known, so the Brownian motion was not linked to atomic or molecular dynamics for a very long time. Albert Einstein in 1905 finally showed that the Brownian motion of pollen particles is due to the million million times faster motion of molecules. There I was in 1973 observing these incredibly fast dynamics for the first time, using an old bench with a hole cut in it, a borrowed interferometer, and a primitive computer. As the rotational velocity correlation function took shape it dipped below the zero line and gradually climbed back again to zero. Sometimes it oscillated and looked very much like the interferogram being punched out on the paper tape machine behind me. That was switched off and I had forgotten all about it. My ears were given a rest from incessant pounding and there were no further attempts to blow me to pieces or have me gassed. All thought of career was pushed to the back of my mind. It was an interference in thought and all that I really needed was a minimum amount of personal organization, a way of keeping myself from starving and out of the coal mine. The beauty of nature was all around, on the verdant green bank outside the window, on the bench on a piece of graph paper, and on the distant mountains. Vincent van Gogh must have felt like this in Arles in Provence.

There were graduate students of many nationalities in

Cwrt Mawr, more realistic and able than the undergraduates at the digs of Aberystwyth. There was one from Iran, an infinitely careful man used to the worst regime in the world. We decided to walk up Cadair Idris with one other student, a fluent Welsh speaker, from Minffordd on the road from Machynlleth and just above Tal y Llyn, and I did my five thousand metres on the track in the early morning. It was another fine day luckily, and I was wearing my red track suit. The path climbed up steeply at first through trees, then out to the bare mountain above the tree line. I felt the exhilarating freedom of the mountain and left the other two a long way behind. Not the sanest thing to do, but the beauty of nature was everywhere. I was unaware of any danger on the Minfforth path as it is called now, around a small lake of ancient beauty, Llyn Cau, up and around a steep cliff with Llyn Cau far below, to Pen y Gadair, the summit. I waited for the other two there, keeping a careful eye on their progress. Eventually they toiled up and there was an infinite expanse of beauty across Abermaw and its long rail bridge to the Irish Sea, and surrounded by mountains in all directions. They had been using my red track suite as a guide. "You could see this guy anywhere". Far below lay Tal y Llyn, and we made our way directly down towards it. It could all have happened yesterday. I drove them back to Cwrt Mawr and made myself something that looked like stew. The spoon stood up in it in amazement. There was stale bread and strong tea, and a good night's sleep.

About this time Pete Deft was drinking heavily in Cwrt Mawr and it was very painful. He was a quiet, dedicated student to whom Mansel Davies had given a typically impossible task. By that time the latter did not supervise, if there was any supervision going it was delegated, in Pete's case to someone in Bangor. I remember that he was transferred to room 262 at some point, so the room was filled with high voltage. His sample cell suffered from a design problem so it sparked and this pitted the electrodes. The workshop was very slow to respond and time ticked away. Mansel Davies bellowed insanely at Pete in his office one day, a foot or so from my face, completely enraged and out of control, spewing ugly hatred - not a humanist at all. Alun Price tried to calm him but the damage was done, Pete never recovered, his Ph. D. was destroyed. That set me on the road to independence and I look back in anger. That incident illustrates the knife edged existence at EDCL, so I enveloped myself in discovery. With a system like that, who needs Henry VIII, famous for sudden judicial murder? That academic system was a mediaeval court. With all my self control I remained as aloof from it as I could, and have remained so to this day. When a sow eats her piglets and when an honest student is destroyed before one's eyes, one never forgets it. It must have happened many times over, and the bellowing anger of the system is ever present today, but in electronic disguise, the stalkers, the cowardly haters who lie all the time. The latter have the same effect on me as Mansel Davies, which is no effect at all. Pete fell apart completely and I drove him back to Liverpool, reaching a drab brown and grey street in Liverpool five. That was the last I saw of him, he disappeared through the door, into internal exile.

CHAPTER FOUR

With that first glimpse into the world of moving molecules, I knew that years of discovery were possible if only the system would disappear, or remove itself as far away from me as possible. I quickly built up a library of rotational velocity correlation functions. These functions are built up from the rotational motion of the molecule, a value at some initial time is correlated statistically with a value a time t later, giving an evolutionary record of the super fast molecular dynamics. The beauty of my discoveries of that year 1973 is that the complete correlation function was given by a simple Laplace transform from the far infra spectrum. I had a collection of rare specimens that Darwin could have collected on the Beagle. The next step was to find out how a particular theory coped with the new species on my laboratory bench top, the only thing that the EDCL contributed - the only thing it could find as an office. I just got used to my bench top, which was decorated with packs of cards and paper tapes. Sometimes when in deep thought I could lock the double doors from inside - lock out the politics. It was necessary to do a lot of study and research to find a contemporary theory that could cope with my new specimens. There was certainly no theory of natural selection to be seen anywhere on the horizon. The Debye theory failed catastrophically, it just gave an exponential decay and failed completely to give any detail vividly apparent from my discoveries. It was just a much vaunted theory that painted a bird with no feathers, or armadillo with no rings. Up to that time the Debye relaxation theory was regarded as the classic theory of molecular motion, or "relaxation", at all frequencies below the microwave. My new correlation functions showed that the theory could only give a vague idea of the molecular motion, a badly blurred photograph.

I hunted around for suitable theories and found a few examples as described in Omnia Opera Five of www.aias.us: theories by Lassier and Brot, Gordon and St. Pierre and Steele. I realized that these theories could be tested directly with the new correlation functions. Most of them failed miserably. Later I devised an even sterner test by extending the far infra red data to lower frequencies, and using a combination of techniques. There is still no theory that adequately describes the complete data range and this was the first paper to show this fundamental limitation of knowledge. It was eventually submitted for publication on 21st January 1974, and published in the Journal of the Chemical Society Faraday Transactions II, 70, 1620 (1974). It has remained an acknowledged classic to this day and was the first of many papers that earned me the Harrison Memorial Prize and Meldola Medal of the Royal Society of Chemistry in 1978 and 1979 respectively, recommended by the National Physical Laboratory. Mansel Davies did not know about the Medal procedure in either case because he was too volatile and could have destroyed my chances. I always hoped that the Aberda^r side would prevail, but it never did and the incident with Pete Deft killed off almost all respect. I still try to have some respect for his better side, and it is sure that he was a highly intelligent man. There were some at the EDCL who were far worse than Mansel Davies. He did not know anything about my Thesis of Scientiae Doctor, submitted in secret in 1977 and awarded in 1978. I am the youngest recipient of that degree in modern history and the second youngest in the entire history of the degree from the year 1860, when it was brought into existence in the University of London as a distinction higher than a full professorship.

I cannot recall how I met Graham Hall, but it must have been in 1973 because in the September of that year I drove him up to Oban in Argyll. He had been a geology/ chemistry student so knew all the staff at the EDCL. He was a typical product of the seventies and used the vivid slang of that era, freaking out all over his guitar. To my delight, many years later, I found that he had learned Welsh and was a lecturer in the medium of Welsh. He earned his doctoral degree in mathematics as a mature student. In 1973 he looked like an owl, with large glasses and long hair. He was a geologist who had worked near Ben Mhor on Mull for an undergraduate project. I also met Gareth Kelly and Christie O'Donovan Rossa, who had bright red hair and would speak to me only in Welsh. He had a deeply scarred face but I never asked him how he got the scar. He was a descendant of Jeremiah O'Donovan Rossa of the West of Ireland, and a fluent Gaelic speaker. Gareth Kelly was a Yorkshireman and a member of the Communist Party at that time. He worked on one of Beynon's contraptions, a radio telescope of some kind situated between Aberystwyth and Borth. These three became mountaineering companions, the most unlikely imaginable. The most dangerous trip was made with Graham Hall up to Nant y Moch reservoir and up to a savagely different Pumlumon. This was at a time of year when mist and rain could turn to snow. The idea was to walk up to the summit from the Nant y Moch side, so that the huge unnatural reservoir would gradually shrink into a small puddle below us. Nature that day had other ideas, and was wearing a savagely coloured coat. We were wearing clothes through which the wind tore very easily. With mindless determination we followed the stream called Nant y Moch and left the car near the road. The idea was to reach the summit of Pumlumon, but very suddenly we were enveloped in driving snow and began to walk in circles. The cold became bitter and it was a great effort to keep going. I had the idea of looking for falli g ground and by luck this led back to Nant y Moch. Otherwise I would not be writing this now. Pumlumon was a merciless punisher of the foolish and unprepared. Its great beauty it reserved for those who deserved to see it, and there is a Hyddgen type battle going on now against invaders who wish to destroy it completely with wind turbines. The human species will destroy itself soon if it destroys nature at this pace and no one will go to its wake.

In September 1973 I decided to take a break and go to Oban with Graham Hall, who had lived in the Youth Hostel there as a student on Mull. This trip turned into a pilgrimage to Iona of the Book of Kells. It meant a four hundred mile journey across Wales and up the M6 to Glasgow and in to the Highlands. We set out very early with Graham's bicycle and pack. The journey was completely unprepared, and by luck the old car did not blow a tyre or otherwise give up on the way. The first part of the journey was over the mountains of Wales towards the north east, through Bala and across the border into the flat country of Cheshire and in to the industrial greyness of Manchester at early morning. Once on to the M6 I drove fast in the third lane into the ancient Kingdom of Rheged, past Helvellyn alongside the railway line. I recognized the second half of the word, "Felyn" meaning "yellow" in the ancient language of Cumbria. For the first time I was seeing the island of Great Britain. North of Rheged lay the ancient Kingdom of Ystrad Clud or Strathclyde, the outflow of beautiful water. In 1973 however the border with Scotland flashed past near Carlyle or Carlisle and we drove into agricultural country with well ploughed furrows. This was the country of Hugh MacDiarmaid, another predecessor of mine on the Civil List, and the greatest poet of the twentieth century from Scotland in Scots and English. We turned off the M6 towards Paisley and Erskine and on to the north shore of Strathclyde. On the right was the mass of greyness known as Glasgow, Glas Gae, the green field.

The south bank of Loch Lomond was at first a magical sight, but as mile after mile of beauty flashed by Graham said that beauty is boring, and it can be after a four hundred mile drive. He meant that there was such stunning beauty, and so much of it, that the mind could not take it in. What is really boring is human nature, and of course the whole area has now been destroyed by turbines, temporarily or permanently depends on return to sanity.

Loch Lomond ended at Inverarnan and wild moorland took over to a village called Crianlarich, which means the low pass. This is Rannoch Moor - the fern moor. Raineach in Gaelic, Rhedyn in Welsh. Once again I felt a free spirited nomad as the influence of humanity receded and we turned off towards Oban following the railway line from Glasgow. Suddenly we were across a bridge with a small falls underneath it and I saw a wine coloured sea in the northern sunset, decorated with many fishing boats. The Youth Hostel was a solid building which in that era was primitive but adequate. Now it is advertized on google as a five star hotel, but I don't believe it. I was taken on by the Hostel keeper as a temporary assistant sub warden, the lowest rank imaginable, and I think that Graham became sub Warden. I was so fascinated by the sea and the town that I took a twenty mile bike ride around it that evening, borrowing Graham's bike. I noticed that the tide was coming in and the water under a bridge had started to flow in the opposite direction. The bunks were adequate and part of my duty was to clean out the kitchen, which I did with great alacrity until everything shone for a magpie.

Opposite Oban is the island of Kerrera around which the ferry navigated for Mull and the village of Craignure. I wondered if I could get across to Mull to see the island described by Kenneth Clark in "Civilization" as the place from which he used to visit Iona of the Book of Kells. I wondered how such great beauty could be scribed in such wild landscape. The latter would surely guard its beauty and keep it for itself. So after a few days cleaning out stoves and doing some road running around Oban I asked Graham if I could borrow his bike and tent and set out on the MacBrain Ferry "Columba" to the dark island of Mull. The ferry set sail around Kerrera and soon docked at Craignure. The bike was heavy with a pack and tent and it was tough going through Salen Forest, with the dark Sound of Mull on the right, and the wild coast of mainland Scotland across the Sound. The road was narrow and this is what it was like in the time of Columba (Colm Cille. 7th

Dec. 521 - 9th June 597) and Kenneth (Choinnich or Cainnech) one thousand five hundred years ago. Colm Cille arrived on Iona in 563 A. D. and Cainnech of Aghabee (515 / 516 - 600) was his follower. They are documented by Adomnan (or Eunan), ninth Abbott of Iona (who died in 704). Cainnech was ordained priest in 545 A. D. at Llancarfan in Wales after plague ravaged Ireland. On this wild island of Mull flowered the insular style, initiated by my remote ancestor Dewi Sant (St. David, 500 - 589). These intellectuals were responsible for the towering masterpiece of the insular style - The Book of Kells. That was an age in which civilization flourished, so Kenneth Clark, named after Choinnich, opens "Civilization" with Iona, a small island on the opposite side of Mull from Salen. I was in the sixth century and in the company of civilized human beings, beings who created civilization. I had tried to do the same in room 262. The twentieth century of 1973 had been navigated by - a shallow shoal.

In the small village of Salen there was a stop to buy some milk in a pack, the first time I had ever tasted such stuff, and took a photograph of the thirteenth century Aros Castle of the MacDougals, MacDonalds, and MacLeans. It was only a short distance west to Loch na Keal and Inch Kenneth (Innis Choinich) but I set out northwards towards Ardnacross and Tobermory Youth Hostel. Looming on the right hand side were the dark waters of the Sound of Mull, and I pedalled the heavy bike as far as I could, stopping sometimes to push it. On the left were Aros and Salen Forest, with mountains falling steeply to the sea. It was called the A484, but was really a narrow road of the sixth century. There was complete silence and I was surrounded by Gaelic names, reminding me vaguely or strongly of my own language. The sixth century in which I found myself was a stronger more vibrant time, and cyanogen was completely absent. The distance from Craignure to Tobermory is just over twenty one miles, everything can be googled up instantly now, but in 1973, and back in the sixth century it felt infinite, the road had passing places for cars, and they just scraped by the bike. The cars were a noisy intrusion from the shallow shoals of a time that has lost purpose, the late twentieth century. It was a deep, profound silence, the paper tape punch of the twentieth century had been turned off and there was nothing between the mind and nature. The road was never flat or straight for more than a few yards, and very dark cloud loomed in from the vast Atlantic. It seemed that people used to be here, but they were here no longer, the Highland Clearances had left ghosts in the wind, people evicted for sheep.

Tobermory suddenly sprang in to sight, a small fishing town with brightly coloured houses, one of which was the Youth Hostel. It is still there now and advertized as family friendly. I left the bike and tent there and took a walk around. The mainland of Scotland receded in the distance away from the Sound of Mull, a dark and deep trench cut in the Highlands. The sixth century took its leave and sought shelter in places quieter even than Tobermory. I have vague memories of the Youth Hostel, there must have been an atrocious breakfast and I set out in the morning back down to Salen, my destination being Fionnphort and Iona, a distance of just over forty two miles from Tobermory. This time I took the road towards the south shores of Loch na Keal and Balnahard opposite Innis Choinich or Inch Kenneth. It was a small island in the near distance. In the sixth and later centuries it was en route to Iona, the burial place of Kings, or so they say. When the western gales were too fierce, they would be interred on Innis Choinich. In fact these were probably Highland Chiefs, but never mind. I began to feel the power of the western winds roaring in from the Atlantic in the distance past the cliffs of Ulva. I began to see the ruined crofts more vividly, with my eyes and imagination. People being thrown out of their ancient homes for profit and the thought sickened me profoundly. Innis Choinich was apparently a site founded by the semi mythical Choinich from the main site of Iona. There is little trace left of the two sites, but the incredible detail of the Book of Kells has survived. I saw it much later in Trinity College Library.

The road went up past Balevulin to Dererach on the north shore of Loch Scridain on the great shoulder of Beinn Mhor or Pen Mawr in my own language, the large central mountain of Mull. It looked almost black in the distance, bare moorland without trees. The signs of ruined crofts were miserably clear. It was a hard life of farming and fishing that went on for six thousand years. Some survivors avoided the eviction and forced emigration and in 1973, their descendants still spoke Gaelic. I heard some children and teenagers speaking Gaelic near Pennyghael on the south shore of the loch. "Penn y ghael" is half British and half Irish Celtic. I took a rest there for a while at the side of the A849 and listened to the Gaelic, back again in the sixth century until it was shattered by the roar of a car. It was the first time I had heard Gaelic spoken. Then I began the battle against the wind on to the Ross of Mull. This was the route of pilgrims for many centuries, and the route taken towards the final resting place of Highland and Island Chiefs, Iona. The land to the north gave out at Carraig Mhic Thomais, high cliffs carved out by the savage and hammering Atlantic. Suddenly I was knocked over sideways by a lorry on the narrow road, but landed on grass. They looked back but carried on driving. The next village was Bunessan, and I wondered whether I would get there in one piece. I had been cycling and walking for about half the day and looked forward to whatever there was on Iona.

In fact there was great history on Iona, but in order to reach it I had to load up the bike and tent in to a small boat on the jetty at Fionnphort. The ferryman took it in, and we set out across a mile of water to the jetty at Baile Mor, a little village surrounding the new Abbey of Iona run by the ecumenical Iona Community. It was getting dark and semi consciously I headed straight into the Community. I was kindly but firmly told that it was not a Youth Hostel, so I pitched the tent near a looming stone building - the

Infirmary Museum, so named because it was the Infirmary for the Monks. The tent pitching was a miserable failure, and as I became enveloped in wet polymeric wall material I began to search for a drier place to sleep. I got in to the Museum loft somehow, and put the sleeping bag on the floor, right next to a stone statue of a knight encased in heavy armour, I think it was Hugh MacLean of the Ross of Mull. I was attracted by a light and it was a gathering in the Iona Abbey of the Community. I recall a poem recited in Gaelic. Then it was back to sleep in the Museum Loft, hoping that the knight would not awake and use me as sword practice. In the early morning I was surrounded by a subdued but vibrant light, by Celtic crosses and stone carvings of many a century. Iona is I Chaluim Chille in Gaelic, the Island of Colm Cille or Columba. It became one of the most influential of Abbeys after its foundation in 563 by Colm Cille from Ireland. The Picts and the Danish Northumbrians were converted to Christianity from Iona. The Annals of Ireland were produced here up to about 700 and the great Book of Kells in the years leading up to about 800. It was thought that Iona was safe from the ravages that took place after the collapse of the Roman Empire and was founded in a wild and remote place, but a place of profound beauty in all meanings of the word. The Vikings got to hear of the gold casing of the books in Kells, and killed eighty six monks in 806. The Abbey was dispersed to the Monastery of Kells in Ireland and to other monasteries in Belgium, France and Switzerland that it had helped to found. Slowly Europe dragged itself back from desolation as civilization reached it again from Iona.

The Abbots made an attempt to reoccupy Iona but the Vikings raided again in 825 and burned it to the ground. This practice continues to this day in places such as Gelliwastad, but it is carried out by contemporary savages in the guise of affluence. A Benedictine order was established on the site of the original Abbey of Colm Cille but after the reformation it too was destroyed and its books dispersed. This practice still continues today, when books are thrown into skips by people interested in blank nothingness - not in civilization at all. In 1938, the Abbey was rebuilt and restored to its present condition by the ecumenical Iona Community, and in to this I stumbled exhausted in the Autumn of 1973. The first few Abbots of Iona would have attained a much higher degree of civilization than any County Council. The first nine Abbotts were: Colm Cile mac Fedelmtheo died 9th June 597; Baithere mac Brenaird, died 9th June 598; Lasren mac Feradaig died 16th September 605; Fergno Britt mac Failbi died 2nd March 623; Segene mac Fiachnai died 12th August 652; Suibne moccu Fir Thri died 11th January 657; Cunmere Find, died 24th February 660; Failbe mac Pipain died 22nd March 679 and Adomnan mac Ronain died 23rd September 704 who wrote the Life of Colm Cille. The Abbey had already lasted much longer than the University of Wales or the EDCL back in Wales. It did not take Vikings to destroy them, they decayed from within and died of cynicism. The accurate dating of those times reveal a high degree of organization and hope for the future. The existence of an Infirmary reveals a high degree of compassion, the Vikings reveal themselves a murderous savages of the type familiar in our times. One cannot define civilization very easily, but as Kenneth Clark wrote, one can see barbarism very clearly and with immediacy. Civilization takes great effort, barbarism is the flick of a sword or matchbox. In the cold of early morning I found myself crossing the mile of sea back to Fionnphort and back to Craignure, a distance of thirty five miles. The wind was behind me so I hoped to get back quickly to catch the Columba again to Oban. I drank some liquid in Bunessan which was advertized as milk. The Friesian must have given up. Then it was back as quickly as I could to the Aird of Kinloch where the road begins its ascent up the shoulder of Beinn Mhor, the towering mountain was bleak and black on my left, with patches of sunshine. On my right lay many a desolate pile of stone that used to be a living hearth. The ascent was just possible without pushing the bike, which had the saturated remnants of a tent in trail. Ben Bhearnach loomed above on the left and the road twisted its way suddenly into Craignure, a small village with a pier. I had cycled about a hundred miles around Mull and visited one of the most profoundly influential sites of early mediaeval Europe. It was a fine day and I waited for the Columba back to Oban and cycled slowly in to the Youth Hostel and handed over to the dismayed Graham Hall a sodden pack of fabric, the remains of a tent. My time in the sixth century had been as much of an influence on me as Colm Cille on his contemporaries, and it was difficult to adjust to materialism again. This took the form of haggis and chips near the town centre. I woke after two days or so to find that the Warden's wife had taken care of me, and I must have been very ill from some kind of food poisoning. Graham suggested that it was Vietnamese chicken disease picked up from a fishing boat. Whatever it was I went out photographing Loch Glean a Bhearraidh to produce a tortoiseshell pattern of light. That cured me in an instant and I enlarged the photograph to give to my parents. My photographic slides of that trip have all been lost. They would not have been in the Abbey of Iona in the sixth century.

Before beginning the long drive back to Aberystwyth Graham and I took a drive to Clencoe, across Connel bridge where I had seen the water flow both ways as the tide came in and out on the road to Glencoe. We planned the ascent up to Bidean nam Bean and the nose (sron in Gaelic) of Aonach Dubh and as usual the great excitement of mountaineering took over and I left Graham far behind and below. I could always see him so there was no danger. Nearing the summit the western isles were thrown out like pearls on the horizon but although the summit was in easy reach I decided to go back down to meet Graham, and we walked back to the car before the weather turned nasty or it got too cold. Civilization was found on the nose of Aonach Dubh (the black ridge), it was found on Iona, but now it was time for the M6 again, where civilization is not so apparent. The first few miles across moors to Crianlarich were the best, then civilization gradually faded away. Only a small remnant of it was to be found in Aberystwyth, Room 262. The best thing about the M6 was to get off it, and that led to the mountains of Wales and Aberystwyth. It was time to pay a short visit to my parents, who did not approve very much of the trip to Oban. I never got used to the new house, 91 Lone Road and I was well and truly back in the twentieth century. I thought that I had better get back to work again in Room 262, where I had trapped a piece of civilization on a laboratory bench. The car was given a check and I started out for Aberystwyth.

The record on the Omnia Opera of www.aias.us shows that my work and understanding developed very rapidly after my return from the short holiday in Scotland. Several more papers were submitted and I was also working on my Ph. D. Thesis. I realized that the correlation function method could be applied to collision induced absorption in the far infra red. This type of absorption occurs in molecules which do not have a dipole moment, which is a kind of asymmetric distribution of charge that acts like an antenna for radiation. These papers were entirely my own work and Mansel Davies allowed me to publish on my own. This was the best thing that he did during the Ph. D. and I appreciate that. These papers reached an acknowledged higher standard than anything else being produced at the EDCL. They were: Omnia Opera (OO) 7, submitted on 8th March 1974; OO8, submitted on 25th May 1974; OO11, submitted on 10th June 1974; OO10, submitted on 9th October 1974 from Oxford but prepared at Aberystwyth; and OO9, submitted on 13th Nov. 1974 from Oxford but prepared entirely at Aberystwyth. My Ph. D. Thesis is OO6 and was submitted on 9th July 1974. There were ten papers and a Ph. D. Thesis published as a student, refereed about thirty times and examined externally by Prof. John Rowlinson, head of the Physical Chemistry Laboratory at Oxford. These papers pioneered the use of the rotational velocity correlation function to test models and theories of various phenomena as described in the original papers in the Omnia Opera. They made an immediate impression internationally and piles of reprints and reprint requests began to accumulate in Room 262. I was naively delighted and gave some reprints to members of staff who had tenure, but who were relatively unknown and unproductive. The effect was to produce envy which raised its ugly head as soon as 1977. Most of the people of that era are deceased and almost all are retired, so it is time to talk plain history. The problem is that civilization is prone to barbarism and the coat of many colours has that effect. From the vantage point of April 2013, almost forty years later, it is possible to write objective history without fear of further reprisal.

One out of several good parts of Mansel Davies is that he did not suffer from envy, which can occur in a Ph. D. supervisor. He became very enthusiastic about my work and began to advertise me. This is all very well, but to do that one needs to understand the work, otherwise one cannot defend it against envy. Similarly John Thomas began to advertise me but probably never read my work. John Thomas did not code a computer and could not produce theory. He was and is an organizer. That may be needed in science but it is the opposite of an artist. If these two had been genuine, which they were not, they could easily have appointed me to tenure at the lowest level of tenured research associate in the summer of 1974. The Omnia Opera shows that I would have been very productive and that productivity would have helped get them funding and all the rest of it, the exigency of the system in which they lived. To me, the system is and was something that happens to exist, the accidental result of a type of organization, an accident that has nothing whatsoever to do with original thought. One may as well try to organize the thought of Vincent van Gogh or Dylan Thomas. They simply did not make the simple effort to organize tenure on my behalf, while advertising me at the same time. That is shallow hypocrisy, and again it made me want to go my own way. The academic system of that era or any era does not recognize merit, it is a system in which powerful people dominate. They just made sure that their own groups were tenured, and all of that was very primitive. It was so primitive that they hung on to their salaries long after the EDCL was dead.

As 1973 drew to a close there had been a few more mountaineering trips: I made an ascent of Snowdon three times, from both sides, and ascents of Carnedd Dafydd and Carnedd Llywelyn, with Christie O'Donovan Rossa and Gareth Kelly. Christie told me that he was descended from Jeremiah O'Donovan Rossa (1831 - 1915), known as the spiritual descendant of Colm Cille, and exiled to New York City for his views as a Fenian. The O'Donovan Rossa family comes from Cork, the same county as Michael Collins. The Carneddau ascent started from Ogwen Cottage in fine weather but we were soon enveloped in fog and cold again. After a while I listened for a stream and we went directly down to Ffynnon Lloer to Tal y Llyn Ogwen and Gwern Goch Uchaf and back along the road to the car. We were foolishly unprepared and I saw that Gaerth Kelly was shivering from cold, and that the wild red hair of O' Donovan Rossa had turned a shade of snow white. Listening for a stream is one way of getting off a mountain, but with the Carneddau one has to be prepared with real mountaineering gear. I made one ascent of Snowdon alone from Gorphwysfa and the miners' track and up to the railway in a severe blizzard. That route is usually a safe one. Kelly, O' Donovan Rossa and myself also made an ascent from Ffridd Uchaf on the other side of Snowdon and one ascent from Gorphwysfa and down the railway and around back up Llanberis Pass. We were always glad to get back to Cwrt Mawr, but the mountaineering relieved some of the anxiety I was beginning to feel as my Ph. D. drew to a close because there was no mention of tenure or a post doctoral. By about September 1973 I must have applied for the three post doctoral fellowships that I was awarded in open competition because they were due to start in September or October 1974.

I must have started with an application for a Science Research Council Post Doctoral Fellowship and must have obtained the signatures of both Mansel Davies and John Thomas. My own wish was to carry on working at Aberystwyth, but the system would not allow it so I must have written Oxford at random. At that time I did not know Rowlinson at all. It is obvious now in April 2013 that the creative stage of my life was beginning to come into full force, and any reasonable administration would have recognized it with minimal support. The great weakness of the academic system is that it places creativity at its mercy, but it is not in itself creative. Mansel Davies eventually suggested that I apply for an ICI European Fellowship and a Canadian NRC Fellowship. I went along with this, but with great dismay. Mansel Davies had himself been an ICI Fellow for a year from 1946 to 1947 at Leeds, so this is why he suggested it. I was appalled by the casual way in which he acted, and by an authoritarian and self promoting academic system that had no clearly defined career structure despite its emphasis on career. This is why I have evolved completely away from shallow careerism into a much more profoundly creative life. So as 1974 approached the happy time at Aberystwyth was evaporating. My work was succeeding brilliantly, as it is now, but support from the system was non existent. In the end I had to construct my own way of life and become completely independent. The happy time at Cwrt Mawr was also drawing to an end, and in the summer of 1974 I was shifted in to another room. The disruptions had begun again.

I won all three Fellowships in open competition so I am sure that I should have been given tenure at the EDCL. To my disgust I was asked to go to work with Brot on the ICI European Fellowship and I knew that that would have been a disaster. Mansel Davies was divorced from reality and kept talking about a Fellowship being similar to

Hooke's law, and that eventually I would be given tenure at the EDCL. This was rubbish, and he probably knew it. He wished me to apply for an NRCC Fellowship because in the past, some of his students had gone to Canada. There was only one option left open, to take the SRC Fellowship at Oxford. Mansel Davies became abruptly irritated and asked why I would want to go there. He knew that I do not want to go anywhere. I had to finish my Ph. D. Thesis, which was acknowledged later by Mansel Davies as the best he had produced, the only problem is that he had not produced it, he had almost wrecked it. In the pungent slang of the United States, of which I am a citizen, why didn't they cut out the chicken shit? At the time of writing (April 2013) I realize that I could have taken the SRC post doctoral to physics at Aberystwyth, but there would have been no purpose in it. Post doctorals were just another form of cannon fodder. The Thesis had to be bound in three copies, one for the EDCL Library, one for the National Library of Wales, one for another organization, I forget which, probably the University Registry in Cardiff. The papers that had been published were bound in to the Thesis, whose main part is in OO6 on www.aias.us. It was announced that my external examiner would be Prof John Rowlinson, F. R. S., from Oxford, the internal examiners would be Dr. Graham Williams and my supervisor, Prof. Mansel Davies. The verbal examination was not a problem, Rowlinson asked a few questions about van der Waals forces or similar, the envious Graham Williams fired away but was kept under control because he was hoping for a professorship. I was awarded the Ph. D. but by that time I was in very low spirits. As usual, creativity was an antidote to human stupidity and the exigency of the machine, in the memorable words of R. S. Thomas. It all had to begin again, I had to look for digs again, this time in Oxford, and had to transfer all my computer work to a new computer. Neither Rowlinson nor Mansel Davies coded computers. My studentship ran until about October 1974, so I had time to find digs in some totally anonymous suburb of North Oxford. I think I drove all the way to Oxford to find a place. It was just a dreary room in a dreary suburb. The landlord and his son were both nutters and so I quickly had to leave again for a cellar room in South Parks Road. In that summer of 1974 Richard Nixon was forced to resign, and I listened with complete disgust to what was happening. It was fully apparent that here was a dictator caught just in time.

My undergraduate and graduate days at Aberystwyth were at an end, I had two brilliant degrees but here I was again, looking for digs in a foreign town. The Ph. D. had started very badly, a lot of time was wasted by non existent supervision until I took control of things myself. The trip to France was completely unorganized but I improvised my way out of deep trouble caused by lack of supervision, and learned many new things. The happy time was after my return from France until I was obliged once more to go to on another ill organized journey. If I could have left the system at that time I would have. It took until 1995 until I could finally rid myself of the machine. An artist cannot be controlled by a system.

CHAPTER FIVE

The decade from about 1974 to1983 marked a great development in my work as a chemical physicist as can be seen from the Omnia Opera, but it was accompanied by some of the most severe hardship of my life. The march of ideas on the Omnia Opera gives little idea of the Gulag like conditions at the EDCL during that time. In the summer of 1974 I was moved into another room in Cwrt Mawr and so lost touch with my friends there. After my refusal to go to Nice, Mansel Davies had appeared to wash his hands of me entirely and I was faced with a long journey to Oxford to find digs again. I must have made a preliminary journey to find digs and met one boneheaded relic who told me that Rowlinson must be pronounced Rawlinson, still in the first war era. Digs were randomly found in anonymity. It could have been a dustbin in any alley. I was now a fully independent scientist, and looked back in anger at the smug Aberystwyth institutions who purred and looked after themselves. I worked on my ideas about applying the correlation function method to non dipolar liquids. Three papers were submitted in the first few weeks after arriving at Oxford, Omnia Opera (OO) 9 on 13th Nov. 1974, Omnia Opera (OO) 10 on 9th Oct. 1974, and OO12 on 19th Dec. 1974. These were papers based on work in Aberystwyth and from the drawing I can see that the draughtsmen at the Physical Chemistry Laboratory had been allowed to draw the diagrams. This was the first time I had had any help of this kind. All three were refereed and published and made the usual big impact in terms of reprint requests. In OO9 and OO10 I implemented two methods of obtaining the correlation function from data, and these resulted in excellent agreement: Simpson's rule and the Fast Fourier transform, giving essentially identical results and giving great confidence in the method.

As the time for transferring to Oxford approached I

must have gathered together the packs of cards on my desk, and all the papers I could take with me. The paper tape rolls and computer paper output were left in Room 262, stacked up on the floor and bench. I was being betrayed very cynically by the system, which could easily have appointed me to tenure. All this waste of time and built up resentment could have been avoided. The basic problem was all too clear, I was in the hands of people who did not and did not want to know what I was doing. At the same time I was being advertized as a whizz kid in public and cold shouldered in private. It was perfectly disgusting, so I did not feel the need for any goodbyes. I must have spent a little time with my parents and made for the infinitely boring M4 motorway and the infinitely remote little town of Oxford with which I had nothing in common. Rowlinson knew all this perfectly well, and knew all about the system at Aberystwyth. He had no real intention to force me to comply with his ideas, to his credit. I recall that the first time he saw me was in a short interview at the PCL, where he had his office as Dr. Lee's Professor and Head of Department. Later he became Prof. Sir John Rowlinson, and was already an F. R. S. He was nervous but seemed to be quite friendly, somewhat to my surprise. In the by then accepted fashion he didn't know what I was doing there, other than Aberystwyth had done the dirty. That was well known throughout Britain already. Authority outside Aberystwyth was not pleased to have their fellowships hocked around because some greedy head of department wanted to use tenure to build up his group at the expense of all others, Government included. I think that this is what Rowlinson was trying to say.

I was led to another benchtop, this time in a dark laboratory under the control of Prof. Sir Harold Thompson, F. R. S. of St John's College and the Football Association. He was a short, fat Yorkshireman who smoked a cigar all the time. His laboratory was empty and unused and situated outside the Physical Chemistry Laboratory (PCL) in South Parks Road. Then I was on my own again, wondering again what I was doing there. This was probably the bleakest time of the spectacularly successful decade 1974 to 1983, with no sign of success on the horizon. The first problem was to find a computer, which turned out to be an ICL in the computer unit at Oxford (International Computers Ltd., 1968 - 2002). A large amount of work had to be done to convert the code from the Elliott 4130 to the ICL, and this meant many long walks past Keble College on to Banbury Road until the code was working again. The walk cut through the natural and life sciences complex of buildings and the Pitt Rivers Museum, full of long toothed skeletons of various kinds, then back to the PCL. Also, I had to find a new athletics track and new athletics routine. This was the Iffley Road running track, to which I walked over the bridge near Magdalen College. Erasmus had spent some time at Magdalen and had met Sir Thomas More before writing "In Praise of Folly" in which he swept away the hypocrisy of his own time. I thought that there was no greater folly and hypocrisy than the present, what was I doing here in the damp bog caused by the confluence of the Cherwell and the Thames? Iffley Road had a small stadium and a changing room, and was a broader track than that at Aberystwyth. My wallet was stolen there and that is the most vivid memory I have of Iffley Road. I did about five thousand metres every day, sometimes as it was getting dark so I could see the lights of the backs of the Colleges in the distance, one of them being Merton College. It was a cinder track, and one day I was passed by Bannister, Brasher and Chattaway training there for the last time before it was torn up for a tartan track. They wanted to relive their triumphant four minute mile in the fifties. Bannister completed the mile in 3 minutes 59.6 seconds, hauled around for three and a half laps by the others.

The digs began to cause trouble almost immediately, the landlady was of Welsh origin and spoke Welsh, but was under the thumb of a violent nutter of a Yorkshire husband and a rather weird son, a thirty five year old adolescent who hated Latin being pronounced in a Welsh accent. This was indeed the city of lost causes. One day the landlord grabbed a hold of me and began to lift me off the floor in a bear hug, a form of greeting no doubt. I was about to make a strong formal protest when the landlady intervened. After a few weeks of this, and of driving and cycling down to the PCL, I looked for new digs. The PCL itself is a large complex of offices, lecture theatres, laboratories and one large common room. I ran in to a tradition there, coffee in the morning and tea in the afternoon. There was also lunch where I could get a little to eat, and in the evenings it was again fish and chips on the way back to North Oxford, as if anyone would want to go back to North Oxford. So it was just a transfer of the same existence. I was in to my work independently, and had to suffer gladly the fools who had put me there. Rowlinson was no fool but was resigned to the system. Both of us were already thinking of the best way out of this. I did not meet many of the PCL staff but soon discovered the presence of a coffee and chocolate machine. It looked to be exactly the same as the machines in the EDCL and near the computer unit at Aberystwyth. Even the coffee was the same, a liquid whose molecules eluded analysis.

The original part of life was always the same, the world of ideas. This meant that I could be back in the scriptorium of Iona and work independently of the passage of one thousand five hundred years of time. It did not matter what I was doing there, or anywhere. Academic organization did not exist, but the world of ideas was as vibrant as the ink in the Book of Kells. So for this reason and this reason alone I could tolerate being transferred to a bog after six years of very hard work. Once again there was no input from my nominal supervisor, my first post doctoral supervisor, but by that time it did not matter, and it has not mattered ever since. Ideas cannot be supervised. At some point I was given a proper office or part office at the PCL, and noticed that it had a small library. The main library was the Bodleian, which was a short distance away, a copyright library with a vast collection of volumes. During the third and final year of my Ph. D. at Aberystwyth I had worked with G. J. Davies at the Post Office Research Centre at Dollis Hill in North London and had written and submitted a paper on 16th July 1974. Graham's part was minimal. This is recorded as Omnia Opera (OO) 13 , implementing the tremendously complicated theory of Frost, an Australian visitor who thought that he had wasted a year with Mansel Davies and filled in the time with this Clebsch Gordan theory. I had recorded spectra with pressures as high as one hundred and fifty atmospheres and had designed a new 137.6 cm gold plated cell. I drove up to Dollis Hill with this cell. As usual there were no preparation for my visit, I had to sleep on the floor of Graham Davies' flat in a bag. So it was again the non existent organization versus the inconvenient and enquiring mind. The only reason for the trip to Dollis Hill was to extend the spectrum to 2 wavenumbers (60 GHz). Dollis Hill, according to Graham, was the real world, but to me it was a pit like dump to get out of through miles of traffic jam to Clapham Junction and the M4. In early 1975 this dubious and one sided cooperation was renewed from Oxford. I was getting used to motorway driving and could drive up to London and back in one day with ease, on one occasion to get a Rollin detector from the National Physical Laboratory for Mansel Davies, a kind of postman and messenger boy combined. He began to complain about the cost of liquid helium so the Rollin detector may as well have remained in London.

On 19th Dec. 1974 the first multi technical paper was submitted from Oxford, a submission long delayed by the failure of Daniel Canet to deliver his results from Nancy. This was the paper and technique that was to lead to the European Molecular Liquids Group and its Project Delta. I must have spent some time with my parents at 91 Lone Road, but I could never get used to this terraced house on the side of a road after the magic of "Pant y Bedw", now a gaunt ruin. Compared with the awful digs at Oxford it was home of a kind for a short while. The drive back to Oxford was made in dreary mid winter and I do not remember much about it. The mind blanks out the blankness of mere existence. Oxford was a mere existence, materially, and my first problem was to get away from an unstable landlord. So I found a damp, mould covered cell in a basement off South Parks Road, near St Cross College and opposite Balliol College. The underground room stank with decay and mold, and this is often the reality of Oxford because of its low lying, swampy situation. There was a place to make food, and I must have had some means of keeping dry. This was preferable to being assaulted by a nut. The Jericho district of Oxford for example is an outright slum, situated near the prison, and one day I met a distraught young woman who asked me the way to it. The pity of that stays in the mind. On 6th February 1975 Omnia Opera 14 was submitted with Alun Price and Rafik Moutran from Aberystwyth. This was another late submission of work done much earlier. Rafik was a quiet Egyptian Coptic Christian who sadly lost his mother during his stay at Aberystwyth. Another image I have in mind is of Rafik rushing from a telephone call along that long cold corridor, tears streaming from his eyes. No doubt he too was wondering what he was doing there. I could not give him any answer, the pity of it overwhelmed me.

I attended all of Rowlinson's research seminars, and they introduced me to the type of liquid phase study for which Rowlinson was known. He had developed this work at Imperial College London before moving to Oxford. Completely by accident I met Dominic Tildesley, a Ph. D. student who had come to work at Oxford from Southampton. I think that both Tildesley and Rowlinson were from the north. Tildesley had a generous and open nature and was later to describe the academic system as a loonie bin. He became a Chief Scientist at Unilever. He began to talk of computer simulation. In those days Monte

Carlo and molecular dynamics computer simulation were being developed for atoms, Konrad Singer of Royal Holloway College being a pioneer. I was very interested when I found that the technique could produce time correlation functions because it could produce the correlation functions that I had pioneered from the far infra red. My work was already known internationally and showed the severe limitations of analytical models in the far infra red, and the complete collapse of the Debye relaxation theory. I had also showed that chemical physics had shied away from the challenge of describing the far infra red combined with lower frequency data, and had shied away even further from the challenge of describing data from many techniques in a self consistent way. Chemical physics still has not solved that problem because my work was deliberately wrecked by Howard Purnell when I refused to become his errand boy in Swansea. That was also well known all over Britain. Tildesley was a near contemporary with whom I could talk. This was a relief because people like Brian Smith were inviting me to talk to people instead of remaining locked in my office. Brian Smith was a mountaineering companion of Rowlinson. I found my office to be more fascinating, the new correlation functions taking shape before my eyes like a photograph in the development tank.

I was also more interested in memory functions than coffee and tea with biscuits. I was the first to apply the memory function to the far infra red and found that it was the cure for the Debye relaxation theory. The latter was an imaginative theory in its time and described the interaction of molecules with friction combined with a random force. At Oxford in late 1974 or early 1975 I found that its failure in the far infra red is due to the fact that the friction coefficient is too simply described. It had to be replaced by a memory function, a mathematical function that describes the memory of past encounters in the zig zag motion of molecules caused by collisions. Much later I animated this motion with Chris Pelkie at Cornell, and the animation is on www.aias.us. The animation shows that the molecular dynamics computer simulation code works perfectly, code that began to be developed in those pioneering days at Oxford. I was also working on the technique developed during my Ph. D. and one of the best papers on this was submitted from Oxford as OO15 on 29th April 1975. The correlation functions in this paper were again produced in two ways, using Simpson's rule and the Cooley Tukey fast Fourier transform program that I developed independently. The almost exact agreement between the two methods was deeply satisfactory. This is a fully mature paper of its type, no theory was able to match the data, even when restricted to the far infra red. OO17 was submitted on 2nd May 1975 from Oxford after another visit to Dollis Hill in winter. I recall the bleakness of the countryside in winter, and again nothing had been prepared, so I just slept on the floor again. The data in this paper stretched down to 2 wavenumbers and again this is a classic paper of the pre memory function era.

To my surprise, Mansel Davies invited me to give a research lecture at Aberystwyth in the winter of 1975 and I drove there from Oxford past a great pile of stone called Blenheim Palace, through Woodstock and eventually in to the Wye Valley. The lecture seemed to go well and I decided to drive back that evening. I may have given the first results from the memory function technique in that lecture, but shortly later there was a conference organized at Gregynog attended by George Wylie. There was snow on the ground outside and at that conference I recall giving a lecture on the memory function approach. This was interrupted by some clown from Bangor who asked me what I was talking about. Obviously the proceedings were well beyond him. I thought of spam and chips, but replied by stating the obvious, I was talking about memory functions. Mansel Davies was out of his depth and wondering whether to save his own reputation again by joining in the attack. George Wylie mentioned laconically that it was a brilliant lecture and that the memory function technique was a wonderful discovery. That saved my skin and the kinder side of Mansel Davies invited me to stay at his home, reputation strengthened by a prodigal. He suddenly became very friendly and showed me a copy of his second edition of Principia by Newton. I asked if he had read it and he said of course not. The first paper on the memory function was submitted on 17th July 1975 from Oxford with a new Ph. D. student of Mansel Davies called Gareth John Evans, who had been awarded the Mathews Prize for the best first year results in chemistry and held a studentship on an S. R. C. Grant to Mansel Davies.

So I must have met Gareth Evans in the time between the Gregynog Conference of the winter of 1975 and the Spring or early summer of 1975. For the first six months of his Ph. D. he had apparently been told to mend a paper tape punch, which is a worse fate even than the synthesis of cyanogen. On the 22nd August 1975, OO21 was submitted from Oxford with Graham Davies, another classic paper which showed that the far infra red absorption of non dipolar liquids could be described perfectly by the memory function technique. That is still a high point of knowledge in this area of chemical physics. Between winter and summer of 1975 however I applied for a Junior Research Fellowship of Wolfson College Oxford purely to get out of my damp underground cell. To his credit, Rowlinson supported this application and I was short listed for an interview. There were probably many other candidates. The interview was conducted in a building which I eventually found at the end of Linton Road off Banbury Road. This was and is Wolfson College, founded in 1966 by donations from the Wolfson and Ford Foundations in typical sixties concrete style. I found myself in a room at the focus of a mirror made up of the President and Fellows, who fired away with many questions of no relevance to memory functions but which meant something to them. The President was a retired High Court Judge called Sir Henry Fisher (1918 - 2005), son of the sometime Archbishop of Canterbury. So I waffled and answered as best as I could and was duly elected Junior Research Fellow. This was the first time I had established a formal link with Oxford.

Life at Oxford improved dramatically in the material sense and I moved in about the summer of 1975 to my own modern room with proper heating. It was and is a mixed graduate College. It has no high table and no undergraduates, and I was entitled to battels, which means an evening meal self service. I was situated in a curving wall called the Berlin Wall from the first President, Sir Isaiah Berlin. There was also a good library on two levels in which I found a book on Newton. Summer in Oxford in 1975 was quite tolerable, South Parks became a pleasant sight. I also met an Indian friend with a cut glass English accent who was due to do a post doctoral or post graduate with Bruce Berne in New York City and was invited to dinner at his College, Merton College, one of the oldest Oxford Colleges. I was also invited by him to his graduation ceremony which took place with champaign on the lawn. The best graduates in Latin and Greek were destined for the diplomatic service. To my consternation, Mansel Davies asked me to supervise Gareth Evans, perhaps not in so many words, but that was the intent. In retrospect this is outrageous, especially as nothing had been arranged, par for the course. I suppose I was expected to pay double, for a room in Wolfson College and a room in Aberystwyth, but I could not afford it, very obviously. It also meant using two different computers and oscillating like a rusty spring between Oxford and Aberystwyth, training in two different places, and all the rest of it. There was no communication between Mansel Davies and Oxford. The latter might get up tight because I was supposed to live within a few miles of the centre of Oxford.

So the only solution was to sleep on the floor of room 262 in a sleeping bag. I thought that this was fine if no one objected. There was a precedent in that Monk had done so during his time in the Soddy laboratory, and there was also a caretaker's flat which was used as domestic quarters. The floor was concrete and the flashing light of the interferometer was difficult to contend with. I suppose that Mansel Davies was talking about tenure at the EDCL. I got up very early in the morning and was at work before the day started and must have been allowed to fire up the Elliott 4130 again. Gareth Evans was looking back in anger at six months wasted on a paper tape punch. I could see another Ph. D. going down the drain as in the case of Pete Deft. So I decided to invite Gareth on to the pioneering OO20 as co author and had to leave for Oxford before my absence was noticed. During the summer of 1975 a few more papers were submitted: OO18 on 11th August 1975, in a scruffy journal called Advances in Molecular Relaxation and Interaction Processes. The journal published the manuscript, which is of acknowledged high quality, but looks like a hay stack. I also started work with Rowlinson on OO16, my first review article, "The Motion of Simple Molecules in Liquids". This was at the invitation of Rowlinson who told me that he had to have something to show for my presence, or more accurately, semi-presence. The memory function technique is reviewed in this article. OO21 was submitted on 22nd August 1975 from Oxford, with Graham Davies at Dollis Hill; and OO22 was submitted on 27th Oct 1975 from Oxford, also with Graham Davies at Dollis Hill and also used the memory function technique to great effect. In the summer and autumn of 1975 I decided to start work on computer simulation, and was given a pioneering program developed in various groups in Britain that could deal with diatomics. This was handed over to me by Dominic Tildesley as an immensely long pack of cards. That began the great adventure of computer simulation, which I pioneered at Aberystwyth, many years before others eventually started to use it.

It was taken very carefully to the back seat of the car and driven back to the EDCL, and placed carefully on the bench in room 262. I locked the double doors and settled down on the concrete floor, as ascetic as Colm Cille. In the bright light of early morning (or it could have been in the hammering of rain), it was taken up to the computer unit where an incredulous staff loaded it on to the computer using magnetic tapes. It was to be used on the new remote link to the CDC 7600 at the University of Manchester Regional Computer Centre (UMRCC) and was written in 128 bit single precision FORTRAN. It had to be run on zero priority, which meant that a turn around would average a month. From the perspective of today's hyperfast computers it was a ridiculously slow process, barely possible, but with great patience and determination I got it to work. It would take a couple of years before I got the first results, first with Gerard Wegdam, then with my post doctoral Mauro Ferrario, later Prof. Mauro Ferrario, Director of CECAM in Switzerland. On one of those visits from Oxford, in the summer of 1975, I saw by accident an advertisement for the Ramsay Memorial Fellowship competition of 1976, and got the necessary bureaucratic signatures for an application, just in time for the deadline. Obviously the story of 1974 was repeating itself, I was being asked to supervise someone else's student at the EDCL, but there was no effective effort for tenure on my behalf. I was not allowed to apply for tenure, and there was no objective measure of how tenure was awarded. A future career depended entirely on tenure. At any time, it could have been awarded to me at the EDCL, and very easily. Once more I was the puppet in someone else's cynical career play.

Mansel Davies had pushed his luck too far and Oxford objected to my use as a surrogate supervisor. Nearly forty years later I know clearly that this was entirely unethical. I was the fall guy and was hauled in to Sir Henry Fisher's office for a judgment, or so it felt. He turned out to be a kindly man and accepted my waffling explanation. Rowlinson also had a kind side to his character and agreed to co sign my S. R. C. application for a new interferometer. After all if I was successful he could keep it when my fellowship ran out. He had tenure, I did not. So all depended on the result of the application for the Ramsay Memorial Fellowship of University College London - probably the toughest Fellowship competition of all. I had already been put on the treadmill of Fellowships, which had to be won every few years in the toughest of competitions. The carpenters who made the treadmill were comfortably tenured and avoided all competition for as long as they could. From this perspective this was an outrageously cynical way to treat acknowledged talent, and unforgivable. I was inwardly angry and outwardly polite as ever. I was not so young any more and still being made to apply for lecturer. I am not sure what Gareth Evans did when I was at Oxford, but being an experimentalist there was little he could do. Without a paper tape punch he could do nothing. I was hoping that this farcical waste of Ph. D. time could be remedied temporarily by theory, and ultimately by new equipment. On 4th February 1976 OO19 was submitted to a letters journal called "Chemical Physics Letters", and accepted for publication as announcing work of importance on the memory function. By that time I was careful to spend more time at Oxford. OO23 was submitted on 9th February 1976 with Gareth Evans invited as co author on data that I had obtained on compressed ethylene. Although he had no equipment his Ph. D. was already quite safe with two published papers. OO25, submitted on 7th April 1976, mentions the award of an equipment grant. This was a new interferometer awarded at Oxford.

I had also been awarded a Ramsay Memorial Fellowship and was allowed by University College London to take it up at the EDCL. Mansel Davies notified me of the award in the long corridor of EDCL, where my fate was so often determined. He told me that I had won it by a mile. I was still snatching sleep on the concrete floor of Room 262, and did not know what I had achieved, I did not know that the Ramsay was a prestigious Fellowship. I got back to Oxford and asked Rowlinson if I could transfer to the EDCL and if he could allow the new interferometer to be set up in room 262. He readily agreed because he knew that I had been forced to hock the fellowship in the first place. Everyone in Britain expected me to be tenured at the EDCL. The Americans were especially disturbed that I wasn't. OO26 was submitted from Oxford on 15th Oct. 1975 and published in "Spectrochimica Acta" edited by Prof. Sir Harold Thompson. This paper is one of several that used the memory function to reproduce far infra red spectra of dipolar liquids. The memory function theory was the best theory by far at the time and its use was always limited to three variables at most. OO27 was submitted on 6th Nov. 1975 from Oxford and developed a fine theory of line broadening based on the memory function. I was very pleased with this paper because the theory could describe all stages of line broadening from sharp peaks to broad bands. This was again published in Spectrochimica Acta. The relative stability at Wolfson College Oxford resulted in work of acknowledged originality. All of these papers were published in the best journals, and all were refereed two or three times. They were the result of very original thought, working outside a large group, and essentially on my own. The unstoppable development of imagination can be seen in them very clearly. Wolfson College represented the modernist Oxford and there were none of the traditional trappings, no silver plate, servants or gallons of wine. After I had explained to Sir Henry Fisher what was going on at Aberystwyth life was fine there. The traditionalist Oxford was represented by Merton College, where I dined once. It was long, fussy affair with servants. At Wolfson College I just got my own food on a tray and enjoyed eating it after a long day at the PCL and training on Iffley Road. The graduates were interesting and the library was good, and the surroundings were comfortable.

So why bother with Aberystwyth at all? It had shown itself to be duplicitous and corrupt. It was well known to be corrupt, even in the Aladdin workshop back in 1968.

The EDCL administration acted as if they owned it and could do what they liked to the lives of other people. They were ruthless careerists and not particularly talented. They blew their own trumpets deafeningly. At Oxford excellence was taken for granted, rightly or wrongly. The antics back in Aberystwyth had got me into trouble at Wolfson, and I had wriggled out of it. Why should I supervise someone else's student? I would not get any credit or pay for it, and why should I have to snatch a few hours of sleep on the concrete floor of a laboratory when I had comfortable quarters at Oxford surrounded by intellect and international enlightenment? From this distance I should have stayed at Wolfson College by applying for a lectureship at Oxford. Strike when the iron is hot. It was already clear to me that the EDCL administration would never be honest enough to give me tenure. I had got through the roughest part of moving to Oxford, and had made the mistake of choosing wrong digs, but now things were fine as a Junior Research Fellow, won in an entirely honest way in open international competition. I was beginning also to attract grant money from the Science Research Council. The answer is that the Welsh language was and is of paramount importance to me. Those in Wales who profess to support the language often turn out to be shallow hypocrites, but there are enough honest people to keep it going. I should have taken up the Ramsay Memorial Fellowship at Wolfson College, giving two years in which to try for a lectureship and Fellowship of Wolfson. Having annihilated all opposition in the Ramsay competition, there was an excellent chance. I was told by Mansel Davies that I had won by a mile, and I believe him in this case, not out of shallow arrogance but from objective assessment of peers in the profession. In fact the EDCL was a pit to g back to, on the edge of being closed, run by a ruthless careerist who was able to channel all funds into the furtherance of his own career. That could not happen in Oxford, or any other University of any note. There had been ominous signs of envy in the EDCL among the mid career people who wanted no competition from real and younger talent. So the ludicrous stupidity of "publishing too much" began to echo in a very ugly way. It was pure stalinism, "enemy of the people". All kinds of abuses could and did occur very shortly at the EDCL.

In April 1976 however I felt fine, OO25 was submitted on 7th April 1976 from the EDCL, with G. J. Evans and G. J. Davies, so I was back there by then. I had just packed my stuff in to a new Mini that my parents had kindly bought for me in return for the second or third hand car. This car cost much more than the money they got for "Pant y Bedw" but it was a much appreciated kindness. I remember one of the PCL technicians looking at me packing the car in puzzlement. That must have been in about March 1976. Out of habit I was still snatching a few hours of sleep on the floor of room 262, waiting to rent a house in Tal y Bont in the autumn of 1976. OO25 is a very good paper that balances theory and experimental data over a range down to 60 GHz, and by that time Graham Davies had moved to Martlesham Heath with the Post Office. So I helped him get the data there and Gareth Evans began to produce data on the shining new interferometer that had been set up by Grubb Parsons in Room 262. The interferometer arrived in well crafted wooden boxes, with a set of beam splitters and other accessories, and above all, a new paper tape punch. So Gareth Evans was relieved of the burden of repairing a paper tape punch and took charge of the interferometer. At that time he was due for his half term verbal examination, half way through his Ph. D. OO31 was submitted on 21st April 1976 with G. J. Davies and G. J. Evans. All these papers were written and organized by me, and I also did the drawing, theory and computing. Gareth Evans and Graham Davies contributed to the experimental work. OO31 was peer acknowledged to be an excellent paper that reported data on the liquid and rotator phases of carbon tetrabromide and by that time the Ph. D. of Gareth Evans was guaranteed provided that he passed the mid term verbal examination and wrote up to an acceptable standard. This was a dramatic change from six months spent repairing a paper tape punch. He had a supervisor who actually supervised and made sure he would not land up like Pete Deft.

OO28 was submitted to "Chemical Physics Letters" on 30th April 1976, with G. J. Davies, and achieved an almost perfect match of theory and data. I am not sure what G. J. Davies contributed to that paper, from this distance it seems like my own work. Sometimes I was overly generous to co authors, having a generous nature. Later at IBM I came across the fact that powerful people like Clementi could demand to have their names included in a paper. I didn't like that at all, but it was either comply or be sacked. There was none of that kind of pressure from G. J. Davies, to his credit. I recall that the nervous Gareth Evans was given a grilling by Mansel Davies in his half term examination. I did not like this but could not do anything about it. If you almost wreck the Ph. D. prospects of a student by non supervision, you have no right to grill him when supervised by someone else. However Gareth Evans got through this and was still on his feet at the end. The last paper submitted from Oxford was OO30, on 25th Feb. 1976. This became a very popular paper because it explained the dynamics of water when diluted in a solvent, freeing the water molecules from H bonding. The memory function theory produced a perfect fit with data, as can be seen in OO30 on www.aias.us. When Gareth Evans and I decided to test the memory function theory (or Mori theory) with a greater range of data it did not succeed so well, other theories failed completely. This method was the beginning of the multi technical approach that led to the Delta Project of the European Molecular Liquids Group (EMLG). I prepared the Delta Project entirely on my own, and it was brought into being on 19th June 1981 at the National Physical Laboratory. Shortly afterwards, in September 1983, my career was destroyed deliberately by corruption at the peak of its early success, and the Delta

Project was never implemented. So knowledge in that area of chemical physics had remained frozen to this day. After 1983 my life was put into turmoil and took until about 2003 to stabilize again.

Although he had no authority over me, Mansel Davies asked me to represent him in the 1976 Gordon Conference on "Dynamics of Molecular Collisions" at Holderness School, New Hampshire, 26 - 30 July 1976. It was not really a question of being asked, it was a question of being told. He had tenure, I did not. Ethics did not enter in to the matter at all. Is it really ethical to ask a post doctoral to open a Gordon Conference on behalf of a full professor? I had to open it and that was that. I had never been to the United States before, so prepared for the journey by expending my meagre savings on a plane ticket. This would be reimbursed if and only if I attended the conference to do someone else's lecturing. This ticket was bought at a travel agent's in Aberystwyth, and as with all bad things, it is clearly remembered. I do not buy the argument that Mansel Davies was trying to do me a favour. If he was, all he had to do was arrange tenure, I would do the rest. He had had plenty of time and plenty of opportunity. It looks to me that he was using me as an example of what he could produce, and had lost touch with reality. It was clear to all that he had not produced the memory function theory, he did not even understand it. If he did not want to go to the conference he could just have declined the invitation. As summer drew on I submitted OO33 on 19th July 1976 on high and low frequency torsional absorptions of a liquid crystal, with G. J. Evans who took the spectra. This was the BBC Hall of Fame Group beginning to do its famous work despite the lunacy of its surroundings. Then it was a matter of hauling myself out of Room 262 to Heathrow Airport and boarding a Boeing 747. It was a very large tube, much larger than a Comet. It took off slowly and gradually headed for the skies. The flight was about seven hours to Logan Airport Boston, and we were stuffed with food of all kinds. It was very boring, sitting there, but eventually I found myself queueing up at immigration control, grasping a passport. I was waved in to the United States at about late afternoon my time, morning Boston time.

There was a group of people from the National Physical Laboratory near the bus stop to Holderness School, and that included George Chantry, who proceeded to tell me all about America. The bus drove on the wrong side of the road but had shaded windows. It rolled through the very flat and wooded countryside of Massachusetts. It looked to me like one great forest, with occasional towns and buildings. In New Hampshire there was a prohibition on alcohol, which could be bought only from special stores. It did not affect me at all, but I saw some participants loading up when the bus stopped outside one of these. In any case I did not know where I was from jet lag. I was scheduled to open the conference the very next morning and very early. The hills of New Hampshire gradually became high mountains in the distance, one of which was Mount Washington, with Lake Winnipesaukee below. Holderness School turned out to be a collection of buildings with accessories like an ice rink. It was the equivalent of a public school. The accommodation was school accommodation for pupils, luxurious compared with a concrete floor, but very warm and humid. It was past midnight my time so I tried to get some sleep, making sure that all my slides were in order and so on. In the early morning local time I went for a run around the American football pitch, about three miles in all, and bumped into Prof. J. H. Van Vleck of Havard, who was shaving. He was catatonic and mumbled that it was "awfully early, isn't it". If it was early for a native, it was certainly early for me. He was a small man well into his seventies. He was awarded a Nobel Prize shortly thereafter, and that finished him off from surprise. The breakfast was made up of pancakes and maple syrup, which almost finished me off too, and it was a matter of launching desperately into the talk on memory functions and the far infra red, being eagle eyed by Americans all aligned in the front seats. The slides were in order, and the lecturing technique took over. I was not inter upted by any questions and to my surprise the audience seemed interested. It was over suddenly and I fielded a few questions and the conference broke up for a very crowded and noisy coffee break. The cups were decorated with 1776 symbols, it was the 200'th anniversary. I talked to Prof. Robert Cole of Brown University, Rhode Island, who had a shock of white hair and when I got outside I found myself surrounded by tall trees and a new land. I was elated that I had got through the talk without being chewed into sawdust by theoretical termites. J. H. Van Vleck mentioned that I was doing some very fine work. Whether he meant it or not is not known, but it was nice to hear. He had made many notable contributions, including the development of ESR and NMR and was a good lecturer.

Prof. Lars Onsager was a Nobel Laureate at the conference but in very poor health by that time. He died shortly later. He tried to give a talk, but it was a disaster, with small writing and face turned to the board all the time. Later on I sat directly opposite him at the Conference dinner but he did not utter a word. He had intensely blue Norwegian eyes and it looked to me as if he had had a minor stroke. He was not happy with the heat of Florida and wanted to return to Yale. I don’t think he ate very much either. Either he was ill or did not want to talk to a young upstart. One of the envious mid career EDCL people was there, Graham Williams. He had been my teacher but was now my enemy. Animosity and envy is part of human nature, and should be expected. He had tenure, I did not, and he wanted to keep it that way. I met his wife and himself and she was glad to see me, but he more or less ignored my presence. I had never been insolent or impolite to him, and he had kept my laboratory books as a star student. I was well used to being ignored in the EDCL corridor, which now extended as far as the ex colonies. So I politely greeted them both and made my way into the conference to hear his lecture. This was mediocre to the real experts, and he came under fire from an American. Suddenly I saw how vulnerable he was to criticism, and how nervous. I was not going to do anything to him, I was just going to work in my office and bother no one. I did not question him after his lecture. He was well known for one thing only - a minor empirical adjustment to dielectric theory. I wandered off for a walk in the wilderness and as usual got carried away with nature, and was told by one of the Americans that the place was well known for mosquitoes. It must have been out of season, so I was lucky. A few of us walked up to Mount Washington and I rushed ahead of them with exhilaration. This was an entirely new landscape and a very high mountain with a large blue lake spread out below. In the distance were many more mountains stretching to infinity.

I got my money back from an irritated accountant and that mattered a lot to me. I was never paid very highly, and for a lot of the time not at all. There was some discussion and a violent thunder storm, and as usual for the Gordon Conferences there were morning and evening sessions. Apparently I had just opened one of the most prestigious conferences, but in reality I was asleep from jet lag. I just made sure to catch the bus back to Logan Airport and waited for the plane with one of the staff from the National Physical Laboratory. It was an overnight flight during which I got little sleep, and emerging from customs I found that my father and two friends had driven up to meet me. They did not understand jet lag, so I drove them home half asleep, arriving in one piece. At the EDCL Mansel Davies asked how things had gone, I cracked a joke but he was not amused. I explained that things had gone very well, and that made him feel that his reputation was not in danger. On my return he asked me to open another conference on his behalf in August 1976 at the Dublin Institute for Advanced Studies, and again it was matter of being told what to do. He refused to go to Ireland and this was one of his many prejudices. I was sympathetic to the

Irish Republican cause but rejected all forms of violence, being brought up as a Welsh speaking Baptist. I did not really know anything about Ireland, but there I was again, this time my parents drove me to Abergwaun or Fishguard for the ferry to Rosslare. The sea was completely calm in high summer. Ireland was astonishingly green, and the train journeyed its way up the east coast through some very beautiful country, especially the estuaries. It ground into Dublin late at night and I made my way to a posh hotel, reserved for Mansel Davies. So I found out how the other half lived. There was time for a run in the morning before I had to open the conference with a review talk. I was also scheduled for an individual lecture.

On the walk to the Institute in 10 Burlington Road, I asked the way and was asked in turn whence I originated. "That's not very foreign" came the friendly reply. The Institute itself is a small concrete pile in a Dublin suburb and prides itself as having had a famous first director, the Nobel Laureate Erwin Schroedinger. At that time its Director John Trevor Lewis had just been appointed, and looked like a bony long haired owl. The conference was attended by Brendan Scaife of Trinity College Dublin, who looked like a Dublin Viking minus a battle axe. He later offered me a lectureship at Trinity College Dublin, provided I was well dressed. There were more members of the DIAS staff: Rev. Prof. James McConnell and one other. Those invited included Wylie, Calderwood, Powles, Madden, Tildesley, Schroer and Coffey. It was a small conference with only nineteen participants in all. All went well until the lecture by Scaife, when he suddenly drew a savage cross through a well known theory. This came across as weird. Scaife's superficial friendliness evaporated there and then. I declined his offer of a lectureship because of this, and Trinity College was not my style, it quickly became claustrophobic because most of the appointments at that time were made without competition. William Coffey looked like a public schoolboy and was dressed in a cravat and blazer. For some reason he invited me to walk over to Trinity College Dublin, of which I had never heard. It turned out to be a very long walk, until the green central area of the College suddenly appeared through a gap in a grey wall. He had just been appointed a lecturer without competition after being appointed a lecturer without competition at Salford. He was and is a capable mathematician, but a difficult character. He may have mellowed up a bit by now. He told me he was afraid of growing old in Trinity College, which is precisely what happened. Trinity College was quite interesting, having been founded by my ancestral cousin Elizabeth 1st., but I had to get back to DIAS. My talks seemed to go well.

In the hotel there was a small book which contained photographs of the people executed in the 1916 Easter Rising, these included Patrick Pearse, James Connolly, Joseph Plunkett and thirteen others. Being a Welsh speaker I was sympathetic to the Irish Republic so innocently took a photograph back with me to the EDCL of some of those executed. I had at last been given a half part of a very small office with no windows so I taped the photograph on the wall above my desk. I was verbally worked over, black and tan style, by Mansel Davies but kept the photograph there. This was the thanks that I got for deputizing for him. He had only a short while to go until he retired in 1978 and then the working over began in earnest. It took them five years to finally get rid of me in 1983, they lost the EDCL in about 1988, and they have vanished into total obscurity. The University of Wales was never their concern. OO29 was submitted on 1st Sept. 1976 with G. Wegdam and G. J. Evans. Wegdam was on leave from the University of Amsterdam. This is one of my favourite papers because Gareth Evans had obtained a first class and very original, high quality spectrum which revealed the individual rotational lines of hydrogen bromide dissolved in the liquid state in sulphur hexafluoride solvent. This was interpreted with a memory function theory and a theory due to Frenkel and Wegdam. Daan Frenkel later became an F. R. S. at Cambridge. OO34 was submitted on 8th Sept. 1976 on the memory function theory applied to Rayleigh scattering and some results from computer simulation. This method was greatly extended in the Delta project, whose challenge has been ducked for many years. So that era of the late seventies and early eighties was a high point of civilization.

I was worked over once again by Mansel Davies for snatching a few hours of sleep in Room 262. This was a low point in hypocrisy in contrast to the high point in civilization. I had been asked to supervise Gareth Evans after all, but this was forgotten. I was a danger to the insurance policy of the EDCL. One day I saw him walk into my office, place a note on my desk, and walk away. It was a scribbled note stating that if I did not vacate Room 262 he would do nothing more for me. In fact he had never done anything for me. I did not tell anyone about this disgusting note, but that was effectively the end of communication with him. I spent about three weeks at my parents' house and fortunately managed to rent a house in Tal y Bont from Martin Beavers who was scheduled to go to Australia for a year and moved in there as soon as I could, in the autumn of 1976. The method of placing notes on my desk was used extensively by Jeremy Jones from 1978 to 1983, each telling me to leave, for Oxford, or anywhere. Jones told me that Purnell would cut his head off if I stayed, a loonie bin indeed. There is nothing that concentrates the mind so sharply as repeated threats of career destruction. Later at Trinity College, Scaife whispered in my ear: "This is a nut house, you know". This was on my first official visit to Trinity College. At the time Coffey was in the habit of screaming down the corridor: "Vij!,Vij!" This was not a vegetable but his colleague Jagdish Vij. Echoes of the Raj. I thought that Coffey was either crazy or playing around and evidently, Scaife had been subjected to this for some time so was wondering what he had appointed without competition.

The last paper of 1976 was submitted on 2nd December,

OO35, with Graham Davies and Gareth Evans. This was the first paper in which the range of data was extended sufficiently to lower frequencies to show up the limitations of the memory function theory, and indeed all other theories. Today in 2013 there is still no theory or computer simulation method that can match a sufficiently broad range of experimental data. The interval from autumn 1976 to autumn 1977 was again a happy time, because there was stability and because the group was coming together so well. Mansel Davies had forgotten about the note and I had not admonished him for behaving in such a stupid way. Gareth Evans was nearing the completion of a more or less guaranteed Ph. D. and was soon to be joined by Colin Reid. We had new equipment, computer simulation was about to get off the ground, and the multi technical approach to liquid phase study was also being developed rapidly. In 1977 I was to submit my Scientiae Doctor Thesis in an entirely innocent way. Quite simply, I had found that such a degree existed and that I could submit a Thesis. It was not a careerist conspiracy, it was a celebration of knowledge. For a very short while, things seemed good again at the EDCL.

This was the first time I had been able to rent a house, in the village of Tal y Bont north of Aberystwyth. I was very lucky because a beautiful lady from Clwyd, a fluent Welsh speaker, began to bring me some food sometimes, and ordered a newspaper for me. This is it at last I thought. I had never had a taste of such luxury and such kindness. It was a pleasant drive in to Aberystwyth and the house was surrounded by beautiful countryside. It could not have been a greater contrast to "Brig y Don" or 8 Powell Street. The former was boarded up on my last visit about two or three years ago. The little house in Tal y Bont was a stone house with an open hearth fire, so I bought some coal for the winter nights. If I had been the Head of Department at the EDCL I would have tenured my entire research group, and that would have saved the EDCL from closure. A level of stability is needed for civilization, and I had already been a nomad for too many years. The house belonged to Martin Beavers, who went to Australia for a year. From this perspective it is obvious that Mansel Davies should have arranged accommodation if he wanted me to supervise Gareth Evans. If it had been possible to work like a van Gogh, in a frenzy of ideas, I would have done so, the administrative organization of the EDCL was non existent in any case. The new interferometer was set up in Room 262 and with Gerard Wegdam I began to develop a routine for computing correlation functions of various kinds by molecular dynamics simulation. I had succeeded in getting the program to work on the link to the UMRCC CDC 7600. This produced the data for analysis with time correlation functions.

The production of the data took about a month on what was known as zero priority turnaround. A correlation function program was written by Wegdam and myself to analyse the data in terms of auto and cross correlation functions. This type of program was improved later in work with my post doctoral Mauro Ferrario at the EDCL and later in work with Keith Refson at IBM Kingston, New York, where it became very efficient. The first paper reporting this technique is OO36, which must have been submitted early in 1977. It was published in a very scruffy way by Orville-Thomas in his journal "Advances in Molecular Relaxation and Interaction Processes". He would simply take manuscripts from me and publish them without reading them, and was a short red haired man with a ridiculously patronising attitude. He would tell me later that I would never be given a job because I was truthful, and what idiocy! How could people like that run an academic department or a bubble car? His bland acceptance of corruption infuriated me, but I remained outwardly polite as usual. Jeremy Jones, who finished off the EDCL, was his abusive student. OO37 was also published in this journal, but unfortunately he printed them so badly that they are barely legible on the Omnia Opera. They are available however in copyright and other libraries. This journal took an immensely long time to publish articles, one review article, OO40 submitted from Wolfson College Oxford on 6th January 1976, was published in mid 1977. This article uses and analyses data from different sources, and is a prototype for the Delta Project. OO43 was submitted with Gerard Wegdam and Gareth Evans on 17th Feb. 1977 and published in Molecular Physics. It is the first mature paper on computer simulation, the correlation function program was working perfectly and produced results for diatomics which could not have been obtained in any other way. OO38 was submitted on the 9th March 1977 and uses a combination of computer simulation and an immensely complicated analytical theory. It was already obvious that the theory could not keep pace with the simulation. At this time I was working on my Scientiae Doctor Thesis, OO44, "Intermolecular Dynamics in Fluids and Plastic Crystals", submitted on 23rd April 1977.

This Thesis bound together the first forty two or so articles on the Omnia Opera and epitomizes the overwhelming power of ideas. The purpose of the Thesis submission was furtherance of knowledge. I had no idea that I was to become the youngest in modern history to earn the degree, and had no idea that it was meant by the University of London in 1860 to be a distinction higher than full professorship. At that time there was no google of course, only a set of rules which I found by accident in the EDCL library. The rules stated that two years had to elapse between the award of a Ph. D. and submission of the D. Sc. and that the Thesis had to be bound in three copies. I did not need the signature of a bureaucrat however, so I just went ahead and had it bound, prepared an introduction, and submitted it. By that time I had lost all trust in Mansel Davies and John Thomas, as time went on, people would be suddenly tenured, but no sign of tenure for any of my group. The reason was clear, tenure was being used in furtherance of the career of the head of department. In some way he could influence the College to award tenure without any kind of assessment. All appointments to tenure from 1969 to 1978 were for his group and no other group. There was no assessment, no competition, no nothing. I knew that my D. Sc. Thesis submission would have been prohibited if I had talked about it. The Thesis was examined and assessed by outsiders, and there was no verbal examination. It was awarded in early 1978 for work of outstanding quality recognized internationally, and for that reason I had a clear claim on tenure. In fact I should have been promoted full professor, but the system evaded its duty, and that is unforgivable corruption. What remains is the obvious quality of the work, the bureaucrats have disappeared into obscurity.

Tenure is a mediaeval concept that was used by the EDCL administration to evade duty to the Government and other assessors. For example, my Science Research Council Fellowship awarded in 1974 was won in open competition, I attended a testing interview in London before being awarded it. The type of post doctoral Fellowship awarded at the EDCL was the uncompetitive type, from a grant awarded to a supervisor. If there is to be any meaning to tenure, there must be an objective selection process. Usually only one post doctoral fellowship is needed before a tenured lectureship is awarded. The fact that I was invited to a lectureship at Trinity College Dublin and at Swansea means that tenure should have been awarded at Aberystwyth . In addition I won an ICI European Fellowship, an NRCC Fellowship, a JRF of Wolfson College, a Ramsay Memorial Fellowship, an SERC Advanced Fellowship, two prestigious medals and earned the D. Sc. Degree, all in the span of five years from 1974 to 1979. The post doctoral record of others appointed to tenure by J. M. Thomas from 1969 to 1978 is as follows. Dr. J. O. Williams took up one post doctoral fellowship before being appointed to tenure. There is no record of a post doctoral fellowship for Dr Eurwyn Evans. Both were appointed directly to tenure in 1969. There is no record of a post doctoral for Dr David Parry other than that given to him by J. M. Thomas himself and there is no record of a competitive post doctoral for Dr. John Adams. The post doctoral fellowship awarded to Dr Gareth Evans late in 1977 was the grant type of fellowship, not a competitive fellowship. However under my supervision he was awarded a University of Wales Fellowship in open inter subject competition, and a prestigious SERC Advanced Fellowship in open competition. So he should also have been awarded tenure. My other post doctoral assistant Mauro Ferrario attained the rank of full professor. The University authorities have never been able to answer these criticisms. Looking carefully at the record of Mansel Davies he won only one competitive fellowship, an ICI Fellowship in 1946. He was a post graduate student at Cambridge but no more than that. Under my guidance, Gareth Evans won a University of Wales Fellowship in 1979 and a SERC Advanced Fellowship in 1981. There is no doubt that my group was destroyed by endemic corruption that spread throughout the entire system. Some individuals such as myself survived by adherence to the principles of science. It is very important to reform this corrupt system completely, or otherwise cease funding it completely. A system that awards tenure and career arbitrarily is no system, and must not be tolerated.

At about this time I was also working on my second review article, OO39, "Correlation and Memory Function Analyses of Molecular Motion in Fluids", a review which contains some molecular dynamics simulation results, theory and experimental data: the three corners of the Delta Project were experiment, theory and simulation. OO41, submitted on 17th May 1977, was the first paper in co authorship with William Coffey, who had telephoned me from Trinity College Dublin arguing that his planar itinerant oscillator and my three variable Mori theory were the same theory. He had already been given tenure by invitation, without competition, so had the advantage over me in some respects. In retrospect I should not have cooperated with Coffey, because it turned out to be a one sided affair in which he tried to take advantage of my untenured career for his own gain. He was the complete opposite of me in all respects, a heavy drinker and a kind of latter day unionist who referred to his fellow citizens as Bog Irishmen, despite being a Catholic himself in a Protestant College, Trinity College. I recall that I had to take his telephone call in the lowest level of the EDCL in the corridor, an outburst of tedious hubris. For some reason I accepted his invitation to visit Trinity College Dublin and was put up in the guest room. The most interesting part of that visit was a book of essays about Yeats, one of them was by Hugh MacDiarmaid. Both are predecessors of mine on the Civil List, and MacDiarmaid wrote of the Celtic narrowing intensity. Yeats' work was very well known to me and his Abbey Theatre was just around the corner. It was an uncomfortable visit because of Coffey's habit of dragging guests around his drinking dives after finishing Commons at Trinity College. This is a long drawn out dinner at which the Grace is said to my ancestral cousin Elizabeth 1st in Latin.

There were some gruesome eccentrics on that High Table, including one Ulsterman who never stopped talking in an incredibly tedious way. They retired into the Senior Common Room, where there all kinds of luxuries, leather chairs, tables, and mountains of newspaper. Coffey had been arbitrarily appointed to this set up. I was able to do some athletics training on the track inside Trinity College and got away from Coffey for a while to look at the Book of Kells. It was as vivid as if it had been written yesterday on Iona. That brought some serenity into an otherwise crazy scene. A post doctoral called Jagdish Vij seemed to be under Coffey's thumb. Later on Coffey would bellow like a buffalo of the Raj down the corridor at Vij in a place called the Printing House, the Department of Microelectronics and Electrical Engineering. Jagdish Vij seemed to be fresh from India and initially referred to me as Sahib. What am I doing here I thought to myself again.

It was a relief to get back to Tal y Bont. Coffey could be tolerable in his calmer states of mind, but otherwise he was very tedious, with his talk of the Raj, his half colonel grandfather and so on. OO41 is an excellent paper which I wrote myself with minimal input from co authors. The planar itinerant oscillator was mildly interesting but could not stand up to the test of data when the latter were observed over a sufficient range of frequency

OO45 was submitted on 27th June 1977 and tested the itinerant oscillator with data from the far infra red and computer simulation. Coffey's type of analytical theory had had its day, and was still based on techniques developed in Langevin's time. He continued in this rut throughout his career and never seemed to learn how to use a computer. The severe limitations of his theory began to show themselves in OO45. Being a planar model with several loose parameters, it had no right to be in the presence of a three dimensional computer simulation, or a general theory of statistical dynamics such as the three variable Mori theory. OO51 was submitted on 15th August 1977, and was the first paper with both Gareth Evans and Colin Reid. The Coffey Calderwood Itinerant oscillator failed qualitatively, and no variation on that type of theory has succeeded since then. For years, theoreticians have ducked the challenge of data over a broad range of frequency, combined with data from other techniques. OO47 was submitted on 19th Sept. 1977 with A. R. Davies of Mathematics, after many months of delay waiting for Davies to finish his work. The happy time was drawing to an end again, Beavers and his family were due back from Australia and I had to leave Tal y Bont and its beautiful surroundings. In retrospect I should just have looked for another house in the same village, or got married to the beautiful Welsh lady and left the lunatic academic system altogether. Sadly for me she was married already.

About this time a sinister letter was delivered behind my back to Mansel Davies by a Cambridge don called A. D. Buckingham. The letter asked Mansel Davies to make me publish less, and this was like one of those midnight telephone calls from Stalin. I had published only three times in Buckingham's journal "Chemical Physics Letters", each time on different subjects, each time being refereed positively. So this was my first taste of the unethical attempts at control extended from Cambridge toward Aberystwyth. Buckingham's personal animosity was countered by the National Physical Laboratory group, who knew my work in all detail, and later by SERC CCP5, but Buckingham kept his talons in me until he retired, to no effect whatsoever. Mansel Davies showed me the latter and said nothing. I took no notice at all of Buckingham, who continued to accept my papers in his journal. This was a very nasty experience, showing the extent to which personal envy could corrupt. "........ For now I see /

Peace to corrupt no less than war to waste." I suspect that Buckingham has never coded a computer in his life, so does not even know that any theory must be precisely correct for it to work on a computer. Whatever he was thinking, he was grossly out of order, and his action would be sen now as a violation of human rights, so would be the hideous verbal abuse by Mansel Davies. All of that stuff must be cut out of society, if it still goes on. It goes on underground of course, via stalkers and haters.

I was very loathe to leave Tal y Bont but finally had to shift myself in a hurry, back to the worst hole in the ground I have ever lived in, including the cellar at Oxford. It was a place called Eastgate, which happened to be occupied by a graduate student I knew at the EDCL. Its kitchen stank, and I had an odorous room with peeling wallpaper without window glass. This was a very stupid move made in a hurry, especially as I was trapped in this disgusting hole until I managed to rent a flat from a technician called Mansell Davies at three pounds a week in Borth. The move was forced on me by the worst piece of corruption I have ever encountered, one which led to ferocious animosity and disrupted my life until 2001, when I finally settled back here in Craig Cefn Parc. I lived in that windowless room throughout the winter of 1977, my excellent athletic fitness keeping me going. The ingrown nature of the academic system gnawed at my attempts to work throughout those revolting months and well in to 1978. My work of late 1977 shows no sign of this turmoil caused by a violently disfunctional system. The last paper of 1977, OO53, was submitted on 22nd Dec. with Gareth Evans. It reaches a new peak of sophistication with theories by Bogoliubov and Morita being tested rigorously. The acknowledgement shows that Gareth Evans had been given a Fellowship by Mansel Daives, and had completed his Ph. D. His final examination took place in the presence of the external examiner Wilkinson from King's College London, Mansel Davies and myself and he had produced an excellent Ph. D. Thesis.

CHAPTER SIX

In the autumn of 1977 Mansel Davies walked into the now busy laboratory in Room 262 and mentioned casually that I had been offered a job in the then University College Swansea by a man of whom I had never heard: Howard Purnell. My first instincts were to refuse, because I expected tenure at Aberystwyth. I remember Mansel Davies' exact works, because they infuriate me to this day: "The job is yours if you apply". This is a form of grotesque corruption that has probably been prevalent in the University for years. Either you offer a job, and that is that, or you advertize it fairly. J. M. Thomas had been busy appointing all his group to tenure without a single instance of open competition. No head of department would be allowed to do that today. Obviously I was being pushed out of the EDCL because J. M. Thomas wanted to appoint inferior performers to bolster his group and further his own career. The Department was being used for his career, notably Fellowship of the Royal Society, as if that meant anything. The University administration seemed to allow him to do this without any constraint. They were inferior because their post doctoral record was greatly inferior to mine, in some cases non existent. They were all being pushed in to lifelong tenure through the back door, undermining Government policy and all pretence of fair competition. J. M. Thomas himself was appointed to tenure at Bangor without competition and without competing for a single post doctoral, straight from the Atomic Energy Authority. So Academia is a system that does not appoint the most talented people. It is a form of blatantly false authority, the untalented push out the talented. I know now that J. M. Thomas and Howard Purnell had arranged this transfer between themselves. Later they co authored two patents. Unfortunately for them they had neglected to consult yours truly. Mansel Davies had probably sleazed with them behind the scenes. I was never going to be a pawn in someone else's careerism, I was a scientist used to open and fa r competition, and as an athlete, detested smoke filled rooms.

I was told to telephone Howard Purnell, taking care not to use too much departmental money on a long call, and to accept his offer, and by the way, there was going to be an interview. Taking care not to throw up all over the conspiracy I kept concentrating on my work and pushed Swansea to the back of my mind, where it has remained ever since. This was a time when the group was developing strongly, and there was no time for career, only for thought and work. At the time I was vaguely aware of appointments to tenure being made, and knew that I was being quietly by passed and at the same time trumpeted. I shared the general feeling of contempt among the post doctoral staff and post graduate students for what was going on. I had done what Mansel Davies had asked me to do, to go away for a couple of years and then come back. I had waited a year for him to fulfill his promise of tenure and of course it never materialized. It was an inherently corrupt system and it had always been that way. From the very beginning there was only one way for me, and that was to produce work to the best of my ability. Those appointed to tenure without advertisement at the EDCL in the J. M. Thomas group include the following: J. O. Williams. E. L. Evans, J. M. Adams, D. A. Jefferson, D. E. Parry, J. L. Hutchison, and later S. Evans by W. J. Jones. W. Jones was appointed to tenure at Cambridge without advertisement and was able to stay there his whole life. So there is no exceptional merit in Oxford and Cambridge. There was not a single competitive post doctoral fellowship between them, in contrast to seventeen won in open competition by Gareth Evans and myself. The kind of work they were doing was routine, it could have been done in any capable department worldwide by any technician. Having been appointed to tenure in this way several were able to stay there all their lives, having never faced open competition at post doctoral level. Tenure also means the opportunity of applying to the Science Research Council for funds. G reth Evans and I were denied this opportunity all our lives, greatly damaging science thereby. Jefferson and Jones went to Cambridge with Thomas and got in the back door. Despite Thomas' professional Welshness none of these appointments were to Welsh speakers with the exception of J. O. Williams and E. L. Evans. The Welsh language was just not a consideration.

In that autumn of 1977 I forgot about Purnell for as long as I could. I know now that he published with J. M. Thomas in 1978 in number 254 of Thomas' list of publications, in reality the organized work of many others. So it becomes clear that Thomas and Purnell decided to shovel me out of the way to Swansea, where I was supposed to earn a lot of money for Purnell's department. This was not my style at all. I had had some experience of Thomas' methods at undergraduate and at post doctoral. They were not particularly interesting and I was annoyed at the long delays in the workshop, which was used to build models for his lectures. I did not think that this was right, the workshop was for the whole department. His lecturing style was far too oratorical, one found that at the end a lot of work had to be done to make sense of it. He had little mathematical ability, no computing ability, and did no experimental work with his own hands. I cannot imagine a renaissance master in Florence not being able to paint. A real scholar spends all his time at work. The system is secondary and has no right to interfere in scholarship. I also had the experience of Thomas bursting out of his office one day to tell me to be quiet, I was whistling a tune in the post room after one of my papers had been accepted. Perhaps he was tone deaf. On another occasion he asked me in the post room to do some work for him on simulation, but I declined because I was not interested in it. He was very angry but that was his problem, I had other things to do as a scientist. The contemporary British Government ACAS website shows very clearly that much of all that would be considered now to be a violation of human rights and of the rules of the work place. To block promotion and try to force a transfer is considered now to be harassment with recourse to ACAS and in law. To be told to shut up for whistling is a form of bullying. Mansel Davies' verbal blasting would have got him dismissed these days. Fixed or laundered job advertising is of c urse a kind of fraud, which ought to carry a prison sentence. In those days I was wholly at the mercy of the system. The slightest objection would have got me thrown out. So the academic system defeats itself, it does not respect or support scholarship and tolerates only routine ideas. It is the archetypical cult of personality, the antithesis of reason. This is why Erasmus wrote "In Praise of Folly".

At my instigation, the Information Commissioner recently obliged Aberystwyth to reveal that Howard Purnell was on the interview committee that appointed Jeremy Jones of the chemistry department in Cambridge to head of department of the EDCL in 1978. So it seems overwhelmingly likely that the job for Jones was another arrangement in a smoke filled room, an arrangement that was taking place at about the same time as the arrangement for me to move for Swansea. It was arranged that J. M. Thomas would take up a post at Cambridge and it was arranged that W. J. Jones would fill the vacancy at Aberystwyth. Purnell had also been at the same department in Cambridge, and Buckingham was situated in the same department. I suspect that Buckingham's pressure to make me publish less was an attempt to make the denial of tenure easier. This attempt failed. Such pressures today are illegal, they would be considered to be intimidation at work. Cambridge in the guise of Swinnerton-Dyer of thatcherite days finally intimidated Aberystwyth into closing EDCL. For this he was made honorary professor by the rival physics department, which had been allowed to remain open to no purpose. The appointment of W. J. Jones in 1978 marked the beginning of first degree harassment of my group, harassment which lasted for five years, from 1978 to 1983, and came to an end because Aberystwyth breached contract and allowed my SERC Advanced Fellowship to run out. That destroyed Project Delta and wasted about half a million pounds in Government funding in today's money. The EDCL was saved from demolition by the efforts of Gareth Evans, who had it listed by CADW. It is not possible to think of a worse administration than the one which prevailed in the late seventies and eighties at Aberystwyth.

In my pungent room without window glass in the Eastgate slum, I tried to think of ways of getting out of "the Swansea job", as it became known throughout Britain in chemistry. Luckily, Cadman pointed out to me the existence of the Science and Engineering Research Council (SERC) Advanced Fellowship competition. This was the toughest post doctoral competition and was the only way I could stop myself becoming embroiled in the undergrowth of a corrupt jungle. For reasons known only to himself, J. M. Thomas signed the application, for five years at the EDCL, and legally committed the College to give me tenure. The funds were available as all those J. M. Thomas appointments show. Perhaps the arrangement with Purnell had not yet taken place. This was my sixth open international post doctoral competition, having won five already: SRC, ICI European, Canadian, NRCC, JRF of Wolfson and Ramsay Memorial. Even at that point this was a world record. It is all too clear in retrospect that J. M. Thomas deliberately refused to give me tenure because he wanted all the tenure for his own group. Today that would be a form of career blocking, considered by ACAS to be harassment and a violation of human rights. I am a Welsh speaker, so what about all that Welshness to which Thomas regularly refers in his writings? In reality it did not exist, it was all about power and money. So I applied for the SERC Advanced Fellowship in the autumn of 1977. It was clear to many of the EDCL staff that I did not wish to move to Swansea, some were sympathetic. In 1977 the National Physical Laboratory had supported me for the prestigious Edward Harrison Memorial Prize of the Royal Society of Chemistry, which I was awarded in 1978. Mansel Davies knew nothing of this medal procedure because he might well have blocked it. The perversity of his character was unfathomable. This award was for work in theoretical and physical chemistry. Previous winners include the Nobel Laureate Derek Barton, Longuet-Higgins, Carrington, Luckhurst, and Buckingham. In 1978 I had also completed my D. Sc. Thesis and submitted it. It was awarded in early 1978 at the age of 27, another record for modern times. Mansel Davies also knew nothing of this procedure. So being forced to compete for the sixth time was wholly wrong, and completely unethical, especially as others appointed to tenure were of very meagre calibre in comparison. Many of the EDCL staff sensed the injustice acutely, but were completely under the thumb. After all, they had been my teachers.

The day of the false "interview" approached and I felt sick at the blood soaked system, the wasted blood of real talent. It took place in the winter vacations of 1977, and I spent the night before at my parents' house in a state of complete uncertainty. I loathed the thought of being forced into corruption by self seeking mediocrities, and was intensely angry at those who were so arrogant as to think that I would ever go along with their plans. There were four short listed for the interview, three of whom had been deceived into thinking that they had any chance of being appointed. We were told to sit in the corridor of the bureaucratic building in Swansea and I was hauled in. I knew that the whole procedure was false, Purnell asked if I would take the job if offered, as if he had not done so already. I hesitated before this little weasel of a man for a very long time. He became very tense and nervous. In the end I was forced to answer yes with great foreboding of doom. Purnell asked if I liked rugby and this time I could answer no. I was duly offered a bucket of doom, and went back to the EDCL. I had been given half a microscopic room in which were stuffed three desks. To get at mine you had to walk over the top of another. This was infinitely preferable to Swansea, already a decaying campus of blackened concrete sixties style. My hope was that the Advanced Fellowship offer would come through soon, so I could refuse the Swansea offer with honour and dignity. At this time Gareth Evans was a post doctoral, and we had just been joined by Colin Reid, who was doing a Masters degree which I was told to supervise. These two were nominally part of the group of Mansel Davies and could not have moved to Swansea with me. Moving to Swansea meant the destruction of a very promising group, considered in fact as the best in Britain in theoretical and physical chemistry. The truth is that EDCL did not deserve us.

As can be seen from the Omnia Opera on www.aias.us the flow of high quality papers was unaffected by the rotten administration. There was an unusually long gap of about three months between 22nd. December 1977 (OO53) and 20th March 1978 (OO68, submitted to Spectrochimica Acta). This is the only sign that something was wrong. In those months there was tremendous turmoil as I drove back and forth between Swansea and Aberystwyth, setting up my work at Swansea as slowly as I could and continuing to work with the group at Aberystwyth in order to keep it alive. Without my input Colin Reid would never had been awarded his Thesis, and Gareth Evans would have drifted out of the academic world. Mansel Davies was due to retire in September 1978. I have always loathed the campus at Swansea as a concrete jungle. It used to be known as a glorified grammar school. I was given an office and as always nothing had been prepared. Purnell worked in an entirely different area. I know now that he was a mafia boss with considerable power for no reason. He was a small, vindictive man who decided to try to destroy my career when I eventually returned to the EDCL on the Advanced Fellowship. I was not due to start at

Swansea until the autumn of 1978, so had no real need of being there. I was reluctantly preparing for something that everyone knew was a mistake. A "career move" has nothing to do with scholarship. The stinking slum in Eastgate had to serve at home for a short while. From the perspective of thirty five years it can be seen very clearly that this was administrative chaos, all they had to do was to appoint me to a low paid tenure research associate when I was still at Tal y Bont. The perennial pleas of poverty repulsed me with their dishonesty. Of course they had money, not least for their own high salaries.

Suddenly in 1978 I was a Harrison Memorial Prizewinner and a Scientiae Doctor of the University of Wales, a distinction higher than full professorship. So I was effectively a full professor but still being kept untenured. The Principal Sir Goronwy Daniel wrote to congratulate me. He was a former pupil of Pontardawe Grammar School. With reluctance I informed Mansel Davies of these very prestigious achievements but he was merely annoyed. I suppose I should not have expected anything else. I was not even congratulated by John Thomas. What I was hoping for also came through, an SERC Advanced Fellowship, and I was told by someone that I was graded top of my year in chemistry. All they had to do at the EDCL was to award me a tenured research associate, lock me in an office, give me some bread and water and throw the key away. I would have brought in all the money they wanted, and they always wanted money. So I bided my time, accepted the SERC Fellowship and got on with work. I was also supported for the Meldola Medal of the Royal Society of Chemistry by the National Physical Laboratory, and was awarded this in 1979. Any administration with any sense at all would have offered tenure, but all I got were lies about poverty. I was also awarded a large grant by the British Government's Science and Engineering Research Council (SERC). This was a surprise because I had not even applied for a grant. In today's money it was about half a million pounds. The

SERC Advanced Fellowship was roughly equivalent to an associate professorship in the United States, and was fiercely competitive. The British Government's stated aim in awarding this fellowship was that the supporting institute should award tenure as soon as feasible. The EDCL administration signed the application form and committed the College to awarding tenure. I also had the enthusiastic support of Sir Goronwy Daniel but he was due to retire in the autumn of 1978. He was later critical of the administration.

The Meldola Medal is awarded to a chemist under the age of 32 for the most promising publications. So much for Buckingham's "publishing too much", and I won it outright in 1979. Past recipients include Poliakoff, Luckhurst, Carrington, Rowlinson, Robertson, R. H. Jones, Todd and Norrish (two Nobel Laureates), Hinshelwood and Ingold. With Luckhurst, Carrington and Sutton, I am among those who have won both the Harrison Memorial Prize and Meldola Medal. These are the most competitive awards in early career, where competition is really meaningful. I was also judged to be the joint winner of the Marlow Medal of 1978, but it was awarded elsewhere because I received the Harrison Memorial Prize of that year. Again I was supported by the National Physical Laboratory. I was so unlucky to be administered by a bunch of local careerists. The EDCL would not have allowed me to take the interferometer to Swansea, and in any case that would have destroyed the work of Gareth Evans, shortly to become a University of Wales Fellow under my guidance in open inter collegiate and inter subject competition. So nothing had been thought out by Purnell and Thomas. In addition, J. M. Thomas had allowed the student intake to fall to a dangerously low level. There were only five students in the final year of chemistry when he suddenly left in 1978. In that year our group also began to match that of J. M. Thomas in quantity, although we were a much smaller group. Our group was already above the Thomas group in internationally acknowledged quality. I decided to concentrate on my work, and reject careerism, and began to produce the papers that led to the formation of the European Molecular Liquids Group (EMLG) at the National Physical Laboratory. The Pisa group of Paolo Grigolini had also indicated that it wished to cooperate with my group in the area of memory function analysis, and I had been invited to produce my first prestigious "Advances in Chemical Physics " review by Stuart Rice. I was invited by "Accounts of Chemical R search",edi ed at Cornell, to write up the Meldola Lecture, which I gave at Oxford.

On 22nd March 1978 OO61 was submitted to Faraday II and is the first to use the new description of the far infra red as the Zero to THz Profile. This led shortly later to the discovery of the gamma process of the far infra red. OO61 was co authored by Gareth Evans and William Coffey and reports the discovery that spectra can record the time evolution of the dynamics of molecules from picoseconds to years, on a time scale stretching from a million millionth of a second to millions of seconds or more, all in one spectrum. There is still no theory or computer simulation that can begin to understand this process in sufficient detail. The itinerant oscillator of Coffey failed dismally, to his intense annoyance with me, not with nature. On 31st March 1978 OO62 was submitted to "Molecular Liquids", with Coffey. This paper began to extend the analysis to incoherent neutron scattering. Coffey produced a vastly over complicated theory and had not yet learned Debye's adage that complexity is lack of understanding. All these papers were submitted from the EDCL, none from Swansea. On 11th May 1978 OO54 was submitted to a Faraday Discussion meeting with Gareth Evans and Russell Davies. This is the first paper that records work on the interaction of rotation and translation making extensive use of computer simulation. The program that I had struggled with for nearly three years was at last working efficiently, producing a vast amount of new information. Another problem with the "Swansea job" is that it would have made computer simulation almost impossible. So Purnell and Thomas did not even know what I was doing at a time when the rest of British chemistry knew all about our work. I was digging in to my work with all my strength, and Gareth Evans and Colin Reid were also beginning to work to great effect. This is despite the fact that Colin Reid was initially a very difficult student who would be absent from work for weeks on end. On one occasion there was a violent flare up between Colin Reid and Mansel Davies and again I was being made to supervise someone else's student, caught in the middle. I knew that Mansel Davies had only a short time to go before retirement, and I thought I would be free from verbal violence. In reality it was to intensify to near insanity with the arrival of the delightful Jeremy Jones, the last head of department of the EDCL.

Suddenly I was told that John Thomas was to go to Cambridge, shortly after arranging with the BBC to make a fuss over his FRS. I remember feeling a sense of great betrayal, mixed with relief. A new head of department would surely award the tenure expected by the Government. Purnell wrote me a hostile and sarcastic letter from Swansea instructing me not to expect a "personal laboratory". The archetypical scarecrow made to be knocked over. I had not expected anything of the kind. This revealed his true nature, he was a cold blooded crook, and it was only matter of time before I resigned from the Swansea job. On 31st May 1978 OO55 was submitted to Faraday II and was the pioneering paper of the multi technical approach that became the Delta Project of the EMLG. This was immediately acknowledged to be an excellent paper in which high quality data were collected by Gareth Evans, Colin Reid and Ram Yadav, with some low frequency data by Graham Davies. Data from neutron and depolarized Rayleigh scattering were also used. The critically important thing was the fact that data over a sufficient range disposed of theories like dominoes, the most successful one being the Mori three variable theory. That remains the case to this day. For the first time, dichloromethane was used as a model liquid, and this became one of the three liquids of the Delta Project. On 15th June 1978 OO58 was submitted with Gareth Evans, Colin Reid and William Coffey to Buckingham's letters journal "Chemical Physics Letters" and showed the dramatic effect on molecular dynamics of using a glassy solvent. This was followed by OO59 on 10th July 1978 with Gareth Evans and with Kestemont, Hermans, Finsy and van Loon of the Free University of Brussels on the computer simulation of the itinerant oscillator model.

As a Scientiae Doctor and holding a distinction higher than full professor I decided to apply for the advertized post of head of department of the EDCL. This was forced upon me by the need for tenure, but such a job is not suitable for a dedicated scholar. Somehow the application was leaked to Mansel Davies. Although he had no authority over me as a Ramsay Memorial Fellow, I was told to withdraw the application. This was done in a sarcastic, malicious way, "you as head of department!". These days that would be seen as another clear violation of the laws governing behaviour in the work place. It would be seen as deliberately and unreasonably refusing to award well deserved promotion and blocking the chances of promotion. At the time I thought it over and wondered what damage Mansel Davies could do even at that very late stage in his career. So I withdrew the application in considerable bitterness. I know now that some arrangement had already been made to give the job to Jeremy Jones behind the scenes. Other candidates probably had no chance at interview. Mansel Davies may have known this, but denied to me that he had any knowledge of the procedure. One of the candidates was J. O. Williams, who had been given rapid promotion to Reader, but who had refused to move to Cambridge with Thomas. J. O. Williams's application was revealed most dramatically to me in the corridor as he burst out of the interview, infuriated and incoherent, snarling at me in the Welsh language and almost knocking me over in rage.

OO60 was also submitted on 10th July 1978 on current and spin density correlation functions which I evaluated with my molecular dynamics computer simulation program. OO64 was submitted on 3rd July 1978, a short paper to Faraday II. By this time I had already produced the equivalent of the entire output of papers by my supervisor Mansel Davies in his entire career, and had comprehensively out performed him in early career. Yet he was still as patronising as ever. The strangest thing about him is that he kept informing Gareth Evans, with whom he was on good terms, that I was the best scientist he had ever worked with. I could never bring myself to have much respect for him in turn, although he did do some good work. The verbal outbursts, career bending and so on knocked almost all the respect out of me. Having written that, he was infinitely preferable to what the tide washed in next, a little man called Jeremy Jones who had been a student of Orville-Thomas. Most of the EDCL could not believe that such a man could be appointed as a head of department, surely they could have found someone better. Within ten years the EDCL had been closed and abandoned.

J. M. Thomas disappeared in the summer of 1978 and the EDCL porters had to help him pack. I do not know if he had the right to use the porters for his personal affairs. Before he left however he joined in the pressure to make me move to Swansea in a short interview where he very grudgingly seemed to offer tenure again. Of course nothing came of it. Pressures to force me to move to another job would now be illegal. I remember him intoning in Welsh to me that he had heard of my SERC Advanced Fellowship but I was not to refuse the Swansea move. “You’re not supposed to do that” he said in Welsh. I found this to be intolerably patronising so made up my mind to take the SERC Advanced Fellowship. The great output of work that started in 1978 shows this decision to be entirely the right one to make. He should have been making efforts to appoint me tenured full professor in view of my British, Irish and Commonwealth record D. Sc. and Harrison Memorial Prize, both acquired in 1978. The money was available of course, and was always available. In the same interview he told me "I know all about you". I almost replied "Very good for you", but said nothing. So there was obvious personal animosity, and again that would be against ACAS rules these days. It was probably illegal in those days too. The reason is that I helped a technician called Mansell Davies who lost an eye in an accident while doing work for Thomas, and wished to claim compensation. In that summer of 1978 Mansell Davies rented a flat to me in his house in Borth, overlooking the sea, so I popped out of the Eastgate slum like a cork out of a cyanogen lecture bottle. The individual Thomas was nothing like the image, the cult of personality at work. They never are. What is needed in a National University is an intelligent and helpful head of department who shares resources fairly, and above all a fluent Welsh speaker truly dedicated to Wales.

Prof. Mansel Davies (not to be confused with the technician Mansell Davies) remained at the EDCL until the day of the interview for a new head of department. In those days such a process was entirely secretive, but recently the Information Commissioner obliged Aberystwyth to give some details. Howard Purnell was on the interview committee, and there were about twenty or thirty applicants. There was a short list which included Jeremy Jones and J. O. Williams. None of the candidates had my record of achievement in open competition, so stopping me from applying is suspicious, especially as I had the support of the Principal, Sir Goronwy Daniel. It is also blatantly illegal and I would have made a strong candidate. My Civil List predecessor Hamilton was full professor at the age of twenty three, and Heisenberg at twenty six. I was already twenty eight at the time. So the system always slid out of its obligations. The Scientiae

Doctor was meant by the University of London, who founded it in 1860, to be a distinction higher than full professor or personal chair, but this distinction was not honoured by the University of Wales despite the fact that it awarded the degree as a mark of internationally recognized achievement. The administration of the University of Wales was therefore anarchic, it did what it liked because those whose duty it was to control it failed totally to do so. This left a small clique in control, as nearly always in Wales. The Harrison Memorial Prize was a rare achievement, but the University of Wales refused to recognize it. By the "University of Wales" was meant a few untalented careerists, cuckoos in the nest. The People of Wales should not be deceived in this way. The talent and dedication to the language inside Wales is to be found outside the colony known as "The University of Wales" in individual homes and in the best secondary schools. This has always been the case. There was also an exact precedent: Graham Williams had won a Harrison Memorial Prize in 1977, one year before me, and was promoted to a personal chair, without a D. Sc., in 1978. So I should also have been promoted in 1978 to a tenured personal chair because I had a D. Sc. and a Harrison Memorial Prize. If the money was available for Graham Williams it was available for me. So this was illegal prejudice and career blocking. There was no pressure on Graham Williams to move to Swansea. So the system was riddled completely with injustice.

The enthusiastic support for my work from Sir Goronwy Daniel became vividly apparent when I was invited to a reception in late winter of 1978 at the Principal's Mansion with Lady Daniel, formerly the Honourable Valerie Lloyd-George. So I found myself transplanted from the worst slum in Aberystwyth to the resplendent mansion. Being a cold, damp night I put on a borrowed leather jacket over a woollen jumper, and emerged from the slum at a brisk pace. I decided to walk to the Principal's mansion because my car was parked at the EDCL. Sir Goronwy and Lady Daniel were both very pleasant, despite the Principal's reputation for a ferocious nature, and almost his last act as Principal was to hand me my D. Sc. Certificate at the Degree Ceremony of July 1978, where he broke into a broad, genuine smile. He offered me a sherry which I could not refuse, and I remember Lady Daniel's bemused countenance as I started to melt under the combined effect of leather jacket, woollen jumper and sherry, being an athlete and non drinker. She looked like Lloyd-George almost exactly and I looked like a long haired owl. All was going well, and I felt completely at home, "here is appreciation at last" I thought. The whole occasion was spoiled by a pathetic comment from Prof. Sir Granville Beynon, who told me that I was too young. I was about to assure him that he was too old and way past it when Sir Goronwy stared him down. There was deep rooted envy as well as animosity in a small place like Aberystwyth. Nevertheless that touch of kindness by the Principal did me a power of good at a time when I was being beaten up by the petty minded. Sir Goronwy evidently did not know of these pressures, or if he did he kept his diplomatic distance. Some time later he wrote me a latter in retirement asking me to bide my time, and that letter is now reproduced on www.aias.us. Sir Goronwy did more for the Welsh language than John Thomas ever did or ever thought of doing.

That degree ceremony took place at around the same time as the interview process for head of department of the EDCL. J. O. Williams and I were awarded the D. Sc. Degree at the same ceremony and he sat right next to me. To my great surprise he was intensely nervous, while I was just mildly bored. He was visibly shaking, and I wondered why this should be so. In his less ambitious frames of mind J. O. and I got on fine, we always spoke in Welsh of course, and I cannot help wondering what would have happened if he had been appointed Head of Department. He was a far stronger candidate than Jeremy Jones, who was an obscure lecturer, and had no D. Sc. Degree. J. O.

was already a Reader, two steps up in the pecking order and had out produced Jeremy Jones. J. O. was also a better lecturer than Jeremy Jones, and had none of the latter's evil and offensive temper. Finally J. O. had a fluent grasp of the Welsh language and was an enthusiastic supporter of it, while Jeremy Jones could not care less about he language, speaking the remains of Llandeilo patois. Later records show that J. O. was a good administrator, as a full professor in Manchester and Principal of what is now known as Prifysgol Owain Glyndw^r. Jeremy Jones was a complete and abject administrative failure. In his hyper ambitious phases J. O. was less likeable, but he did have a sense of fairness. He was not very enthusiastic about the increasingly nasty campaign to force me to move to Swansea. The D. Sc. is a rarely awarded degree, so there were only two of us there - both from the EDCL, in the D. Sc. Gown of the University of Wales. J. O. had an open character and a sense of freshness and innocence about him, when I started speaking in French to a visitor one day he was greatly surprised and impressed. He did not particularly like John Thomas because the latter was manically ambitious. One can only be ambitious if one leads by personal example, not by putting one's name to myriads of papers by other people. Clementi at IBM was also in the habit of doing that. All those papers at IBM were of course my own work, with some input from Keith Refson and others, but none at all from Clementi.

It is almost certain that Jeremy Jones had been "given the job if he applied" - the Purnell hallmark. So none of the other thirty or more candidates had any hope. This really infuriates me to this day. There may have been a hundred or so candidates for the Swansea job in which they tried to make me into a pawn on a dirty chessboard. Ninety nine out of the hundred would have had no chance, and the short listed would have been hauled down to Swansea and completely deceived. How many times does that happen in the academic system? J. O. Williams clearly expected to be given the job of Head of Department at the

EDCL. I know this from personal experience because the first thing that I knew of the interview process was his rage at being cold shouldered. He was beside himself with fury and burst in through the doors of the EDCL venting his intense anger at me in the Welsh language. I have recounted a little of this already. I made my way back to room 262. I met the newly crowned king when Mansel Davies asked me to have a cup of coffee with Jones and himself. This was a rare happening, Jupiter descending. Mansel Davies always referred to him as “Bill Jeremy”. The latter had made his hallmark by some minor role in the inverse Raman effect as a post doctoral in Canada, and for some reason has been appointed without competition to Cambridge. It is not hard to guess that this was due to Mansel Davies at the peak of his influence. So I made my way to the little common room of the EDCL - then reserved for tenured staff only. Along with post docs I was confined to the coffee machine and its dubious molecular dynamics. Inside was a very nervous little man smoking incessantly. He was floored by the fact that the EDCL graduated only five chemistry students. Obviously the job arrangers had neglected to inform him of this, and he wished that he was not there. I was told to take Friedmann and Jones up to Pant y Celyn Hall for some reason. Friedmann saw a Welsh language poster and sullenly muttered “that’s all I need”. I didn’t bother to explain that Pant y Celyn was the Welsh language Hall, and that William Williams of that name was our greatest hymn writer. “This is great start” I thought to myself, and indeed it got worse very quickly.

I was summoned by his majesty to attend court that evening in the Sze Hing Chinese Restaurant opposite Aberystwyth Pier, near the alley of a thousand dustbins. Here, over wonton soup and a china spoon, I was told to go to Swansea, Jones had brought his cracked record with him. Friedmann was there, and remained silent. He had just been appointed to tenure at the EDCL without competition. So “here we go again”. Within two or three years Friedmann had gone because he could not do anything at the EDCL from lack of technical support and a large lecture load. What a mess. Friedmann was quite a pleasant man, or seemed to be, but he had just been transplanted into a culture and language of which he knew nothing. Jones told me that "Purnell will cut my head off" if I didn't go to Swansea. I have never met an individual who thought so much of himself. There was no use protesting that public executions did not happen near Aberystwyth pier any more. I was just thinking of fish and chips, because wonton soup was not much of a meal. Very shortly thereafter I resigned the Swansea job, and took up the SERC Advanced Fellowship. I had been a lecturer at Swansea for a few months and resigned because it was my duty to do so. This was the honourable way out. None of those corrupt people had any right to interfere in my decision to build a group at the EDCL which from 1978 to 1983 out performed the other staff combined. The source documents are all in the historical source document section of www.aias.us. Shortly thereafter a large grant came through from SERC of about half a million pounds in contemporary money. With a sense of huge relief, I emerged from the Sze Hing and Jones and Friedmann made their way back to Pant y Celyn. The ugly, menacing tone of the interview was washed away with fish and chips and coca cola. Thus began five years of warfare between Jones and the rest of the staff. This destroyed the EDCL completely.

At the time, Room 262 was a busy laboratory doing work of international renown. I occupied it with Gareth Evans and Colin Reid, and Gareth Evans and I were given two desks in a microscopic office with no windows opposite the laboratory. On 10th November 1978 OO66 was submitted to Faraday II with Gareth Evans, A. H. Price and Eugene Schwartz. Alun Price was one of those who had refused to join in the go to Swansea scene. On 17th Nov 1978 OO66 was submitted to Molecular Physics with Gareth Evans, Yarwood, P. L. James and R. Arndt on the molecular dynamics of acetonitrile, developing the multi technical approach further. I had just discovered the gamma process of the far infra red, that was reported in OO67 submitted on 11th October 1978 and secured Colin Reid's M. Sc. Degree. He was able to go on to a Ph. D., supervised by myself. I was not given any credit for this supervision because I had no tenure. OO67 reveals the intricate nature of molecular dynamics of a small molecule, dichloromethane, dissolved in a glass. The spectra were obtained in the far infra red and at low frequency, so the evolution of the dynamics could be observed from picoseconds to years as part of the same, immensely protracted, evolutionary process. In rough analogy, this is like observing the geological evolution of the earth in real time. So here was an individual with a distinction higher than full professor, and a Harrison Memorial Prizewinner, being denied credit for supervising an excellent Thesis. I paid a visit to Trinity College Dublin at about that time, and the result of that was OO63, submitted on 1st December 1978 to Chemical Physics Letters with William Coffey and J. D. Pryce of Bristol University's School of Mathematics. On my return from Trinity College I met an Italian physicist called Paolo Grigolini of the University of Pisa who had visited the EDCL in order to start a cooperation on mutual interests. That resulted in his student Mauro Ferrario becoming my post doctoral assistant under the newly acquired SERC grant. The first class technical ability of the Pisa group strengthened my own group as can be seen from the Omnia Opera. The first paper with Ferrario and Grigolini was submitted on 25th May 1979 as OO76 on the interaction of rotation and translation in molecular dynamics. Both Grigolini and Ferrario became full professors, and Ferrario became a Director of CECAM.

As soon as he heard of my resignation Jeremy Jones wrote an illegal letter from Cambridge trying to force me once more to go to Swansea. His judgment had already collapsed, because he was prepared to give up a half million grant and the most talented British group in molecular dynamics for the sake of neurosis. Purnell would not destroy his department, Jeremy Jones would destroy it himself. That strange, menacing letter is to be found in the historical source documents of www.aias.us, written with a fountain pen on Cambridge notepaper. I was to receive many strange little notes from 1978 to1983. All of these notes would be illegal today, because they were all aimed at getting me out of the EDCL as soon as possible, a clear case of prejudice and career blocking. Nothing else mattered to the little man from Cambridge. To the rest of British chemical physics this was an obvious disaster. Here was an unknown bureaucrat with the arrogance to set aside the opinion of an entire profession. The incoming Principal in the Autumn of 1978 was a nonentity who could not even speak the Welsh language, so with his appointment Aberystwyth ceased to have anything to do with Welsh speaking Wales and meekly accepted colonization. I ignored the pathetic letter from Jeremy Jones, so afraid of his own shadow and completely unsuited for any position of responsibility. He was a peculiarly offensive man with the attitude of an occupying Gauleiter of Cambridge, sent down to sort out the peasants. Some thought he was appointed to close the department, nearly all found it impossible to accept the appointment. There were no ACAS mechanisms in those days, there was a Trade Union but it was almost wholly ineffective. The EDCL was at the mercy of tyranny.

In the autumn of 1978 there were secretive promotions to full professor of J. O. Williams, H. Heller and G. Williams. No one knew how these promotions were assessed. Being a D. Sc. I already held a distinction higher than full professor, but of course with the new jackboot in place there was unilateral government by personal animosity. I was allowed to attend only one staff meeting, at which Jones threatened almost immediately to close the department. His exact words were a little different, he said that the department would be closed, but we all got his meaning. He sat very nervously at the head of a table in some staff common room in Laura Place. He had been an undergraduate at the EDCL in the same class as Graham Williams, and both were awarded tenure without any form of open competition. I sat silent and contemptuous of the entire farce. John Adams (also appointed to tenure without competition) made some remark that everyone thinks he is a Nobel Laureate, and was put down with false authority by Jones. The latter uttered the one truth of the meeting, that he was not of Nobel Prize quality, whatever that is. So the staff were treated like schoolboys by a chain smoker. All were going to be set to work campaigning and scouring for students, never mind the quality, feel the width. The Welsh language and Welsh culture were not present at the meeting, having been deemed as not capable of attracting funds or sufficient student numbers. I felt hungry after this gathering of the gods, got some fish and chips and went home to Borth. The advantage of Room 262 was that it was right at the end of the corridor, a long way from Jones, who could be ignored if the moon were not full. It was a long way from politics, a name for professorial dog fights. After that one meeting I was never invited to another because an edict came down from Olympus - the untenured are lepers, only those with random and unearned tenure would be allowed to attend staff meetings of the EDCL. Scientific achievement did not matter. Again this would be illegal today because it is a form of discrimination and career blocking. In the case of a Government S.E.R.C. Advanced Fellow such as myself it was a breach of contract. The Government's clear intention was to tenure the Advanced Fellow. In the case of a D. Sc. such as myself it was a breach of University Regulations, a Scientiae Doctor of the University of Wales has an international reputation and holds a rank higher than full professor. Any head of department in his right mind would value such talent and aportion jobs according to talent, some for teaching, some for research. The gross corruption in the university system in Wales was already apparent worldwide, not only in Britain. People were appointed to lifelong jobs if and only if they were part of a small clique. After tenure, no matter how much of a disaster they were, they were allowed to keep comfortable jobs and salaries, all paid by the Government. The Welsh language and culture were not factors in the game. So the University betrayed its origins utterly.

It was already obvious that Jones' sole intention, regardless of any merit or productivity, was to get me out of the EDCL, because otherwise he would be decapitated by Purnell, by axe on a block near the pier, or if Purnell was in a good mood, by sword. It is impossible to believe that a National University could ever be run in this way, and today it would be a multiple breach of human rights, virtually every human right ever dreamed of. So I decided to show what the group of Room 262 could do in the face of disgusting animosity. All around us the island of civilization known as the EDCL was sinking. The planks were creaking and the timbers shivering. Civilization needs confidence, stability and hope for the future, and we had a lunatic in charge, Gaius Caligula had declared war on the sea and had read out his edict on the promenade. The Roman Empire slowly began to collapse from madness and decadence. The first sign of carnage was the sudden appearance of a deeply embittered Cecil Monk right next door to Room 262. He had just retired and had given lifelong service to the EDCL and had founded the spacious Soddy Laboratory for radiochemistry, but had been savagely booted out by the ambitious J. O. Williams and stuffed into a small preparation room. He had been allowed to continue to work at the EDCL, but was denied access to the interminable boredom of staff meetings. He continued to write scientific papers from that small room, which filled with smoke from his pipe. I think that J. O. was in turn booted out of part of the Soddy by Jeremy Jones, who put Friedman to work on some apparatus that was never made to function. John Thomas had vanished to

Cambridge and had gutted the EDCL of apparatus. None of the Welsh speaking technicians of his group moved with him, quite naturally. They had worked hard for him in the expectation that he would build up the EDCL with my help as another Welsh speaker and the youngest Scientiae Doctor in history under modern rules. They were naively unaware of what am ition can do to a man . Jim Jenkins was to pay the price by suicide, and Mansell Davies died some years after an eye injury. Islwyn "Griff" Griffiths died of cancer, but not before declaring his infinite disgust and anger as he saw me about to leave for Bangor. Irfon Williams was transferred to physics and became deeply depressed. I believe he left academia completely. The non Welsh speaking technicians fared very little better, and lived out their lives in a deep pit of bitterness in scenic Aberystwyth by the sunny sea. They actually had to live there without jobs, and it wasn't very scenic in the dole queue. This is what always happens to Welsh speaking or non Welsh speaking Wales, whose history is one of continuous betrayal by manic ambition.

In this eerie, creaky, loonie bin our group began to be very productive and spectacularly successful, while the rest of the EDCL slid into eternal obscurity. OO69 was submitted on 13th Feb 1979 under my own authorship after a dreary visit to Trinity College Dublin which had been marred by Coffey's heavy drinking and weird behaviour with Vij. I think I was offered a lectureship by Brendan Scaife on this visit, but had been put off when he described his own department as a nut house, Coffey turning out to be a liability screaming down the corridor like a banshee. This is a paper on electrodynamical influences in disordered solids published in Faraday II. Earlier in the Autumn of 1978 the National Physical Laboratory had supported me as a candidate for the prestigious Meldola Medal. I had also received an invitation from Stuart Rice for my first prestigious review article, OO75 on www.aias.us . This reviews the work of the time very clearly, and was published in "Advances in Chemical

Physics" by Wiley Interscience of New York. The Americans of course had no idea of the chaos at the EDCL. On 17th May 1979 OO74 was submitted to Faraday II with Alun Price on a new diffusion equation for the dielectric loss of the nematic phase of a liquid crystal and reflects the mastery of the diffusion equation that I had obtained through my own study in Trinity College Dublin. Price was always the careful politician, and survived by doing anything that Mansel Davies would tell him to do. He had switched his allegiance to Jeremy Jones in a grudging type of way, but was already looking forward to retirement. Colin Reid had suddenly decided to work for his living and had produced a lot of spectra which were written up in OO73, submitted on 24th May 1979 to Faraday II. Colin Reid rapidly developed at this time into quite a good theoretician and also developed trust in me as a supervisor. Mansel Davies had just not bothered and had vanished to Criccieth in the autumn of 1978. So I steered Colin Reed through to his Masters degree and then through his doctorate. I was not given any official credit and that would be illegal today. The official credit was given to Alun Price, but it is obvious from papers such as OO73 that Price could never have achieved the theoretical finesse of this paper and was not a co author. So the corrupt system gave credit to people who did not supervise and who were happy to accept credit for work they did not do. Again, this should never happen in a National University.

On 22nd May 1979 OO79 was submitted to Faraday II with Paolo Grigolini and Mauro Ferrario on transient response in a very intense field using computer simulation and followed on 25th May 1979, by OO76 submitted to "Molecular Physics" with Paolo Grigolini and my new post doctoral, Mauro Ferrario. The latter had joined the group and Prof. Konrad Singer had given a copy of the TRI2 molecular dynamics computer simulation code for triatomics. This was a pioneering simulation code able to deal with symmetries different from linear. I had been invited to the department of physics in the University of

Pisa by Grigolini, and had my first experience of flying club class in an Alitalia jet into Galileo Galilei Airport, with the mountains in the background. Some of these flights go low over the marble quarries of Carrara, where Grigolini came from. The Department of physics was situated on the Via Santa Maria on the way to the Duomo with its leaning Bell Tower, and Grigolini's office was in a stochastic condition, situated below street level in a cellar, stuffed with files and paper, with ants crawling on the floor. The department had a small library, but its drainage system was appalling. Over the street there was a small café and restaurant. Grigolini had come over to Aberystwyth in the hope of establishing cooperative work with my group, already well known throughout Europe in its field, and was an able theoretician. He was prone to deep depression and outbursts of temper, being hyper intense and always deeply immersed in thought. In contrast, Mauro Ferrario was infinitely polite and quiet and was one of the new generation of students familiar with computers. He came from a region of central Italy, and later became a Director of CECAM in Switzerland and a full professor. Grigolini became a full professor in North Texas. In those early days though he could be very uncertain and unstable, and once shook his fist under my nose as I was about to leave Pisa Airport. This absolutely outraged his colleagues. I do not know the cause of this incident, maybe some underlying irritation or animosity, or some bout of depression. Apparently he had lost his fiancé when she died in an accident. On another occasion e wrote to me from one of the mid West Universities: "For God's sake get me out of here." I put him up in my flat in Borth on one occasion and was most surprised and ill at ease when he asked me some advice on marriage. I had never been married at that time, and I thought of Handel, throw the soprano out of the window, but kept quiet and did what I could to help because he was obviously unhappy. He seemed to have a nice family when I met them, and once showed me the sharply leaning top of the

Pisa tower with his daughter Silvia playing dangerously close to the railings. I hoped that he was not going to use her as a Galilean experiment. He also showed me the inside of the Duomo with magnificent art by Pisano. After he became full professor he had no further need of being associated with me, a mere post doc., and I never heard from him again. I must say that I did not miss his company.

For OO76 Mauro Ferrario and I had coded up the running time averaging algorithm for a range of correlation functions of many dynamical variables, auto and cross correlation functions that wove a rich tapestry of information which at that time (1979) was entirely new and original. These correlation functions could probe areas of dynamics that conventional theory could not, and much as they tried, neither Grigolini nor Coffey could ever come to grips with the far infra red or with computer simulation and drifted off into increasingly abstract work of the type that solved problems that could be solved, exercises in mathematics. Neither could improve on my early work using the Mori three variable theory in the far infra red, started at Oxford and taken up at Aberystwyth. The severe problems with Jones had already begun to affect both Mauro Ferrario and Colin Reid, and Mauro Ferrario could stick it out until the autumn of 1981 when he won a CNR European Fellowship and later moved to the Free University of Brussels. By the time Mauro Ferrario left however, the correlation function technique had been developed to the point where it became the mainstay of about three hundred papers and reviews of mine in total, in all the best journals worldwide.

On May 30th 1979 I submitted two more papers, OO71 as a single author, and OO70 with Colin Reid. OO71 was on Brownian motion modulated by the atom atom potential, which was used in computer simulation. OO70 used data over ten decades of frequency to describe the molecular dynamics of dichloromethane dissolved in a glass, and developed my slightly earlier discovery of the gamma process. This paper used a development of the Smoluchowski diffusion equation based on methods that I had developed myself at Trinity College Dublin and later at Aberystwyth Colin Reid worked very hard all of a sudden to produce the data. At first I thought he would never produce anything, being absent from work for weeks on end. It may have been the stabilizing influence of his fiancé Jennifer Davies of Aberaeron. They were later married in Brecon Castle just before I was forced to leave for IBM as full professor in Sept. 1986. On May 31st 1979 OO77 with Grigolini was submitted to Molecular Physics on an extension of my earlier Mori theory to try to describe rototranslation, but as can be seen from OO77 on www.aias.us the theory is hideously complicated and cannot come to grips with the simulation. So a combination of the far infra red and simulation is enough to defeat theory already. I began at that point to forge the European Delta Project, because I could see the need to coordinate research all over Europe. This was done with the usual complaints about postage, which Jones used as an excuse to complain to the Registrar as an example of my lack of discipline. So he was a disaster waiting to happen, without vision and imagination, and deeply offensive to science.

On 2nd July 1979 OO90, submitted to Faraday II with Grigolini, I produced a pioneering paper using molecular dynamics in an entirely original way to show that processes in molecular dynamics were in general non Markovian and also non Gaussian. Grigolini attempted to provide an explanation, but both of us agreed that the simulation when used in this way left the theory in its wake. On 22nd August 1979 OO80 was submitted to Chemical Physics Letters with Grigolini and Resca on a hydrodynamical theory generalized with the Mori theory. Grigolini had spent some time at Purdue University and had probably written frm Purdue asking me to "get him out of there". Nevertheless the paper is good work in the frequency and time domains but again shows the characteristic overcomplexity of Grigolini's approach to molecular dynamics. It seems muddy and fuzzy compared with simulation in the necessary three dimensions. On 11th Sept. 1979 OO82 was submitted by myself as sole author to Faraday II on power reflection spectroscopy near the Brewster angle, a technique that I hoped would develop into a new spectrometer. I made some calculations using my own Mori three variable theory which showed that near the Brewster angle, the features of molecular dynamics hitherto confined to the far infra red could be shifted into the near infra red, opening up a whole new area of study. Unfortunately the conditions at the EDCL made this development impossible there, but it could be carried out easily with contemporary technology. On 24th Sept. 1979 OO81 was submitted to Faraday II with Gareth Evans on the effect of an electric field on the far infra red power absorption of liquid aniline, with an extensive theoretical analysis by myself inter relating several different theories as part of the methodology I was developing for the Delta Project. The quality and quantity of the work matched any group in the world at the time with relatively meagre resources under appalling administration.

At about this time I won the 1979 Meldola Medal outright and the clipping of the announcement is on www.aias.us in the photographs section. So I became part of a small elite awarded both the Harrison Memorial Prize and the Meldola Medal. If I had been awarded the Marlow Medal (of which I was effectively joint winner) Iwould have been one of only two nly scientists in history to have recorded the triple : Harrison, Meldola and Marlow. Stretching a point I did in fact do the triple. I am the only member of the University of Wales with this achievement. The University did not recognize this by tenure, and has still not done so. This is therefore a severe breach of human rights, all due to the animosity of one individual over whom there was no control. No organization should be run in this way, an organization blatantly opposed to meritocracy. Not only was this allowed to happen, but no mechanism has ever been able to right the injustice, so from my case it is seen very clearly that society is not a meritocracy at all. Nonetheless I was very proud to have won the prestigious Meldola Medal. The photograph for "Chemistry in Britain" was taken by Jim Jenkins, and what a profound shock it was to receive a newspaper clipping from Gareth Evans in early 1991 reporting Jim's suicide. At the time I was in a small office in the Irchel Campus of the University of Zurich, an office shared with Stanislaw Wozniak. There was no sign of such a tragedy in 1979. I think that Jim Jenkins was made redundant when the EDCL closed, and could not come to terms with the desolation. Jones had vanished to Swansea and by some corrupt arrangement had been allowed to keep his job. Cecil Monk described this with great contempt as "scuttling away" when I last saw him in 1993. There was no attempt by the administration to congratulate me on these prestigious medals, showing up a terminal psychological sickness or iron in the soul. Any normal University department would have trumpeted these awards to the skies, as they do today. So the generosity of spirit of Sir Goronwy Daniel left Aberystwyth with him in Sept. 1978 when he retired, to be replaced by crabby greyness devoid of any connection with the scholarly traditions of Wales.

In addition to these awards and publications a major item of new equipment granted to myself was due to arrive: an Apollo Instruments far infra red laser ordered from California. With the wisdom of hind sight and experience I should have used the grant money to fund more post doctoral staff or extend the terms of the post doctoral staff to five years. In the event Jones had the opportunity of totally disrupting the Government's intentions by deliberately refusing to house the laser, and deliberately wasting the Government grant. This is illegal and could be actionable today in court. The Government should have taken action back in the late seventies and early eighties. ACAS rules these days would interpreted such an act as career blocking, discrimination and harassment. On 3rd Oct 1979 OO83 was submitted to Advances in Molecular Relaxation and Interaction Processes and developed the technique of low angle Brewster reflection spectroscopy for ionic crystals, melts, conducting media, biomolecular systems, semiconductors, gas / solid and liquid / solid interfaces. Unfortunately this was a scruffily produced journal and OO83 is not easy to read on www.aias.us. Nonetheless it is one of my favourite papers of that time. On 16th Nov. 1979 the most incisive paper in molecular dynamics produced up to that point in history, OO78, was submitted to Chemical Physics Letters with Mauro Ferrario and Paolo Grigolini. I was able to show by simulation with the Singer algorithm TRI2 that the statistics of molecules are in general non Gaussian. This was the first time that this had been demonstrated since the nineteenth century. There were so many fundamental discoveries made in that year of 1979 that they must stuck on to paper here like so many postage stamps. It seemed to me that each new discovery was accompanied by a note from Jeremy Jones placed on my desk at midnight complaining about postage, or if he could not think of anything else, about my very existence on this earth. What a travesty of all that is just in society!

On 26th Nov. 1979 OO85 was submitted to Molecular Physics with Colin Reid on the liquid crystal known as K21 and on 4th Dec. 1979 OO86 was submitted with Colin Reid to Molecular Physics and is another very fine paper utilizing a range of data to test theories to destruction. There is still no theory that is able to describe data used in this incisive way. On Dec. 18th 1979 OO84 was submitted to Zeit. Phys. B in sole authorship comparing the results of an incisive new simulation method with Mori three variable theory. The simulation exposed the limitations of the theory. Finally on 21st Dec. 1979 OO87 was submitted with Colin Reid to Spectrochimica Acta on solvent shifts in the far infra red, based on extensive experimental wotk by Colin Reid on the new far infra red interferometer granted to Rowlinson and myself at Oxford and transferred to Aberystwyth, a place to which I was far too generous. In that year of 1979 about seventeen first class papers had been produced and the three legged Delta had been defined: experiment, theory and simulation. These all brought in a pile of reprint requests by post card so Jones had a whale of a time complaining about postage. He did not read any of the papers about which he complained. The system, instead of supporting scholarship, set out to destroy it because one individual was afraid of his career being hurt and all others were afraid of stopping him. That is such an absurd way to "educate" and it had to be shut down of course. By now, thirty three years later, it has become a great pleasure to see all that original thought archived on both sides of the Atlantic and available for all to read open source.

Colin Reid completed and submitted his Ph. D. Thesis in the same year of 1979, and my method of publishing refereed papers in advance pulled him through. He was intensely nervous before the final examination, despite writing up an excellent piece of work of about two hundred and fifty or more pages. He got into an argument with Graham Williams and threatened to pull out, so it took all of my persuasive powers to keep him going. His "official" supervisor Alun Price was way out of his depth, and Colin acknowledged my contribution generously. Graham Williams never read or understood any of my work, whereas Colin Reid had a thorough knowledge of both its experimental and theoretical aspects. He pulled through his final examination and was awarded his Ph. D. In late 1979 I offered him a post doctoral Fellowship which he accepted. So for a very brief time in late 1979 I had built up a group with three post doctoral assistants while being in the wildly anomalous situation of being a post doctoral myself, with a D. Sc. Degree. My work was acknowledged throughout Europe and I had begun work on the Delta Project, published in OO99 in 1981. We still occupied Room 262. Gareth Evans was in the last year of his post doctoral assistantship granted to him by Mansel Davies, and this was also switched to Alun Price. The latter of course did nothing at all to supervise. Around about this time Gareth Evans became worried about his future prospects because we could all see that the EDCL was headed for disaster, and we could all read those revolting notes placed on my desk. Jones would have them typed out by his secretaries, placed in a sealed envelope, which would then appear on my desk very suddenly. We all thought that he was disturbed psychologically. The typed letters would be copied to the Registrar and Principal. Instead of sorting him out, the senior administration did nothing from very afar. This seems to read from this distance in historical perspective that they had decided to close the EDCL. Either that or the were not administrators at all, just there for the salary and pension.

So I encouraged Gareth Evans to apply for a University of Wales Fellowship in open competition in the autumn of 1979, and strangely enough, Jeremy Jones signed the application. I suppose that he did not even know at that point that Gareth Evans was working for me, otherwise he would have refused to sign. The Fellowship application was of course based on our award winning work. Gareth Evans also applied for other jobs, such as that of a Warden and I positively refereed all the applications. He went as far as an interview in industry, but was told that if he did not get a heart attack by age forty he would be sacked. This drivel put him off industry. So the group stayed together and all seemed set fair for Room 262. At that point the S. E. R. C. should have stepped in and demanded tenure for me as an Advanced Fellow from Aberystwyth, but it did nothing. The group felt relatively safe and insulated in Room 262, in which I had been working since 1971. Cooperation had also been forged with the National Physical Laboratory, Trinity College Dublin (part of the Oxford / Cambridge system) and the University of Pisa, and I had begun to forge excellent relations with the

Singer group at Royal Holloway College of the University of London. Despite this, the unstable sword of Damocles was always hanging above us. In a historical perspective it is clear that the corrupt nature of the University of Wales would not tolerate truly competitive talent. It was a small clique made up of individuals who appointed each other and used the system as a springboard for career. They regarded all talk of the People of Wales with disturbed contempt.

Suddenly the sword fell, in early 1980 we were told to get out of Room 262, which was to be handed over to Graham Williams. The group was outraged because Graham Williams already had plenty of room for himself as full professor. This was therefore a deliberate disruption of the Government's intent. For a long time Gareth Evans and I tried to argue that we were expecting the arrival of an Apollo Instruments laser, and that the EDCL was contractually bound to house the equipment. We were told to move into a tiny room directly opposite to Jeremy Jones' office and completely unsuitable for modern equipment such as the California made laser. Jones disrupted things further by having the room "redecorated". So the plan was to disrupt and destroy our group by having its equipment piled up in the corridor, awaiting redecoration. We were forced out of Room 262 but there was no other laboratory available. All of this is illegal, it is harassment and career blocking. All of the strange little notes were and are illegal. At the same time a third desk was jammed into the tiny office occupied by Gareth Evans and myself opposite room 262. To reach my desk, Gareth Evans had to walk out of the room so that I could get in, and then reoccupy his desk. There was no direct lighting. These days that would be a violation of conditions of work. Finally we were forced to move the delicate interferometer into the corridor of the old EDCL, awaiting redecoration. It remained there for months in full view of all staff and students, none of whom dared protest in any way. This was Government equipment which by today's money might be worth about one hundred thousand pounds. The Apollo laser might be worth a further three hundred thousand pounds. Graham Williams did not use Room 262, it was kept empty for two or three years.

This harassment helps to explain the long gap between OO87, submitted on 21st Dec. 1979, and OO88, submitted on 16th April 1980 in sole authorship submitted to Spectrochimica Acta on moment analysis of the depolarized Rayleigh spectrum. On 16th April 1980 a paper with Colin Reid on the Zero to THz Spectra of rotator phases was submitted to Molecular Physics, making clear that this range of spectra challenged theory as never before, or indeed since. There was another relatively long gap to 3rd June 1980, when OO95 was submitted with Grigolini to Physica A. These were all theoretical papers, we could no longer use the far infra red spectrometer. The Apollo Instruments laser arrived in crates from California in the first part of 1980, and the crates were again piled up in the corridor. The "decoration" was taking an awful long time, especially as it was just a coat of paint. From this perspective I should have demanded an S. E. R. C. inspection. These days I would have had immediate recourse to ACAS, the Government's advisory and conciliatory service. On 21st July 1980 I submitted three more papers. The first was OO92, with Mauro Ferrario and William Coffey, submitted to Advances in Molecular Relaxation and Interaction Processes in which computer simulation was used to evaluate theoretical models. The second was OO93, submitted to the same journal, with Gareth Evans and William Coffey on computer simulation used to evaluate short time translational motion, and OO94 to Zeit. Phys. B with Paolo Grigolini, on computer simulation used to demonstrate that molecular dynamics are neither Gaussian nor Markovian. Computer simulation was running far ahead of the theory.

Jones'delaying tactics were beginning to work against him, long overdue criticism of him from increasingly browbeaten staff and technical staff forced him to open the door of the tiny little room in which both the laser and interferometer were somehow to be assembled. There was room only for the laser, which worked with high voltages. The interferometer remained piled up in the corridor, so experimental work on it was stopped as planned. Mauro Ferrario announced that he might be leaving for Brussels on an Italian CNR Fellowship because there was no longer any space available for him to work at the EDCL. No one likes to work in a department in which the atmosphere of animosity could be cut with a knife. The group struggled to forge its own kind of civilization against this cynical harassment and somehow we managed to get the apparatus stuffed into the room. This was very dangerous because the room was completely unsuitable and deliberately chosen to be so. The Apollo Instruments support technician flown over from California could not quite believe what was being done to the new laser. He did his best to get it going on an ordinary laboratory bench. The interferometer must have been crammed on to another bench in the same small room. We were harassed by George Morrison and A. J. S. Williams, who had been set up as some kind of safety officers. Morrison was probably senile and A. J. S. Williams knew nothing about lasers. They did not even notice the high voltages and could have been conveniently electrocuted. Morrison spread cigar ash all over the new gold mirror.

This laboratory was at the opposite end of the EDCL from the microoffice occupied by Gareth Evans and myself and one more post doctoral. This scene would be condemned outright these days as multiple breaches of safety at work, harassment, and career blocking, but in those days all turned a blind eyes as they looked after themselves. In the same way, when Caligula declared himself a god, all agreed that it was obvious. The human spirit defeats dictatorship by ignoring it until it implodes and destroys itself. So OO93 was submitted from a dustbin on 29th. July 1980 with Gareth Evans and William Coffey to Advances in Molecular Relaxation and Interaction

Processes. This document is clearly legible on www.aias.us and records the work being done with Coffey at the time. The paper was essentially all my own work, the itinerant oscillator was already obsolete. Coffey had a free ride all his life because he was given tenure at Trinity College Dublin at a time when it was ingrown and a club of self appointed individuals. Gareth Evans and I donated some old apparatus to Trinity College but it made no good use of it. With tenure there was no need for competition, and life was a leisurely routine of lavish Commons, coffee, and newspapers. After a few years one would get promotion, and settle in to the existence of a nonentity, without risking any new ideas or radical thought. I cannot blame people for liking such an existence, but it leads nowhere in the end. After safely transferring the apparatus Gareth Evans was surprised at the laconic pace of the College, Coffey would drift in at about noon, and on one occasion appeared to be demonstrating Brownian motion in a zig zag path to his office. He was stoned in the middle of the day as Gareth put it. The hyper cynical Vij would say that you can do anything you like after tenure, and that was not far from the truth. In the end though it is a waste of life, you do not build civilization that way, without imagination, and using the work of others. They had the Book of Kells in their midst and that would not have been written by a stoned scribe at high noon. The brilliant and intricate detail needs the steady hand of civilization.

On 20th August 1980 OO97 was submitted to Spectrochimica Acta and reported a completely new type of spectrometer which was built by the group from a combination of the Apollo laser and far infra red spectrometer. It was a Model 560 Apollo laser with Brewster window plane grating generating 85 lines at up to 50 watts continuous wave output. This pioneering paper was the result of work in appalling conditions, and was in co authorship with Gareth Evans, Colin Reid and Mauro Ferrario. Gareth Evans designed a cell with a parabaloid gold plated wall and interferograms were recorded by Colin Reid and Gareth Evans of far infra red induced fluorescence. This paper shows what the group could have achieved in a normal environment. After that experiment the laser had to be shipped back to California because of the damage done to it by Morison's cigar ash and the unsuitable conditions of the "laboratory" opposite Jones' room at the EDCL. The technical staff and the responsible academic staff looked on in dismay as the laser was recrated and shipped back out of the main EDCL doors, three hundred thousand pounds of brand new Government apparatus. Conditions were becoming intolerable in other ways because the group was joined by Prof. Ahmed Hasanein on leave from the University of Alexandria on a Royal Society scholarship. No foreign visitor could believe the conditions, they expected the sophisticated, civilized and enlightened environment of my papers, of my intellectual achievements. They found dictatorship by a small lunatic on the edge of the grey sea, not sunny at all.

The office next to our dustbin had been empty for some months, so I moved into it quite innocently. This allowed more space for the rest of the group, now consisting of three post doctorals and a visiting professor. This office had a window, and eventually it filled with computer output and empty coffee jars. I have been in there for maybe a couple of weeks before Jones appeared at the door and started a stream of vulgar, gutter abuse, watched in disgust be Cecil Monk from his own microspace in EDCL. If Monk had come forward as a witness Jones would have lost his job, or more accurately should have lost his job. These days ACAS would have protested strongly to the College administration. Thirty three years later I take this opportunity to lodge a strong protest, not only against Jones but against the whole rotten set up that passed as a university department. In due course he retreated and left me in charge of the office. By now he was hanging on to the EDCL by a thread, he had insulted too many senior and productive staff. The laboratory next to the office was also empty, so taking advantage of this foothold, the group somehow managed to make him see reason and allocate this laboratory to us. It used to be Cadman's laboratory, and the latter most sullenly allowed us to take it over. Cadman's apparatus was moved out and there was space for the laser and interferometer.

The Omnia Opera betrays none of this vulgar warfare and continues on a high intellectual plane with OO98, submitted with Mauro Ferrario on 4th August 1980 on the cumulant expansion of the orientational autocorrelation function providing a general theoretical method of relating the orientational and angular momentum autocorrelation functions in the asymmetric top. This paper shows the mathematical influence of Prof. James McConnell of the Dublin Institute for Advanced Studies. Even this level of theoretical finesse could get nowhere near to a truly complete description of the computer simulation. As usual I wrote most of the paper, and it is mostly my work. During these months I had also been working on the Delta Project, which was published in OO99 as a long review in Advances in Molecular Relaxation and Interaction processes with J. Yarwood, whose scientific contribution was minimal, but who was interested in helping to organize the European Molecular Liquids Group. OO99 was published in 1981 but there is no date of receipt. The Delta Project grew out of my award winning work of the seventies and is a plan for the systematic evaluation of the state of knowledge in the dynamics of simple liquids using all the resource available: experimentation, theory and computation, especially molecular dynamics simulation and Monte Carlo simulation. OO99 reviews all the relevant material in great detail, and coordinates the experimental conditions. The Delta Project was my conception entirely, and written entirely by me. I wrote to about seventy five leading groups in Europe and got a very positive response. My work was always admired by the National Physical Laboratory so George Chantry eventually agreed to chair the meeting that brought the

EMLG into being. Jeremy Jones had a great time complaining not only about postage but about xerox costs while the rest of Europe ignored him completely. It was apparent to me that the state of knowledge in liquid state molecular dynamics was poor, some theories gave the impression of being able to explain some small parts of the data set. Despite the great improvement in instrumentation and computing power between 1980 and 20 3 , little or no progress has been made on the fundamental level. That would need a new Delta Project and imaginative and energetic administration, and would be far more interesting than anything taking place at CERN.

On 22nd Aug. 1980 OO100 was submitted with Ahmed Hasanein and Mauro Ferrario on the ab initio computation of intermolecular pair and trimer potentials for methyl fluoride. The ab initio methods of Hasanein supplemented the theoretical work by working out from the fundamentals the potentials needed for molecular dynamics simulation. This would also have formed an important part of The Delta Project. This type of work has advanced a lot since 1980. My group's work is mainly theoretical again because the laser had been shipped back to California for repairs. The damage was caused by the unsuitable environment and by the safety officer Morrison damaging the gold mirror with cigar smoke. He was completely unaware of the fact that he was surrounded by high voltage and he could have sent himself into Valhalla, smoking. On 15th September 1980 OO111 was submitted to Spectrochimica Acta with Colin Reid, a paper in which molecular dynamics are mapped from picoseconds to years by use of a vitreous or glassy solvent. This paper reported some of the data accumulated by Colin Reid during his Ph. D. Thesis and before our work was disrupted deliberately. Also during this time OO109 was being prepared by myself, it is a review of about seventy or eighty pages and shows the full extent of the work by Colin Reid. The acknowledgment shows that he was now my post doctoral assistant. Any administration worth anything would have tenured the entire group at that point in time. It was the best group in Britain in its field, and was developing strongly. On 29th Sept. 1980 OO134 was submitted to Spectrochimica Acta with Gareth Evans and Pethig of Bangor, who contributed very little to it.

The group was joined by Dr. Barbara Janik of the Jagiellonian University in Krakow. Although Mansel Davies was retired, he asked me once more to supervise another of his ideas, that of bringing Barbara Janik over from Krakow to the EDCL. The group was augmented unofficially by Dr. Jozef Moscicki of the Jagiellonian University in Krakow. Officially he was Graham Williams' post doctoral but Moscicki regarded Williams with barely concealed contempt. One of the historical source documents on www.aias.us is a letter from Moscicki recording the conditions of work, and the fact that Graham Williams kept Room 262 empty. This proves deliberate disruption of our work beyond doubt, and I regard this as malfeasance. Moscicki was the grand nephew of the President of Poland to 1939, Ignacz Moscicki, a capable chemist in his own right. His wife Katia was a Hapsburg. Janik and Moscicki later became research associate and full professor respectively. On 14th Nov 1980 OO113 was submitted to Spectrochimica Act with Gareth Evans and Barbara Janik and in this paper my Mori three variable theory was developed so that there were no adjustable parameters. Barbara Janik was the daughter of an influential professor in Krakow and her career probably progressed within the family. So she was not much of an experimentalist and this paper is purely theoretical, almost wholly my own work. She was evidently disgusted by the conditions and asked me how I could possibly have won a medal. I think that this remark was an innocent one, meaning that no one forced to work in a pig sty could win a medal. The acknowledgment records the fact that Gareth Evans had been awarded a University of Wales Fellowship in open competition. This was the group's seventh prestigious Fellowship won honestly in open competition, and not be some sleazy arrangement behind closed doors. At that point we had seven Fellowships, two medals and a D. Sc. Degree. All of this meritocracy could be blocked at that time by the poorest administrator in Britain. These days it could not, ACAS would protest and demand fair career assessment. In the light of objective history, it is clear that the EDCL was destroyed by corruption, the appointment by some obscure arrangement of a person wholly incapable of running a bubble car. At that time our group was by far its best group. All the mechanisms put in place by the University constitution failed. There was no control over the most bitter and self blinding personal animosity imaginable, and no senior member of staff would act to save the sinking ship. Indeed they would soon scuttle away.

I was delighted when Gareth Evans was awarded the University of Wales Fellowship for two years, with a possibility of going on to the Pilcher Senior Fellowship. This was a prestigious achievement in his own right, and the news came through in the Autumn of 1980. He had been on the edge of leaving just at a time when he was developing excellent experimental skills. No junior post doctoral could be blamed for wanting to get away from the insane animosity, which was directed by Jones randomly, grossly offending his colleagues. After hearing the news I did my usual training on the Penglais athletics track and gave Gareth the news there. At that time I was doing interval training over two hundred metres on the athletic track, and sprints over a hundred and sixty metres. On Saturday I would do a road run of about eight miles, and on Sundays a five thousand metres on the track. I soon found out that I was no sprinter and no distance runner, but kept training daily for about thirty years. I trained sometimes with Dick Evans, the Welsh 3,000 metres steeplechase record holder at the time, and his group of athletes. He became a marathon runner and has represented Wales more times than any athlete in any sport. Berwyn Price and other real athletes used to train on the track. Dick Evans advised me not to use the track too much because of the possibility of tendon injuries, so I switched to the Vicarage fields next to the EDCL. This was grass running that could be done without athletics shoes. For the road running I used marathon shoes, the lightest type. I was much faster than Dick Evans over any short distance, but over any other distance his superior heart lung system took over and he vanished into the mists.

In August 1980 Lech Walesa started the Solidarnosz Rising in Poland in the Lenin Shipyards in Gdansk. This coincided with the arrival of Barbara Janik and Jozef Moscicki. The Russians massed tanks on the Polish border and the Polish Government imposed martial law. Moscicki and Janik had the traditional anti Russian attitude of the Poles, who expected everyone to agree with them. It was common knowledge in Britain that the Poles had been treated murderously by the Russians under Stalin. I had read a biography of Stalin and probably knew details that the Poles did not because of their authoritarian, censorious system. In the autumn of 1980 Barbara Janik and Jozef Moscicki were cut off from Poland because the telephone lines were cut under martial law. So I had the extra burden of dealing with this and also with our very own dictator in the EDCL. The EDCL staff kept their heads down as usual and looked after themselves exclusively. I had a sense of international responsibility from the Delta Project and was soon involved in getting Edward Kluk out of a KGB prison. The EDCL staff behaved as if nothing had happened to Kluk, none of their business as usual. They had not heard of John Donne, no man is an island. It was all about grabbing tenure and staying there for ever.

On 13th. Nov. 1980 OO101 was submitted by invitation to Accounts of Chemical Research at Cornell University, recording my Meldola Lecture at Oxford: “Spectral Studies of Rotational Diffusion”. This article mentions the need for the Delta Project, and I had been invited by Prof. Bill Steele to advise the U. S. National Science Foundation on the Project. The paper starts with a quote from a poet I had just discovered in Galloway's - Patrick Kavanagh:

> "Until a world comes to life -
> Morning, the silent bog,
> And the God of Imagination waking
> In a Mucker fog."

Two or three Nobel Laureates and many Fellows of the Royal Society have been awarded the Meldola Medal, and I was invited to give the lecture in the Physical Chemistry Laboratory at Oxford. I drove up to Oxford and gave the lecture in one of the main lecture theatres. The audience included John Rowlinson who handed me the medal. I decided to drive back to Aberystwyth that winter evening in my Mini and stopped on the outskirts of Oxford for some coffee and cake. Then I headed rapidly past Blenheim Palace and through Woodstock towards the border. I celebrated with fish and chips and pickled eggs and a pie in Llandrindod Wells, having driven in the gathering darkness through the home country of my direct paternal ancestors, the Wye Valley. Near Rhaeadr it began to snow quite heavily but I kept to the main road and stopped for a while at the high point on the shoulder of Pumlumon over which I had cycled as a freshman undergraduate, twelve years earlier. It was a snow covered silence with the infinite beauty of nature dancing in the snow all around, and I took out the Meldola Medal and gazed at it, a small piece of crafted bronze in the winter air. With all the remaining shreds of naivety that I could gather in fading hope, I wondered how pleased the EDCL would be at this. The just reaction would have been that of Sir Goronwy Daniel in 1978, an invitation to a reception, or perhaps that long overdue tenure. I arrived in my newly acquired office about eleven in the evening and there was a sealed envelope on my desk. It was an insane note from an insane man. I was told to leave the EDCL for Oxford, where my prospects would improve. Oxford had not been consulted, and I had just returned from there. There were no congratulations, no reception, no tenure. These days a casual glance at Google shows that the Meldola Harrison Award as it is now called is trumpeted by a university department all over the known universe. So the infinitely small man had asked his secretary to prepare this dirt while I was away giving the lectureTand it had been carefully placed on my desk to await my triumphal return. It had been copied to the Registrar and Principal, and again lied about money. These days that would be prejudice and career blocking. I ignored the bile and left the Medal on display for a day on the desk in the Common Room for all to see, or throw up, according to degree of objectivity. This new Common Room was Jeremy Jones' only achievement.

The system had become so corrupt that it could not recognize the highest degree of merit, and so it collapsed into ruin as Rome did before it.

CHAPTER SEVEN

On 18th Nov. 1980 OO110 was submitted with Colin Reid to the Journal of Chemical Physics on the discovery of the gamma process, using a spectral range from hertzian frequencies to terahertz. This paper relied on the wealth of data gathered by Colin Reid during his Ph. D. His post doctoral was wrecked deliberately by the administration, so this is one of the last papers published with him before he resigned to become a teacher eventually in Trinity College Llanymddyfri or Llandovery, a public school that Pontardawe had beaten 103 nil in rugby and also worked at Trinity College Dublin. The complete range of evolution of the dynamics is astonishing, and defeats any attempt at computer simulation to this day. This type of result was one of the main inspirations for the Delta Project. In the narrow range of frequencies of the far infra red, the gamma process looks just like another spectrum, but when that range is extended to hertzian frequencies, an amazing development of dynamics becomes apparent. Computer simulation can cover a range of a few hundred or thousand picoseconds at most, even with the most powerful contemporary computers, but the complete dynamics stretches out to years, over twelve or fourteen orders of magnitude, first developing into the beta process than the alpha process. This became one of the most admired papers of that era and if I were head of department I would have pulled out all the stops to have such a talented and respected group tenured. On 9th Dec. 1980 OO96 was submitted to Physica A with Mauro Ferrario on a theory of the aligned nematic mesophase with considerable theoretical input from Ferrario. The final paper in 1980, OO102, was submitted on 16th December with Mauro Ferrario and Ahmed Hasanein to Advances in Molecular Relaxation and Interaction Processes on the ab initio computation of intermolecular potentials of small molecules compared with the atom atom potential.

In the year 1981 the plans for the European Molecular Liquids Group came to fruition at the National Physical Laboratory, and the Apollo laser was repaired under guarantee in California and re - delivered. It was properly set up on a well insulated brick base made by Gareth Evans' father, a farmer and steel worker who travelled up from Gwent entirely voluntarily. The brick base protected us from the high voltages. In the chaos created by Jeremy Jones we could easily have been electrocuted. So much for the "safety officers" of the EDCL. The work for the formation of the EMLG began in earnest during the latter half of 1980 and is recorded in an extant source document of April 13th 1981 in the source documents section of www.aias.us. I wrote to seventy five leading groups in Europe, and to societies and academies with the intention of carrying out the Delta Project, OO99. This meant the coordination of conditions for research on three carefully chosen molecular liquids under a set of conditions. I could see clearly that only in this way would progress be made and gathered support from all over Europe under a shower of complaints about the amount of postage and xerox I was using. I also tried to establish a new laboratory in Aberystwyth for the EMLG and in this context discussed the plans with Tam Dalyell M. P., the then Shadow Minister for Education, obtained the strong support of the SERC's CCP5 group in molecular dynamics simulation and was invited on to the CCP5 Committee. The three molecules chosen were dichloromethane, methyl fluoride and methyl iodide, and a great deal of background research is recorded in OO99. It was decided to hold a meeting at the National Physical Laboratory on 19th June 1981. The April 13th meeting was preliminary and held at the EDCL but I made the mistake of inviting Graham Williams who disrupted the meeting very badly. Thereafter he was excluded from EMLG by overwhelming majority opinion because EMLG did not want the well known animosity at the EDCL to spread.

The atmosphere at the EDCL was deteriorating rapidly as the crude personal abuse of Jeremy Jones began to take its effect and as staff started to look for other jobs. In that system there was no meritocracy within the department, and appointments were arbitrary. My own group won a total of twenty competitive fellowships compared with zero for the John Thomas group and zero for the Jeremy Jones group. Gareth Evans won a Sloan Foundation Fellowship in about 1980 at the London School of Economics, and was offered a Fellowship by Dr. King at the Cavendish Laboratory in Cambridge. Mauro Ferrario was later won an Italian National Research Council European Fellowship, and I won sixteen competitive Fellowships in total. None of this merit had any effect in that swamp of corruption, as the seventeenth century Levellers would have put it. The EDCL administration should therefore be subjected to the harshest of historical condemnation, and the entire academic system reformed. There should be recourse in law, because to ignore such merit is a violation of human rights. Members of my group were also offered lectureships and all became full professors with the exception of Gareth Evans and Colin Reid, who both left the academic system in contemptuous disgust. In the seventies I was offered lectureships at Trinity College Dublin and University of Wales Swansea, and in the early eighties Gareth Evans was offered a lectureship at the Scottish School of Textiles and invited to apply for lectureships at the Universities of Salford and Glamorgan. I was also offered a lectureship at Salford in the eighties. All this took place in the depths of thatcherism. Later I took up a full professorship at IBM Kingston, New York in 1986, and was offered a full professorship and chairmanship in the State of Delaware. I was forced to take up a full professorship at University of North Carolina Charlotte because IBM cut its funding to Cornell Theory Center. The EDCL closed because of selfish, uncontrolled careerism, sleazy, dishonest methods of uncompetitive appointment, and complete absence of meritocracy, combined with a grotesque level of uncontrolled personal animosity.

I submitted OO114 to Spectrochimica Acta on 15th January 1981, a paper which applied rotation / translation interaction to dielectric spectroscopy. I became interested in this subject after the first results of computer simulation had revealed the existence of the phenomenon through use of cross correlation functions. These were computed with diatomics, the triatomic algorithm TRI2, and later with the SERC CCP5 algorithm TETRA as part of the Delta Project of EMLG. Later at IBM Kingston, Cornell and Zurich I greatly extended the range of applicability of TETRA and pioneered the field applied computer simulation method at Aberystwyth. Our imported lord and master at the EDCL had never coded a computer in his life and was oblivious to all this research. On 20th January 1981 I submitted OO118 to The Journal of Chemical Physics, my first paper to that American journal. This was a paper on mean square torques from far infra red spectra and was part of my analytical work. Preparations for the founding of the European Molecular Liquids Group were accelerating as more and more of the leading European groups joined the effort, including the National Physical Laboratory group under George Chantry, later to attain a high rank in the diplomatic service. By now the EDCL administration had no international credibility and I was being urged to leave Aberystwyth, notably by Chantry himself. My decision to stay at Aberystwyth and to keep the group together is vindicated fully by our spectacularly successful performance in the years 1978 to 1983. We outproduced the rest of the EDCL staff all put together. These were years of gulag existence for me, but of scientific brilliance unmatched until the emergence of the AIAS group in the first decade of the twenty first century.

In order to minimize the danger of further personal abuse from Jeremy Jones I developed methods of isolating myself from him completely. This was made easier by the fact that my office was situated at the extreme opposite end of the EDCL. It was possible to enter the office through a doorway originally meant for maintenance of the air conditioning system of Room 262, designed as a specialist infra red laboratory. In early 1981 it was being kept as an empty room, and housed post doctorals only. After my group was summarily evicted, Graham Williams did not even bother to use it. Jones and Williams had managed to disrupt our work very badly, but had not stopped it. They did manage to discourage Colin Reid into resignation. He was offered a job at Trinity College Dublin for a while but disliked the place intensely. The H block troubles were at their height, and there were bombings in Belfast almost every week. The miners' strikes were getting under way and the country had been torn apart by the grotesquely stupid thatcherite regime. Great Britain as a whole, and Wales in particular, never recovered from that economic catastrophe, which effectively destroyed British industry. Entire communities in the South Wales valleys were obliterated and transplanted to anonymity, to be replaced by English speaking colonists. I was able to spend nearly all of my time in isolation of Jeremy Jones by skillful use of doorways. The danger was that his gutter abuse would make me lose my temper, giving him an excuse to get rid of me. Neither he nor any other of the sleazy cats of the EDCL ever succeeded in making me lose my temper. The rest of the EDCL academic staff probably knew that their tenure would be safely secured in smoke filled dustbins, no matter what happened to the EDCL, so had quietly prepared to abandon it and could not care less for it. They cared only for themselves, their salaries and large pensions. They spent large amounts of time in the glorious new common room. Graham Williams had occupied Mansel Davies' office and I could hear him spending hours on the telephone trying to set up cooperations with other groups in order to obtain funding using their skills. Graham Williams had no computational ability and little mathematical ability, and was described by Jozef Moscicki as "a nothing". Moscicki became a full professor in the Jagiellonian University in Krakow and shared his time with Cornell.

In the entire five years from 1978 to1983 I never knew whether I would have a job the next day, little notes appeared by moonlight on my desk, complaining in an endless whine about triviality. This was not exactly the early renaissance spirit of Florence where man was the measure of all things and all things were possible in an era when the human spirit seeded the flowers of renewed civilization. The latter needs confidence, intellectual honesty, and hope for the future. At the hopelessly cynical EDCL, letters were placed on desks of artists telling them not to paint, so one recognizes the signs of terminal barbarism. The artist is supreme authority, not the corrupt society in which he lives. As my office gradually filled with coffee jars and computer output I injected some music into proceedings via a small cassette recorder I bought for myself and the atmosphere was filled not with cyanogen gas but with classical music. There were two locked doors between the corridor and my office, so here I could play the music unheard by all with the possible exception of Cecil Monk, who continued his research crammed into one small room after forty years of service. He became more and more kindly as time went on, and I remember that he once brought me a collection of apples from his garden. An act of kindness in the EDCL astonished me completely. The music was switched on when I was drawing or plotting graphs, and preparing illustrations. All the administrative help was hogged by the petty bureaucrats, so I did all my own drawing by hand. In times of intense concentration, nothing broke the silence. All the plans and all the coordination of the EMLG were thought out and prepared, and there was essentially unanimous agreement on the need for a Delta Project. The EDCL staff seemed to go from holiday to holiday at this time, and I was especially fond of working in their vacations. Some of the experts would take a vacation, report sick, work for a couple of weeks, report sick and vacate again and there were loud complaints about interminable staff meetings. No great masterpiece of art was ever painted in a staff meeting. I was to get my own experience of the appalling lack of purpose of an EDCL staff meeting on April 13th 1981, when I tried to convene a preparatory meeting for the formative EMLG meeting of 19th June 1981 at the National Physical Laboratory.

On 10th March 1981, I submitted OO115 to the Journal of Chemical Physics. This paper was the first of a series of five in which my new technique of field induced molecular dynamics simulation was brought to the attention of the American journals, and I was soon to be invited to advise the U. S. National Science Foundation on the Delta Project. This part I describes equilibrium properties through time correlation functions computed with a program written by Ferrario and myself as part of the development of TRI2 originally written by Renault and Singer. Prof. Konrad Singer later attended the formative EMLG meeting on 19th June of that year. Field applied molecular dynamics simulation was pioneered in this paper through the application of an external torque. Much later, in 1989 / 1990 at the Cornell Theory Center, the method was animated by Chris Pelkie, and this prize winning animation is on www.aias.us. It shows that the method and code work perfectly. After application of the torque the system was allowed to equilibrate and the correlation functions computed. They show that the liquid develops an anisotropy. The great advantage of the new technique is that it allows very large torques to be applied numerically, so the system can be studied thoroughly, and this method greatly extends the range of experimental techniques such as non linear dielectric spectroscopy. Its value was instantly recognized by such contemporaries as Stuart Rice, Ilya Prigogine and Konrad Singer, and by the SERC CCP5 grouping. A real university is all about such advances in knowledge, but at the EDCL I could work only if fully insulated from bile. One recognizes barbarism as a threat to civilization. If I had moved to Swansea,

Trinity College Dublin or Oxford, none of this would ever have happened, I would have become just another mediocrity embroiled in student numbers. Such was the terrible lack of vision of the bureaucracy, and indeed the bureaucracy of any time. In Florence they drove Leonardo almost mad with rage.

On 30th March 1981 I submitted OO104 to Chemical Physics and in this paper pioneered the use of fourth and sixth spectral moments constructed from experimental data. Konrad Singer liked this paper very much, because using data in this dramatically original way showed that there was not a single theory that could begin to describe the moments, they just failed dismally, and that continues to be the state of knowledge now at the time of writing, May 2013, more than thirty years later. Singer immediately saw the importance of this paper, but pearls of wisdom were cast before swine in the EDCL. On the "Animal Farm" the pigs ruled OK, and ate their piglets. The European world of science anxiously looked on, or otherwise turned a blind eye as human nature is very prone to do. There was no intelligence at the EDCL, no ingredients for a renaissance, no vision, no ability to see the importance of new ideas, or even to recognize them. There were complaints about postage and xerox. In such a pointless wilderness the only thing to do is to produce new art, publish as much as one possibly can as long as each new item is a new idea. Teaching is merely an endless repetition of the same old stuff. On 7th April 1981 OO106 was submitted to Chemical Physics with M. Veerappa and G. J. Davies, developing the new method of OO104. This paper reports work using three interferometers, we had transferred one to Trinity College Dublin, one was situated in the nasty little room to which we had at last been allowed access at the EDCL and one in British Telecom, Martlesham Heath. I remember helping Veerappa take the spectra - again under appalling conditions because there was no fume cupboard and the chemicals used threatened to overwhelm Veerappa. The latter was on leave from

Trinity College Dublin and was a strict vegetarian from central India, so it was very difficult to find anything for him to eat after we finished work around nine p.m. My usual fish and chips dive repelled him - he could not even eat an egg.

Also on 7th April 1981 I submitted OO116 to The Journal of Chemical Physics, reporting the first ever simulation of Langevin functions of various orders. I vividly remember the very first time I realized that my field applied method had produced the Langevin function perfectly. It took some days to twig what was happening, but as I graphed the results one day the proverbial flash of insight occurred. The simulation was able to go far beyond experimentation for the first time in scientific history, and successfully reproduced all orders of Langevin function right out to the point of saturation. I consider this to be one of the best papers that I have produced. Not only is it vividly original, but shows that the field applied molecular dynamics technique can produce a vast amount of dynamical information that neither experiment nor theory can begin to address. From this point onwards in history computer simulation took on a life of its own. From this perspective in time it is amazing how civilization erupted like a spring from such a barren desert, "the pointless, desolate wilderness" of one of my sonnets, the intellectual wilderness that the EDCL had become. About this time I started to write and publish poetry in both languages, Welsh and English. I wrote most of it in the flat at Borth late at night after work and that poetry sums up the EDCL in sharp, critical metaphor. It is in "Autobiography Sonnets" on www.aias.us. The first sonnet sequence was published in the early eighties by "The Salmon" in Galway, Ireland, and they liked it. It is entitled "False Philosophers Fall", and they fell in 1988. At about that time I was short listed for a professorship at University College Galway and on a preliminary trip to Galway from Trinity College Dublin, picked up "The Salmon" and the Classic "Tain Bo Cuailnge" illustrated in black and white ink drawing.

On 13th April 1981, at 10 a m., I convened a carefully planned meeting at the Old Library of the EDCL to organize a summer conference on the Delta Project, OO99. A source document has survived of that meeting, and it shows the very great amount of work I put in to the EMLG. At that time there was no internet, so all communication had to be by letter. The meeting was attended by members of my group but was wrecked with insane malice by Graham Williams, who spent the whole time asking for "terms of reference" which had already been made crystal clear. Thereafter as recounted already he was hastily dropped like a red hot stone. The purpose of that 13tH April meeting was fulfilled on 19th June 1981 in a well attended international meeting at the National Physical Laboratory at which tenured EDCL staff were excluded. At the 13th April meeting national EMLG organizers were proposed: H. J. C. Berendsen for the Netherlands; Alain Gerschel of the Nice group for France; Paolo Grigolini for Italy; A. Bellemans for Belgium, Theo Dorfmuller for Germany, Henryk Ratajczak for Poland, and William Coffey for Ireland. The agenda of the 13tH April meeting was copied to W. J. Orville-Thomas of the European Molecular Spectroscopy Group, Graham Williams of the Dielectrics Society, George Chantry of the National Physical Laboratory, Theo Dorfmuller of ZIF and Karlsruhe, Konrad Singer of the SERC CCP5 grouping and self copied to myself as a member of the Royal Society of Chemistry Thermodynamics and Statistical Mechanics Group that I had been invited to join. I was therefore a member of that RSC group and the British Government SERC CCP5 group (Collaborative Computational Project Five coordinated at Daresbury Laboratory) and attended many meetings and conferences of both groups. I had also discussed the formation of the EMLG with about seventy five leading research groups in Europe, as recorded in point (i) of the 13th April agenda. I also extended my preparatory work with correspondence with the Royal Society and many European scientific societies such as the DFG of Germany, and the European Science Foundation. On one occasion I received a telephone call from the then Shadow Minister for Education, The Right Honourable Tam Dalyell, M. P., and discussed with him the possible formation of an EMLG laboratory in Aberystwyth. I planned the central EMLG laboratory for Switzerland. Since this was an incoming call to a telephone that I had been allocated accidentally, the head of department of EDCL could not complain about the cost of the call, but he had a great time complaining about zerox and postage as usual, and maybe even about the cost of the second hand envelopes that I was asked to use. Periclean Athens was not built with second hand envelopes, but the EMLG was.

On 15th June 1981, OO105 was submitted to Chemical Physics with Mauro Ferrario and William Coffey. In this paper a cosinal potential was used for the itinerant oscillator, and the far infra red spectrum calculated via the rotational velocity correlation function. This was a good enough paper, but OO104 had essentially destroyed the itinerant oscillator model. Coffey never succeeded in developing an analytical theory that could match the experimental data, neither did anyone else. That summarizes the philosophy of the Delta project, it was a plan for a great cathedral of knowledge, but the times lacked the spirit needed for a Chartres or Cluny or Vezelay. Nearly a thousand years ago they were in advance of our super technical times. By 15th June 1981 Mauro Ferrario had won a prestigious CNR European Fellowship, recorded in the acknowledgment of the paper, and was on the way to a successful career. He became a full professor in Italy and a director of CECAM in Switzerland (The European Centre for Computations in Atomic and Molecular Physics, a kind of offshoot of EMLG's computational branch.) On 19th June 1981 the first EMLG meeting was convened at the National Physical Laboratory (NPL) and was chaired by George

Chantry. It was well attended from all over Europe, and importantly for the future of computation, by Prof. Konrad Singer and one other of the SERC CCP5 grouping, Dr. David Fincham. They gave me a copy of the algorithm TETRA which became the mainstay of my later work in computer simulation. At the NPL meeting Chantry volunteered to be first Chairman, Yarwood first Secretary, Birch of the NPL as first treasurer and myself as the first European Coordinator. The plans of the Delta Project were formally taken up by EMLG and a series of EMLG conferences planned. I recall that George Chantry once more urged me to get out of the EDCL. That made plenty of sense to him, but as a Welsh speaker it was my duty to remain in Wales until I was finally kicked out of the University of Wales to IBM Kingston in New York in 1986. Coffey and Rev. Prof. James McConnell of the Dublin Institute for Advances Studies (DIAS) attended the NPL meeting, which made its way into the official history of DIAS. I was duly trotskyized when I was kicked out of the EDCL in Sept 1983, and there is no mention of me at all in the official DIAS history, so here's putting the record straight. I felt that it would take a great deal more work to bring the Delta Project to fruition, these cats seemed too much like experts at attending meetings. A lot of them put the EMLG in to their CV's, but left it at that. They would not have built a cathedral, just a glasshouse in the back garden. On the way back from the NPL, outside the tube station at Teddington, Coffey immediately asked for a leading role in EMLG. He was never slow at taking other people's ideas.

On 7th July 1981 OO119 was submitted to Advances in Molecular Relaxation and Interaction Processes on the computer simulation of a triatomic with TRI2, and this was an attempt to prepare for the simulation of dichloromethane, one of the molecules of the Delta Project. The data for this as for other papers were stored on nine track magnetic tape for further analysis with the correlation function program written by Ferrario and myself. On 30th July 1981 OO117 was submitted from the EDCL to The Journal of Chemical Physics. This is the first paper in scientific history in which an alternating field is applied to an ensemble of molecules in order to study dispersion and induced birefringence, and again the simulation method pushed far beyond what was and is possible analytically or experimentally. So it makes the hyper complicated work of Coffey and Grigolini and similar analytical theoreticians look pointless, or at best, infinitesimal variations on an out of tune theme, the type of thing that makes your publication record look good and ensures promotion, but makes no advance in knowledge. There was no room for that in the Florence of the early renaissance, it would have been seen as painting too much - two coats of pure white in one afternoon. Nevertheless, I was invited by Stuart Rice around this time to write my first monograph, now considered a classic: "Molecular Dynamics" (Wiley Interscience, New York, 1982) and I decided to invite Gareth Evans, William Coffey and Paolo Grigolini as co authors. In retrospect it was a mistake to invite William Coffey and Paolo Grigolini, but Gareth Evans contributed well with high quality experimental data. So a large part of the summer of 1981 was spent writing this monograph, which runs to 880 pages. Coffey merely ripped wads of material from his Ph .D Thesis, taking huge advantage of my invitation, and Grigolini delivered his material in an almost incomprehensible mess, left to me to clean up. After all, both of them had tenure. Jeremy Jones went crazy with postage complaining, because the manuscript had to be delivered by airmail to New York City. Nonetheless I ploughed through all the heavy waves and cross currents of complaint and the frenzied ambition of others, and the MS was duly delivered on time. Then as now I was a professional to my fingertips and never missed a deadline. The monograph is the well studied OO108 on www.aias.us and was described as a magnificent piece of work by Prof. Sir John Rowlinson at Oxford. Whether he meant it or not is a different thing, but it remains a useful review of the work of that era. It was accompanied by a long review with Colin Reid, OO109, where his excellent work is reviewed in detail.

On July 24th 1981 I had submitted OO112 to Acta Physica Polonica. It is a technically brilliant paper, that corrects and extends the Mori theory for which I was awarded the Harrison Memorial Prize and Meldola Medal, but the computer simulation was running far ahead of anything that analytical theory could do. From the perspective of thirty years it seems almost unbelievable that work of such high standard could ever have been produced in the conditions of the EDCL. I must have withdrawn deeply into myself and focused my entire being on abstraction, as if I were writing in the Scriptorium of Iona with only the wild sea for company. The 30th July paper OO117 mentioned above looks much simpler, but the power of computer simulation makes it much more incisive. On 29th July 1981 OO128 was submitted to Physica A with Mauro Ferrario and Paolo Grigolini, who was at the time visiting Florida State University in Tallahassee where he saw Paul Dirac as a "sad old man", but again that paper fell short of the simulation, being hyper abstract and almost unworkable. Grigolini remained in that hyper abstract mode until he retired as full professor in the University of North Texas. On 6th Oct. 1981 OO132 was submitted to Chemical Physics with Mauro Ferrario, and this paper is the first to report our use of the new algorithm TETRA. A five by five Lennard-Jones atom atom potential was developed for the molecule and pair distribution functions are given in the paper. The simulation of about 1989 to 1990 at Cornell Theory Center shows that the code works perfectly. This simulation won a prize in an IBM supercomputer competition of about 1990 for the U. S. and Canada, and is available on www.aias.us. OO132 mentions communications from Ian McDonald of the Singer group, with whom Mauro Ferrario worked later at Cambridge. So Cambridge was keen to work with the post doctorals whom I had trained at the EDCL: Gareth Evans and Mauro Ferrario, and later, Trinity College Dublin and Swansea Mass Spectroscopy unit were keen to work with Colin Reid. Obviously, my entire group should have been tenured at the EDCL and that might have kept the place open. The analysis in this autobiography shows clearly however that the place had no purpose. It had been designed not for research, as it should have been in a small country like Wales, but for attracting students who did not exist. OO133 was submitted by Ferrario and myself to Chemical Physics on the same date as OO132, 6th. Oct. 1981, and is the first paper to compare the results of TETRA with far infra red data for one of the Delta Project molecules, dichloromethane. The simulation did fairly well, and complemented the analytical theory. The basic purpose of the Delta Project was to use simulation, theory and a very broad range of experimental data in a carefully coordinated way. This project was destroyed cynically by the EDCL administration, so the system defeated its own purpose. The state of knowledge in consequence has not advanced since the early eighties. Computer power has increased dramatically, techniques and electronics have improved greatly, but the state of knowledge of molecular dynamics has not. The reasons include careerism, personal ambition, misplaced competition, and poor leadership, and a decline in the quality of society itself.

In mid 1981 several groups across Europe attempted to implement the Delta Project, and some of their efforts are reflected in my papers of this era. OO120 was submitted on 15th October 1981 with Jagdish Vij, Colin Reid, Mauro Ferrario and Gareth Evans to Advances in Molecular Relaxation and Interaction Processes. This paper reported the temperature dependence of the far infra red spectrum of dichloromethane and analysed it with the algorithms TRI2 and TETRA, for whom Konrad Singer is acknowledged. This paper is the first to record a prestigious University of Wales Fellowship to Gareth

Evans, and shows that Colin Reid had moved by that time to Trinity College Dublin. Mauro Ferrario had won a prestigious European Fellowship of the Italian Research Council in open competition. All of these achievements were ignored completely by the EDCL administration, which had probably already decided to "scuttle away" when the EDCL closed, and leave others to their fate. Rats leaving a sinking ship. They never had the slightest intention of being a real administration, and this is where the concept of tenure leads, to corruption, selfishness and mediocrity. OO121 was submitted to the Journal of Molecular Structure about this time, but there is no date of receipt. It is the first paper of Project Delta, dealing with the pressure dependence of the far infra red spectrum of dichloromethane at the three selected state points of the Delta Project. If the project had been completed as planned, data from many techniques would have been used at these same state points. At the time of writing in May 2013 this would be easily possible given the coordination and the spirit of the early renaissance. OO122 was submitted on 30th October 1981 with W. G. Scaife, J. Vij and Gareth Evans to the Journal of Physics D. It was a routine paper on the dielectric spectroscopy of n alkanes which I wrote in my spare time.

OO123 was submitted on 18th Nov. 1981 with Ferrario to Advances in Molecular Relaxation and Interaction Processes, and shows that the computer simulation of dichloromethane succeeds in matching the spectrum of that molecule diluted in carbon tetrachloride, but does not succeed in matching the spectrum of the pure liquid. The use of the far infra red and microwave is enough to show up the limitations of both the theory and simulation. OO129 was submitted on 7th Dec. 1981 to Chemical Physics on the far infra red and Raman spectra of chloroform, one of the three Delta Project molecules with dichloromethane and methyl iodide. This paper shows the strong Polish interest in the Delta Project and I wrote it in co authorship with B. Janik and J. Sciesinski of the

Institute of Nuclear Physics in Krakow, E. Kluk, Director of the Institute of Physics of the Silesian University in Katowice, and T. Grochulski of the Institute of Physics of the Polish Academy of Sciences in Warsaw. Edward Kluk visited me as European Coordinator in the EDCL and was intensely nervous, a frightened man. I knew that the Solidarnosz Rising was leading to the great post stalinist thaw in Eastern Europe but this was a first hand experience of the conditions there. Moscicki and Janik had been cut off from Poland a year before, in 1980, and would wait for hours before they could get through by telephone. Soviet tanks were massing on the Polish border, and Cruise missiles and SS missiles were within eight minutes of blowing each other to pieces, along with the rest of society. As usual the latter turned a blind eye on a macroscopic and microscopic scale. Kluk was ignored by the safely tenured EDCL cats, intent on their pensions, nuclear war or not. These Poles had risked cooperating with "western" science, as Kielich had done before them. Kluk quickly paid the price and was arrested by the Polish KGB shortly after he returned from visiting me at Aberystwyth. I heard that he had been denounced by his own colleagues, but I have no way of proving this. Chantry and I decided to do what we could to get Kluk released from a KGB prison where apparently he had been badly mistreated with cold water in mid winter. Again I have no way of proving this but there is no smoke without fire. Chantry probably used his diplomatic contacts, and we were helped by the fact that Kluk was a U. S. dual citizen. Our letter to "The Times" was published and Kluk was released. He left Poland immediately with his family and found a job n North Dakota. Gradually the tensions on the eastern border of Poland subsided, and the rest is history, Soviet tanks were withdrawn and the Cold War tensions ebbed away.

OO126 was submitted by Ferrario and myself to Advances in Molecular Relaxation and Interaction Processes on 6th January 1982 and this is the first paper in which cross correlation functions were computed from TETRA for dichloromethane. These were computed in the laboratory frame, a few months later I made the major discovery of moving frame cross correlation functions in optically active molecules using an adaptation of TETRA. These cross correlation functions between the fundamentals of motion, translation and rotation, explored completely new territory in a relatively simple way. Any analytical theory of this fundamental phenomenon of physics runs into hyper complexity and many adjustable parameters, but molecular dynamics computer simulation can deal with it easily. I continued to work on this type of phenomenon until the autumn of 1992, when I made an ill judged move to the University of North Carolina in Charlotte under pressure. So the Omnia Opera papers from 6th. January to early 1992 deal with this subject. Contemporary molecular dynamics simulation programs and computer power can build up a vast catalogue of knowledge using these techniques that I developed in the early eighties with the help of Mauro Ferrario and Konrad Singer, and the SERC CCP5 group. This pioneering theme was continued as part of the Delta Project in OO124, submitted with Mauro Ferrario on 1st Feb. 1982 to Advances in Molecular Relaxation and Interaction Processes. In OO124 the cross correlation functions of translational and rotational kinetic energy were computed for the first time in science. Of course, each of these papers report something entirely new to science. There are many of them, and I dedicated almost all my time to science.

OO127 was submitted on 1st March 1982 by Ferrario and myself to Advances in Molecular Relaxation and Interaction Processes and computes correlation times from molecular dynamics simulation. These are compared with data from sources such as quadrupole relaxation, neutron scattering, dielectric relaxation, infra red bandshapes and Rayleigh scattering for dichloromethane. This paper vividly reveals the fundamental lack of knowledge of the liquid state because the experimental correlation times disagree markedly. The Delta Project was intended to bring some order into this fragmentary state of knowledge. Today in May 2013 there has been no advance over this fragmentary state of knowledge in the liquid state because society does not have the will to coordinate science. I think that the waste of time and effort chasing an illusory Higgs boson at CERN typifies the decadence of science, a word which means “knowledge”. On 19th March 1982 I submitted OO135 to the Journal of Chemical Physics as the fourth part of my pioneering series on field applied computer simulation, reporting second order rise transients and comparing them with the analytical results of Kielich - the Kielich functions. Accurate agreement was found between the simulation and the Kielich functions and I was very pleased with this result because I had successfully pioneered a whole new technique of computer simulation. OO131 was submitted with Mauro Ferrario on 29th March 1982 to Advances in Molecular Relaxation and Interaction Processes as a paper presented at one of the earliest EMLG Conferences. This was held at the Dublin Institute for Advanced Studies, School of Theoretical Physics, from 19th to 21st April 1982. OO131 is an impressive review paper, dealing with the computer simulation of dichloromethane and with experimental results from various techniques available at that time, including: inelastic neutron scattering, far infra red spectra, dielectric relaxation, infra red, Raman and Rayleigh bandshapes, NMR relaxation, light scattering, non linear electrooptics and others. The computer simulations by Ferrario and myself produced atom atom pair distribution functions, auto and cross correlation functions of many kinds, and far infra red spectra. Many more techniques are available now in May 2013, together with vastly greater computer power. The acknowledgment of OO131 shows that Mauro Ferrario was funded by the Italian CNR specifically for the Delta Project, so all was set fair at that time, except for the exigency of human nature.

From the perspective of thirty years it is clear that I was associated mistakenly or by bad luck with people who had no real interest in science, they gave a surface appearance of being interested. The most notorious examples were Jeremy Jones and Graham Williams of the EDCL. After being appointed to jobs by avoiding open competition they became experts in keeping their jobs. Tenure made that very easy, so tenure should be abolished in favour of real competition. The DIAS Conference of 19th to 21st April 1982 was almost wrecked by Coffey, who quarrelled badly with Chantry much to the latter's disgust. Chantry described Coffey as "that horrible man", and was not far wrong. At the DIAS Conference Coffey had let me his rooms in Trinity College for the duration, but there occurred an incident which revealed his true self. I accidentally locked myself out of the room whereupon he flew into an ugly rage and would not call the porters to let me in. He walked off and left me locked out. In the event some students helped me climb up to a room and I let myself in through their window and slept on the floor of this empty room. So I was very right not to take up Scaife's offer of a job in Trinity College in the mid seventies. That incident effectively ended all real cooperation with Coffey. Rev. Prof. James McConnell, a priest who was also a professor of theoretical physics at DIAS, helped organize the conference, but was really interested only in money. That was not my scene at all. So after that conference it was already clear that the Delta Project would not succeed, once science gets into the hands of non-scientists it is self evidently finished. McConnell wrote in the EMLG to the history of DIAS but omitted all mention of the names of the first committee: Chantry, Yarwood, Birch and myself, and omitted all mention of the Delta Project. The DIAS history is online and at about that time it was in need of money. There was another EMLG Conference at Taormina in Sicily but that was the last one I attended because I found that there was no real will to explore science rather than the scenery as tourists. At Taormina, Coffey drank the fridge dry in his room and was in general a nuisance. The Italians were more sincere and better behaved, they included Grigolini, and two other members of the CNR research establishment at Pisa, Salvetti and Bertolini. Mount Etna was smoking in the distance throughout the whole conference, after which Salvetti drove us back to Pisa. Shortly afterwards Chantry resigned as Chairman of EMLG and unfortunately McConnell was elected as the new Chairman. That meant the end of the Delta Project and EMLG as I had planned it. EMLG is still going in May 2013 but has still not made any attempt to address the fragmentary state of knowledge revealed by those early and brilliantly incisive eighties papers. They were acknowledged by European science to be incisive, otherwise EMLG would not have been formed.

On 12th April 1982 I submitted the fifth and final part of the pioneering series of papers to Journal of Chemical Physics on field applied molecular dynamics simulation, OO137. This was the first paper in which the various auto and cross correlation functions are evaluated in the field applied condition and this technique was greatly developed later at IBM Kingston, Cornell and Zurich. I submitted OO125 to Advances in Molecular Relaxation Processes on 14th April 1982 on chloroform, another of the three molecules selected for the Delta Project. Orville-Thomas saw the opportunity of taking advantage of my work (not for the first time) and I was told that his journal was now the Delta Project journal, so being naive I submitted some papers to his journal. Rather more accurately I did this in order to get him off my back. He was infuriatingly patronizing, completely corrupt, and was Jeremy Jones' Ph .D. supervisor. On one occasion I applied for the post of Principal at Aberystwyth, but was told by Orville that "I knew I was not going to get it". Did I? That is cynicism at absolute zero and smells like the plague. In 1968 I had accidentally walked in to a disfunctional family which had all appointed each other to tenure without competition:

Mansel Davies, Orville-Thomas, Alun Price, Graham Williams and Jeremy Jones. The last I ever heard from Orville-Thomas was about 1995, when I told him casually on the phone that I had resigned from my full professorship in disgust. He slammed down the telephone and I never heard from him again much to my relief. He died a few years ago back in Aberystwyth. OO125 is again a brilliantly incisive paper that ruined the obsolete analytical methods of just a few years before. The old analytical theorists just kept on going as if simulation had never happened, they were tenured after all. OO130 was submitted on 15th May 1982 with Vij and Reid, with practically no input from the parasitic and barely competent, tenured Vij but considerable input from the hard working and untenured Reid. This paper used a combination of the far infra red spectrometers and Apollo Laser to obtain high accuracy data on some alcohols. The submillimetre laboratory that I had so carefully planned in 1978 and which had been lavishly funded by SERC had at last come to fruition, despite the illegal and very offensive attempts of the EDCL administration to disrupt my work. The tunable Apollo laser delivered several spot frequencies in the far infra red and Colin Reid had come back to the EDCL to do this work. The laser had been set up properly at last on a solid brick base, and its feed gas cylinders were lined up in an orderly manner in the laboratory.

Order had been brought into chaos and order is a kind of civilization. The latter lasts only for a brief time, it is a firefly that is easily destroyed by human nature. Civilization is something beyond the norm of human greed. The submillimetre interferometer was brought back into the same laboratory, and I purchased the first microcomputer to be set up in the EDCL, a Research Machines microcomputer that was interfaced with the interferometer by Irfon Williams and Gareth Evans. It took from 1978 to 1982 to complete my submillimetre laboratory, and it was to last only one year. The disruption by the EDCL administration in my opinion amounted to gross malfeasance. They deliberately wasted very large amounts of Government funds and that is the real reason why the EDCL was closed. At around this time (1982 / 1983) the resignations began. The first to go was Jeremy Jones' own post doctoral, Phil Friedmann, who was given tenure without any form of open competition with the arrival of Jones from Cambridge. He resigned suddenly and Jones's apparatus was left with no one to operate it. I saw it once or twice in the Soddy Laboratory and briefly talked to a completely demoralized Friedmann. He was followed early in 1983 by Prof. H. Heller, and then by Prof. J. O. Williams. The College administration refused to replace any of them. Around 1982 / 1983 I accidentally heard Graham Williams and J. O. Williams conspiring to have Jeremy Jones removed as head of department, and in the very weirdest way, they allowed me to walk in to the room to listen to them. Jones was described with too many deleted expletives to mention here and this was the general opinion of him. Even the most slavish sycophants like A. J. S. Williams tolerated him but no more. I had no time to waste my time. I was untenured and as the Autumn of 1982 drew on, I was forced yet again to compete for Fellowships. So I competed for the University of Wales Fellowship, even though I was already a SERC Advanced Fellowship and a Scientiae Doctor. No on could stop the administrative corruption that led to this kind of repulsive treadmill.

On 23rd May 1982 OO135 was submitted to the Journal of Molecular Liquids with Ferrario, Marin and Grigolini. This paper used computer simulation of dichloromethane under the conditions of the Delta Project to show that rotational and translational dynamics are in general non Gaussian. This fundamentally new result was obtained using well defined types of correlation function at second order. The analytical theory could only address the simulation results in broad outline. So in this era almost every new paper was strikingly original and Jeremy Jones frothed at the pen with postage costs of reprint requests, but by this time he was loathed by all, and had been betrayed by his professoriate. Such were the delights of the EDCL at the time, full of intrigue and malice like a mediaeval court, the innocent being set up for redundancy, the guilty being set up for comfortable jobs and pensions. I suppose that human society is like this all the time and the creative artist does his best to insulate himself from it almost completely. On 2nd June 1982 OO138 was submitted to Faraday II with V. K. Agarwal of Meerut University in India, and Gareth Evans. This was a paper on the liquid and rotator phases of bromoform, and initiated a series of papers and reviews on carefully chosen liquids using the Delta Project methodology - computer simulation and a range of data. This was a very successful series of papers in which the simulated correlation times matched the data well when intermolecular effects were absent. Each molecule was allocated a Lennard -Jones atom atom potential and having tested the simulation against experimental data it was used to produce cross correlation functions between rotation and translation, a method which became an intrinsic part of the analysis, completely in advance of any analytical technique. It was followed a few days later by OO139, submitted on 15th June 1982 to Faraday II with Gareth Evans. This paper was on acetone, the experimental data were measured by Gareth Evans using the interferometer and Apollo Instruments laser at five spot frequencies, both instruments checking each other. Correlation times were again produced by computer simulation and compared with a range of experimental data. This is what I had envisaged in 1978. Most of these papers received excellent referees' reports because they were strikingly new and completely original. In view of Grendel's complaining cave at the opposite and of the doomed EDCL I decided to work as hard as I could to produce this work before being chopped by corruption. Each paper is filled with detail, and can be read as short reviews.

The third paper of this series, OO140, was submitted with Gareth Evans on 22nd July 1982 on tertiary butyl chloride, in which the methyl groups were allocated one atom atom potential each. The Apollo Instruments laser was used by Gareth Evans at two spot frequencies. The simulation produced a range of results and again the simulation algorithm worked very well. The acknowledgment shows that Gareth Evans had won a prestigious SERC Advanced Fellowship and that the competition results had been announced. This Advanced Fellowship was awarded by the Government in the clear expectation that Gareth Evans would be awarded tenure, and was awarded on the basis of my group's work, a group which had a strong international reputation and was at the height of its productivity. Jeremy Jones had cynically signed the application and had no intention of awarding tenure to Gareth Evans or myself. These days that would or should have him dismissed from his position as head of department. My group was the only one in Britain at the time with two Advanced Fellows, roughly equivalent to associate professor in the United States. This paper was received with great enthusiasm by a referee as the acknowledgment shows. The fourth paper of this series was OO141, which I submitted on 27th July 1982 to the Journal of Molecular Liquids on acetonitrile. This was a review with eighty five references in which TETRA was extended to a six by six site model. A broad range of correlation times was used and the simulation was more successful with some than others. In view of the fact that the EMLG had been taken over by people like McConnell who had no idea of Project Delta, I had decided to implement its methodology inside my own group, with very successful results. The fifth paper of the series was OO142, submitted on 6th Sept. 1982 with Gareth Evans on methyl iodide, one of the Delta Project molecules. Gareth Evans again obtained experimental data with the laser and interferometer and this paper is again a short review with seventy four references.

The sixth paper of this series was OO143 on chloroform which I submitted to Journal of Molecular Liquids on 17th. Sept. 1982. It was optimistically described as an EMLG study document and is a review with one hundred and forty two references, using again a range of correlation times to evaluate the simulation program. By that time the EMLG was already defunct, but these papers are more than adequate as a substitute. On 8th September 1982 OO150 had been submitted with Grigolini and Marchesoni to Chemical Physics Letters using simulation to test some of the rather obscure aspects of the analytical theory by Grigolini. Fabio Marchesoni was his student at Pisa, and later became a full professor in the Italian system. Very few could understand the hyper abstraction of the theory by Grigolini but I spent hours trying to make sense of his manuscripts and devising methods of testing almost incomprehensible theory by simulation. In retrospect this was not the optimal use of my time because the simulation was well ahead of the theory and I had devised my far more incisive Delta Project method. There was always the feeling that these tenured visitors would use anyone and everyone for their own ambition. On 20th Sept. 1982 OO149 was submitted to Chemical Physics Letters with Grigolini and Marchesoni on some aspects of relaxation after a liquid has been subjected to very powerful external fields. The acknowledgment shows that I had been awarded the first of my two Nuffield Foundation grants. About this time I submitted my University of Wales Fellowship application in order to stay within the University of Wales. I won two of them in 1983 so my group was unique in winning two SERC Advanced Fellowships and three University of Wales Fellowships against fierce international competition. The EDCL administration looked at these paintings and burned them in envy. From the perspective of thirty years I would not associate with these people at all. My time was wasted on trips to Catania in Sicily to attend a conference that was said to have some elements of the EMLG left in it. At that conference I caught one full professor plagiarising one of my graphs but otherwise there was little of interest. Clementi happened to give a lecture there from IBM in the United States. On another occasion I was persuaded to travel to Bologna by train and on other occasions to the Universities of Lancaster and Glasgow to chase up some of Grigolini's contacts. I should have been at the EDCL chasing up my own thoughts before they were going to destroy my group.

On 7th October 1982 OO144 I submitted a paper on the molecular dynamics simulation of liquid and supercooled ethyl chloride to Faraday Transactions II using the Delta Project methodology and n Nov. 2nd 1982 two papers announcing my major discovery of new fundamental dynamics in optically active molecules. The first was OO146, on chlorofluoroethane, which I submitted to Chemical Communications, and the second was OO147, on bromochlorofluoromethane, submitted to Physical Review Letters. OO146 shows that the dynamics of a mixture of right and left handed molecules differs from those of a liquid made up of a right handed molecule or a liquid made up of a left handed molecule. The dynamics of the left and right handed liquids are the same exactly. The root cause of this difference was traced to a hitherto unknown dynamical process caused by the interaction of rotation and translation. OO147 showed that this phenomenon shows up only in a frame of reference that moves with the molecule. Cross correlation functions in this frame were opposite in sign for the two mirror image molecular liquids, and disappeared in the 50 / 50 mixture. These supremely elegant results were found by computer simulation, a triumph for the methods that I had developed in the hostility and philistinism of the EDCL and a triumph of the computer simulation method in general. On 5th Nov. 1982 these announcements of new and important results were followed up by a paper to Faraday II, OO148. The effect of rotation on translation in liquids was defined precisely in terms of moving frame correlation functions and the appendix of this paper shows that they were measured experimentally by Gareth Evans and announced in OO151 submitted to Chemical Physics Letters on 16th Nov. 1982. A few days later, on 29th Nov 1982 OO152 was submitted to J. Molecular Liquids with Jan Baran and Gareth Evans, augmenting the far infra red data with those from inverse Raman scattering. Jan Baran later became a full professor in the Polish system and worked for Jeremy Jones. Obviously Jones had no control over the intellect of members of his own group. OO156 was submitted with Jan Baran and Gareth Evans on 20th December 1982 in 4 methylcyclohexanone using the same combination of molecular dynamics computer simulation, far infra red data and inverse Raman scattering. Finally for 1982, OO160 was submitted to "Molecular Physics" with Vij and Reid, also on 20th December. Colin Reid used the new Research Machines 380Z microcomputer interfaced with the Grubb Parsons interferometer, and also used the Apollo Instruments laser at six frequencies on a visit from Trinity College Dublin.

CHAPTER EIGHT

In the new year of 1983 the stark hostility of those little notes were symptoms of a disturbed mind. They reverberate out of tune to this day. I was suddenly forbidden to apply for any further grants, and again that would be seen these days as completely illegal career blocking. People like Howard Purnell and Jeremy Jones are only worth writing about in order to try to ensure reform and compared with the intellectual achievement of the Omnia Opera, the system in which they worked was worthless. The really sensible thing to do is not to get embroiled in such a system at all and to try to anticipate trouble from afar. The idea of a university was made into a cynical joke by laughing lunatics, and everyone laughed with them. Around this time Phil Friedmann resigned very suddenly from Jones' group, so his best staff was gone. There was seething discontent throughout the entire EDCL, especially at the way in which my own group was treated. My own publishing career advanced rapidly and about this time I was preparing my second Wiley monograph, again commissioned by Stuart Rice: "Molecular Diffusion and Spectra". I reluctantly invited Coffey and Grigolini as co authors, and it was published in 1984 as OO161. This time the contributions by Coffey and Grigolini were better disciplined but the theory could not match the results pouring out of the new computer simulation technique. I was also invited by Prigogine and Rice to edit volumes 62 and 63 of "Advances in Chemical Physics" as special topical issues (OO178 and OO179).

Mauro Ferrario had left for the Free University of Brussels and Colin Reid spent a year at Trinity College Dublin before resigning to take up a teaching post at Llandyfri College, a public school at which Gareth Evans had earlier been offered a headship of chemistry. There were frequent complaints to me by tenured staff about the heavy teaching load imposed by Jones, and about his gutter abuse, and I had sharply criticised him in “The Cambrian News”, a local newspaper. So his time was also limited although he did not know it. My first monograph “Molecular Dynamics” (published in 1982) had appeared and I donated a copy to the EDCL Library, where it was secretively consulted by Jones sycophants keen to get rid of me. The librarian by this time was Mrs Heyes, who was sceptical of all to do with academics and was fond of telling me how she watched them knife each other in the back. In this idyllic atmosphere the proofs of “Molecular Dynamics” stood three feet tall on a desk in the laboratory outside my office, now lined with empty coffee jars and stuffed with computer output. So that made Jeremy Jones sick with postage costs. I was in the habit of working over Christmas, and had lighted a candle in a tiny and private celebration, but was reprimanded for a breach of departmental safety rules. A. J. S. Williams had been tipped off about the candle and burst into the office to snuff it out. Such was merry Christmas at the EDCL. I had become friendly with Jan Baran and his wife, and they often invited me in to the EDCL flat for some Polish food and a game of darts, at which Mrs Baran excelled dangerously. On one occasion I did a tour of Trinity College and Pisa and was away for about two weeks, so they probably thought I had gone permanently. Much to their dismay I reoccupied my Mini car. Every time I visited Trinity College Dublin my briefcase was searched at Holyhead, but they found no weapons, only intellect, and each time I was waved in by the customs on the Irish side. These ferry crossings became rou her and rougher so by the time I landed I weighed only half as much as I did at Holyhead.

Gareth Evans and I, the two British Government Advanced Fellows, were all that remained of the group in the Spring of 1983. Gareth was safe until 1987, but by this time it was clear to all that the EDCL administration was rotten with cynicism, so would get rid of me by letting my contract run out in September of 1983. This is malfeasance, career blocking and prejudice, but at the time the Association of University Teachers under George Boterill was pathetically ineffective. Again, all revolved on tenure, and they would not fight very hard for untenured post doctorals, and again irrespective of merit. There was another Advanced Fellow in the EDCL, Stephen Evans, who was hired over the heads of Gareth Evans and myself, but resigned a few years later and left the academic profession. On 7th March 1983 I submitted OO145 to Journal of Molecular Liquids describing three of the major discoveries I had made with my own field induced computer simulation method: field induced decoupling, transient acceleration and rotation translation interaction. Orville-Thomas had improved his publication quality, so OO145 is easily legible on www.aias.us . Its challenge to liquid state theorists remains unmet at the time of writing (June 2013). Obviously, the administrative system at the EDCL was in a state of collapse and illegally refused to support these discoveries with tenure. So the university system of that time ruined itself, and I have devised my own hugely successful system with AIAS. The feedback to my work was also very positive in those days, but could only be measured by reprint requests, letters, positive referees' reports and so on. On one occasion I lectured in the University of Newcastle upon Tyne at the invitation of the Vice Chancellor, David Whiffen, F. R. S. He told me that my work was the best since Debye and that that was the general opinion in international chemical physics. I was destined for F. R. S. and maybe a Nobel Prize but the entire scene was painted in green by vandals: Jeremy Jones and Graham Williams. This should never have been allowed to happen.

On 24th March 1983 OO157 was submitted to J. Mol. Liquids on rotation translation interaction with Gareth Evans providing experimental data. The abstract of this paper mentions how computer simulation was causing a quiet revolution in the understanding of the liquid state and again this was the opinion of international science. I mentioned this opinion to Jeremy Jones, but he snarled like a wolf and howled. A real wolf would have been more intelligent. There is a gap until 19th May 1983 when I submitted OO154 and OO155 to the Journal of Molecular Liquids. These are two pioneering papers of high quality on rotation translation interaction in chiral molecules, following up my earlier announcement in Physical Review Letters. This is a long and detailed paper well worth study, and was the precursor to many incisive papers of this type at IBM Kingston, Royal Holloway College, Cornell Theory Center and the University of Zurich in the era 1986 to 1992. The prize winning animation of the code, made in 1989 - 1990 by Chris Pelkie and myself from Cornell Theory Center appears, on www.aias.us. The acknowledgment to OO154 mentions the library of code being set up by CCP5 at the British Government's Daresbury Laboratory, and about this time I was invited to the CCP5 Committee and organized several full scale conferences, including one at Aberystwyth. OO155 followed up with a simulation near the melting points of the mirror image molecules (enantiomers) and the 50 / 50 (or racemic) mixture of enantiomers. On 23rd May 1983 OO153 was submitted to Journal of Molecular Liquids on the trans 1, 2, dimethylcyclopropanes, whose symmetry leads to different patterns of cross correlation between rotation and translation. Knowledge of the liquid state was being advanced dramatically by simulation on the computer available to me in that era, the CDC 7600 at the University of Manchester Regional Computer Centre (UMRCC). By that time I had perfected the computational method with help from Mauro Ferrario and Gerard Wegdam. OO153 was the last paper I submitted from the EDCL.

The axe fell. On a dismal day about this time I was told in one of those little notes to attend an "interview" with Jeremy Jones and Graham Williams in the former's office. This turned out to be a verbal common assault which lasted almost three hours. I was infuriated by these pathetic pseudopeople but kept my temper under control during the whole revolting experience. I wrote a poetic account of it in "Dream Elegy on Human Bondage" available on www.aias.us and written in the style of Samuel Beckett. It was published in "The Spectrum", a poetry magazine from University of Wales Lampeter. I was subjected to his usual odorous verbal abuse by Jeremy Jones and told to move anywhere and quickly, maybe Oxford, and to stop publishing. There was no Speaker like George Thomas to shout "Odour, Odour" and evict the swearing member. For five years he had been trying to stop me publishing, winning inconvenient medals and higher degrees, and becoming well known. All that was to be reprimanded as ill discipline. His temporary sycophant for the occasion, and former undergraduate class mate Graham William, joined merrily in the reprimand of new science, sensing a method of getting rid of a rival for all time. Only a few weeks earlier I had listened in amazement to Graham Williams and J. O. Williams complaining bitterly about Jeremy Jones and plotting his assassination, making no attempt to conceal the rebellion. So is science about truth? Are scientists honest? Can bad politicians be made of worse pseudoscientists? I began to argue back and they were driven behind a wall of stupidity, so finally I was told to go to hell. I suppose they were familiar with the place. All this was done before a cracking fire and a portrait of Jones' mother on his desk. They were both fully aware of the merit of my work, but never mind the merit, feel the tenure. I had refused to fall to their level, and now I was going to be have to pay for it. I was going to be unemployed for the rest of my life because I had refused to be involved in a fixed appointment by Howard Purnell back in 1977. So much for the People's University.

After almost three hours of butting a brick wall they looked at their watches and found that they were busy men, so I was told to get out and have a nice day. In popped Harry Heller and announced his resignation as full professor. This floored Jones with a flank attack and for a couple of minutes I enjoyed see him begging Heller to stay before finally taking my leave with grace and a deep bow. I went back to work publishing yet another paper. Gareth Evans saw me emerge from Grendel's cave in what he thought was a shaken condition, but I was already thinking of racemic mixtures and washing the dirt out of my mind. I just drove down to the prom and sat there for a while in my car to let myself get back into equilibrium. There should be recourse in law against such blatant violations of human rights and verbal common assault (known as "bullying"). Both of these cats should have lost their jobs, and should be regarded historically in that light. Even if they were Nobel Laureates they should have lost their jobs. If they had committed that assault in the street, they would have been arrested as Teddy Boys, being of that generation. The University College of Wales should be regarded in the light of history as tolerating and harbouring a verbal common assault. Obviously the EDCL had to be shut down, and it was, and by now the University has been chopped up into little pieces by colonists. Obviously it was not a university, it was a place in which careerists from shady dustbins dreamed of a large, inflation linked, pension, and beat up inconveniently honest post doctorals.

My routine at that time was to drive in from Borth and train in the afternoons on the grass of the Vicarage fields, which I could reach through a side door and embankment. The tough two hundred metre intervals kept me in excellent physical health, so I could stand up to the pounding. I worked in to the evening, often with Dr. Cecil Monk working away across the corridor, and got some food in a fish and chips dive just before it closed at about ten p.m. I ate these items of ammoniacal fish and spud black protein sometimes with a pie or pickled egg. Usually they were eaten from newspaper in the car park at Cwrt Mawr, and I spent a couple of hours in the T. V. Room there before driving back to Borth. In the harsh winter of

1982 my car was buried in snow in Bow Street and so I walked in to the EDCL, spending the night in my office. I had tried to walk back to Borth but was driven back by a fierce blizzard, described in some poetry published in "Poetry Wales" - "In Snow Drifts - Bow Street, Dyfed " in the original Welsh and my own translation into English. The snow was a white matador ready to finish off the unwary traveller with a length of steel and the poetry was modelled a little on Jack London's "To Build a Fire". I warmed up in the TV Room of Cwrt Mawr and made my way back to the office at the EDCL and managed to walk back to Borth through Clarach. The car was dug out and normality resumed. I had become acquainted with my later biographer, Kerry Pendergast, and we discussed the evils of Freemasonry. Stephen Knight's book, "The Brotherhood" had just appeared and showed that the whole of British society and democracy was riddled with masonic corruption. Some of it was cleaned up but it still goes on to this day. The EDCL was a kind of masonic lodge, quite obviously, with weird signs and handshakes for the tenured inner circle. Kerry came in to the TV room one evening and asked for a talk, so I wrote a recommendation for a job. Despite being beaten up quite often by sealed notes and interviews, I was always ready to help others, even obviously ruthless careerists such as Coffey and Grigolini if they showed any sign of talent. I suppose that this was weakness but it helped contend with the monotony of the sinking EDCL. Kerry returned the favour with a biography bu the other two became ossified academics. Kerry also arranged for me to see his local Council in order to try to build up support for the EMLG, and they kindly showed me the Aneurin Bevan Memorial out on the wild moorland.

In the summer of 1983 I became engaged to be married to Elizabeth Riby, who was a 26 year old nurse from Llanelli. This put some optimism into my dreary existence at the end of a five year interval from 1978 to 1983 which was saturated with crude hostility. My first choice had been that beautiful lady from Tal y Bont who would bring me some food sometimes and who spoke Welsh in a magically clear accent of north east Wales - the accent of my ancestral cousin Owain Glyndw^r. She was probably just being kind but I came instantly under her spell. I made the mistake of inviting my fiancee Elizabeth to see the EDCL, and that had a predictably negative influence on normal people. She was trained in psychology so recognized a loonie bin when she saw it. My father would sometimes visit the EDCL unannounced, and would bring me some food. This act of normality was described by Monk as "coming in here waving a chicken", so one would have to be wary of the inmates all the time. They could always turn on you like rattlesnakes. Mansel Davies was fully aware of the evils of the EDCL regime, but appeared to do nothing except write increasingly bizarre papers. One of these was on how he had dosed himself with mescaline following the example of Aldous Huxley. He had gone to Criccieth to be near Lloyd George, or what was left of him, and on one occasion invited the technicians to join him as a gesture of working class solidarity. They were each offered a quarter of a cold pie before starting the long journey home. Mansel Davies met my father on one occasion and conversed a little in Welsh outside the EDCL. All went well until Davies mentioned out of the blue that I would do well provided my health stood up, omitting the words "to verbal assault". That insulted my father and made him coldly angry and the interview drew hastily to an end. Luckily for him, Monk never bumped into my father or the alleged chicken.

So I took a long overdue break in the summer of 1983 and there were no papers between 23rd May and 24th Nov. 1983 when I has already been at Bangor for a month. Shortly after being terminally interviewed by Jones and Williams I won two University of Wales Fellowships, one for Bangor, and one for Swansea. This double was probably achieved for the first time in history, each fellowship had to be contested for independently in international, inter subject competition. I did not feel in the least bit happy or elated, and in one final bid to stay at the EDCL I applied for a vacant position there that the College had been forced to advertize. I was just told to "go to hell" by Jeremy Jones. I knocked on his door and must have given him an application, he came out and uttered these words of excommunication. There are no witnesses but this again is a multiple breach of human rights, notably the right to equality of opportunity and meaningful assessment, the right to work, and the common law right not to be verbally harassed. It should be clear to all by now why the EDCL was closed, it was not Thatcher, Purnell or student numbers. The advertisement was again synthetic or fraudulent, the job had already been promised to Stephen Evans, a monoglot English speaker who had been part of the group of John Thomas. He was well below Gareth Evans and myself in actual qualifications.

With that stroke of the crozier my days at EDCL were numbered. After a long hesitation I agreed to go to Bangor, as the lesser of two evils. I just signed the contract and left it at that for a while. At this point Gareth Evans announced that he would not be transferring to Bangor, which from the perspective of thirty years was probably the right decision, because physics at Bangor was the worst department in Britain and was closed in about 1986. Gareth had spent a long time trying to come to a decision, and was renovating a cottage on the road between Aberystwyth and Aberaeron. Bangor probably pressurized me into transferring all the apparatus there, so less than a year after the laser had been set up it had to be dismantled again, and again shipped out of the EDCL to Bangor. This was deliberate wrecking of Government sponsored work, and it is not hard to guess that the Government was not entirely happy. So the laser was dragged out into the corridor again and placed on a trolley strong enough to take the weight of its granite base. We did everything we could to protect its delicate mirrors. The gas cylinders and electrical apparatus also had to be shipped to Bangor and I intended to take up the interferometer in my car. Bangor saw this as an opportunity to get free apparatus and a post doctoral whose salary was also paid for it. Its department of physics was run by a completely unlikeable individual from Ulster called Peter Boyd, a crony of William Coffey, and who knew nothing about Wales. All my computer work had to be transferred to Bangor and reloaded there for the same UMRCC CDC 7600 computer. The move to Bangor was of course completely pointless, and that was obvious to all at the time. I was in the habit of eating a pork pie and cream slice for dinner (or "lunch" as they called it) sitting on a bench in the park below the EDCL, and on more than one occasion I was told there by the junior tenured staff and technicians how expletively deleted they were with the whole rotten scene. Strangely e ough they included Stephen Evans. Griff Griffiths the head technician broke into a towering rage in the Welsh language, raging at the injustice of foreign rule in our own People's University and at my shabby treatment. How right he was. He died shortly later of cancer.

As the autumn arrived I suppose I had to search for digs in Bangor, putting the clock back to 1968, and starting all over again as a junior post doctoral. This was a damp and pungent cave in the peculiarly icy atmosphere of Bangor. I soon left it for a Hall of Residence and left Bangor altogether as soon as I could. On the night of 26th September 1983 I was working late as usual in my office, preparing to leave the EDCL as slowly and reluctantly as possible. Walking to the second floor library I heard a small bang and crack so started to look for the cause. There was an intense fire inside the store room on the second floor and the heat had cracked the glass of the door. Smoke started to pour out. I pushed the laser through the fire doors and alerted Jan Baran who called the fire brigade, then returned to fight the fire with cylinders. I used up every fire extinguisher I could find but they had no effect, smoke had already filled the second floor laboratory and I was almost killed by the fumes. The fire brigade arrived and used high pressure hoses to put out the fire. The fire was broadcast by the radio and soon the EDCL staff began to arrive. Although I was badly choked by the fumes I was "reprimanded" by the so called "safety officer", A. J. S. Williams for not closing the fire doors quickly. This idiocy enraged me but I just ignored him. This man managed to hang on to a job at Aberystwyth well in to his eighties and was the most unpleasant individual at the EDCL.

Gareth Evans arranged for a reporter to interview me outside the EDCL and I was a hero of the moment, the most unlikely hero of all time, and then I was told to get up to the Bronglais Hospital for a check. I was intact and drove home to Borth. My photograph appeared in "The Cambrian News" the following day and Jeremy Jones grudgingly offered me a biscuit. Nevertheless I must leave on 30th September or the police would be called in all probability to have me evicted, D. Sc. and all. The laser was shipped off and on the evening of 30th September I rolled out the interferometer and loaded it into my Mini. Thus ended my time at the EDCL. One or two of the worst bigots tried to accuse me of starting the fire, but David Parry admitted to causing it accidentally with a faulty heating tape. One of the last images of the EDCL I have in mind is that of Graham Williams in wellingtons brushing out the corridor in a gesture of porterly solidarity. There should be recourse in law for false accusation, but they are all old men now, many of them deceased. There is no doubt that I saved the new wing of the EDCL, and probably the library, from complete destruction by fire. To my surprise Gareth Evans appeared in my flat in Borth just as I was about to leave for Bangor, and I explained that the apparatus had been granted to Rowlinson and myself at Oxford and was on loan from there. This left Gareth Evans without any apparatus for a while, but I soon transferred the interferometer back to him from Bangor. I had to leave all my packs of computer programing cards at the EDCL and intended to return for them the next week. I was apparently accused of theft of my own apparatus, but that one fell through because it was on loan from Oxford. The EDCL colonists really meant it, and would have had me arrested if they could. Their blatantly false and malicious accusations should have them arrested but they are about to leave this world if they have not already done so.

My Mini made it to Bangor through the mountains and drew up outside the main door of the Tower on Deiniol Road. As usual nothing had been prepared and Boyd was nowhere to be found. I had been told that there was a laboratory ready for me, but to my great dismay and profound anger I found that the three hundred thousand pound Apollo Laser had just been dumped on the floor of a lecture theatre. I had to set up the interferometer in a small dark room described as a "laboratory". I had been allocated an even smaller office on the corner of the top floor of the Tower, through which the wind howled and twanged like a demented string theorist. This was a floor occupied by Applied Mathematics. The political Boyd had managed to get himself headship of both Physics and Applied Mathematics, and was also Dean, but was nowhere to be seen. He was loathed by the Welsh speakers of the mechanical workshop and by just about everyone else, English speaking tenured staff included. I had to find myself a new training ground and had to get acquainted with a new computer unit, had to reload all my programs and start all over again with no group and no apparatus. I found my digs and it was a truly revolting place. This is what I got for refusing to be corrupted. So there was only one thing for it: " .... for the trumpet shall sound and the dead shall be raised incorruptible, and we shall be changed." as in Corinthians and Handel's Messiah. I determined as ever to work on science and provide the world with new knowledge.

After a week I had managed to load up as many programs as I could and asked the staff at the Bangor Computer Unit to help me access the CDC 7600. This would enable me to restart my computer simulation work. So I drove back to Borth on a Friday evening and intended to collect my packs of program cards from my office. The next morning I found that the office had been looted - all my cards had been thrown out or shuffled, and the office was already occupied by either a student or junior post doctoral. No attempt had been made by anyone to stop this happening. If I had not backed up the programs on to magnetic tape the entire output of years of work would have been destroyed quite deliberately. So that is a metaphor for the EDCL, a pack of shuffled computer cards. Monk was there, but had made no attempt to interfere with this destruction. He was retired, but took it upon himself to tell me to return to Bangor, omitting the words “or else”. There were no signs of Florentine renaissance so I left for Bangor to resume existence there, taking as much as I could with me and retaining the flat in Borth for a while as a refuge from the awful hole in Bangor. I managed to get the laser shifted off the floor before it was trodden and trampled by undergraduates, and set up in the new laboratory. It would take some weeks and another Nuffield Foundation grant before it would be restored to anything like its working condition. Gradually I got all my programs working from the Computer Unit in Deiniol Road Bangor, a short distance from the Tower. I could relax a little and watch Bangor City from my office because I knew that some kind of work was now possible - on computer simulation and on the preparation of “Molecular Diffusion”.

Those first few weeks in Bangor were very dismal but on 24th Nov. 1983 I submitted OO173 to The Journal of Molecular Liquids on rise transient dynamics in sec butyl chloride. This paper was probably prepared using the Bangor computer unit and signals to history the fact that the many and varied personal assaults of 1978 to 1983 had not stopped my work in any way. The achievements of the Omnia Opera were made while defending myself against numerous violations of human rights. At about this time I was awarded a Nuffield Foundation grant which enabled P. Rosselli and Colin Reid to visit me in Bangor and set up the laser and interferometer. So I once more fulfilled the terms of the Government grants to Rowlinson and myself and had once more constructed a working submillimetre laboratory in Bangor. This was recorded for history in OO164, submitted to the Journal of Molecular Liquids on 21st January 1984 with P. Roselli and Colin Reid. This paper used a combination of computer simulation, laser and and interferometric spectroscopy on the lactic acids and fluorochloroacetonitriles, once more thoroughly researching the role of rotation to translation interaction. The papers began to flow once more. On Feb. 6th 1984 I submitted OO167 to Physica Scripta on the first direct observation by computer simulation of the fundamental rotation / translation interaction of chiral molecule through correlation functions that could be observed directly in the laboratory frame of reference. This was another major discovery in conditions at Bangor that were poor but still tolerable. I submitted OO168 to the same journal on the same date as a companion paper on field induced acceleration of fall transients in chiral liquids. On the following day OO165 was submitted to Journal of Molecular Liquids with Gareth Evans on the computer simulation of induced translational motion in order to try to explain some effects of crystal growth that Gareth Evans had discovered at Aberystwyth using apparatus that was constructed to his own specifications by the mechanical workshop there. This is again an excellent paper that pushes computer simulation of field induced effects to a yet higher plane of discovery. In this paper both a static and circularly polarized electric field were used producing many new results.

I had also found a place to do my athletics training at Bangor and applied for and was awarded the Wardenship of St Mary's College Bangor, founded in 1893. This brought some first hand civilization into my life because the College had original oil paintings by Kyffin Williams, later Sir Kyffin Williams. I was greatly impressed by their dark and stark simplicity and sense of reality and I would spend a long time gazing at them. They showed the influence of Vincent van Gogh and I felt that I was in my right element at last, not stuck in the top corner of an Applied Maths Department or a cyanogen filled room full of intrigue. The College served excellent fish and chips and I was allowed free board and food. So for a very short while, civilization was once more restored. Something was bound to go wrong, and it did. The first sign of trouble appeared in the shape of Dr. Jan Abas, who was a tenured lecturer who hated Peter Boyd pathologically. To be fair, so did everyone else. After complimenting me for a while on my output of papers he began to rail at Boyd, whom I had not yet met. This was disappointing in the extreme because I thought I had got away from dictators. Jan Abas claimed to have set up the first computer system at Bangor but complained bitterly about lack of credit. I did not see him again for a few weeks. Gareth Evans suddenly turned up from Aberystwyth and suggested that we both demand full professorships. Objectively this was a reasonable suggestion, but reason had no place in the EDCL. Gareth had already been singled out for the chop simply because he was associated with me, a ghastly piece of stupid prejudice and wholly illegal.

The axe fell. I was suddenly told to get out of my office by a Scot called Cunningham who was a Boyd sycophant. The only problem was that no new office was available. This arrangement did not impress me by its mathematical logic. The only thing I could do was to move into a junk room. There are photographs extant of this junk room on www.aias.us. So here was a D. Sc. and University of Wales Fellow working amid discarded trash, feeling a little like junk himself. This time I did protest strongly to the Association of University Teachers, which was again wholly ineffective. These days this procedure of removal into a trash bin would be actionable by ACAS, and Boyd's job would be in danger. I still had not seen him, and was working in a completely independent way. The Nuffield Foundation grant was administered among the junk and I soon made it more comfortable by building up piles of computer output around me. On 13th February 1984 I submitted OO166 to Physical Review A. From a distance of thirty years this reads like a very fine paper, in which several major discoveries were made and it is well worth reading on www.aias.us. I made some obligatory references to theories such as those of Marchesoni, but in reality the simulation was leading the theory, the former predicted things that the later could not. On the following day, 14th February 1984, OO170 was submitted to The Journal of Molecular Liquids with Reid, Vij and Roselli on the measurement of power absorption coefficients with the now fully functional Apollo laser and interferometer at Bangor. They all looked on at the junk surrounding my existence and had walked into another loonie bin. The Nuffield Foundation was acknowledged for a grant, which was used carefully to bring over visiting personnel and to try to reconstruct an experimental capability that had been deliberately ruined at the EDCL. These deliberate attacks on best quality science were insane, and negated the purpose of the EDCL. So it had to close. This is very clear to history, and at the time another staff member, J. O. Williams resigned to take up a professorship in Manchester. This left Jeremy Jones with his only buddy, Graham Williams, and the EDCL was virtually emptied of research apparatus.

On 29th February 1984 OO171 a long delayed paper was submitted to The Journal of Molecular Liquids with Ahmed Hasanein. This must have been written or prepared at Aberystwyth but submitted from Bangor. On 16th April 1984 I submitted OO169 to Physica Scripta on barrier crossing theory to try to explain the appearance of entirely novel far infra red peaks of the liquid state reported by Gareth Evans. This means that I had already transferred the interferometer back to Aberystwyth by that date while the laser remained at Bangor. I myself remained in the junk room while the AUT argued with Boyd to give me an office. This he never did and again I had run into mindless despotism. Physics at Bangor under Boyd was closed only two or three years later, having been found to be the worst physics department in Britain. By that time the EDCL under Jones was probably the worst chemistry department in Britain, and I had outproduced the lifetime output of Boyd and Jones combined. With a system that like, who needs chaos? On 10th May 1984 OO183 was submitted to The Journal of Physics D with Fabio Marchesoni, (later a full professor), who had just obtained a tenured position of the Italian system in the University of Perugia. The Nuffield Foundation grant was used to support his analytical work on extending the one particle theory of dielectric relaxation in an attempt to explain my pioneering simulation results on rise transients. The analytical theory was not very successful, and the way in which I used computer simulation was entirely new and able to simulate the effect of very strong external fields. The theory was restricted to weak perturbations and go not go any further. On 29th May 1984 OO190 was submitted to Physica Scripta with S. J. Abas, Gareth Evans and Colin Reid on the solution of the Kramers equation for far infra red peaks. Colin Reid's address is recorded as "Mile Stone Cottage" near Pont Seni and he was either working at or about to take up a job in the chemistry department of Llandyfri College. S. J. Abas had become interested in helping with graphics. This paper, OO190, is an impressive attempt to explain the claim by Gareth Evans of far infra red peaks.

The experimental claim of far infra red peaks was contested shortly later as aliasing, and appeared to be abandoned for a while by Gareth Evans who was isolated and working alone in the eerily empty EDCL. Later he went back to the view that the peaks are real, and not artifact. Computer simulation produced them in OO184, and they appear under well defined theoretical conditions. Gareth Evans is an excellent experimentalist and the interferometer had been interfaced with the microcomputer, so presumably he was able to obtain good data at the EDCL. It is well worth researching into this major discovery of far infra red peaks with the improved methods now available. It should be possible to remove any possibility of aliasing so I regard this as an exciting area of research and a new instrument and laboratory would settle the matter. On 6th June 1984 I submitted OO187 to Physica Scripta, another important paper which introduced a method of observation of cross correlation functions with electric field induced birefringence. A lot of thought and effort went into this paper, as with all my scientific papers of that or any era. On 14th August 1984 I submitted OO181 as a follow up paper on this subject to Physical Review A reporting the discovery that an applied electric field produces the fundamental cross correlation between rotation and translation directly in the laboratory frame for all molecules, not only optically active molecules. In the absence of an electric field the cross correlation vanishes. The undated OO180 submitted to Physica A and B is another important paper on this topic which must have been submitted at about the same time. Many fundamental discoveries were being made while buried in a pile of output in a junk room. In other words the Bangor administration in the shape of Peter Boyd was in terminal decay, cared nothing about what I or anyone else was doing, and had no idea of what anyone was doing. There is therefore no need for such a university system in Wales, or anywhere else in the world, and the appointment of senior administrators needs much tighter control. Any university system worth the name would have provided the support to follow up these pioneering papers. In the event they were followed up and greatly developed at IBM Kingston, Cornell Theory Center, Royal Holloway College and the University of Zurich, showing that the papers were of great importance and were pioneering papers in the true sense of the word.

On 28th June 1984 I submitted OO174 to Molecular

Physics. This is again an important paper that uses diffusion theory to produce a pattern of peaks in the far infra red spectrum of liquids. The paper also shows the effect of an external electric field is to shift and split the peaks. Gareth Evans had begun to publish his own papers in Faraday II and other journals on his discovery of crystal growth effects and far in far red peaks in molecular liquids. So by this time he was in charge of the interferometer at the EDCL. I rarely returned to the EDCL after that shuffled card experience, which revealed that the EDCL administration was prepared to destroy science deliberately. They managed to destroy an awful lot of science and ruined many innocent lives. History condemns them by their own actions. On 15th August 1984 I submitted OO172 to Physics Letters on phase angle fluctuations in the Josephson junction, having found that the theory of far infra red peaks could also be used in the Josephson junction. At about this time the undated OO193 must have been submitted with Reid, Abas, and Gareth Evans. This paper contains a lot of graphical material that shows that barrier crossing theory using a cosine potential can produce either broad band spectra in the far infra red, or the claim by Gareth Evans of far infra red peaks. The acknowledgment of this paper shows that Colin Reid was working at the time in the chemistry department of Llandyfri College after I had helped to get him a job there. Llandyfri College prides itself as a leading public school in Wales, and earlier, Gareth Evans had been offered the headship of a department there. On 3rd Sept. 1984 OO186 was submitted to Journal of Molecular Liquids with Abas, and shows in great detail how the broad band far infra red spectrum can evolve into a spectrum consisting of absorption peaks. This was followed up on 25th Sept. 1984 by a paper which I submitted to Physical Review A solving the Kramers equation or Langevin equation for any potential, again producing a pattern of far infra red peaks. This paper was produced after consultation with Grigolini, Zambon, Leoncini, Ferrario, Abas, Marchesoni,

Reid and Gareth Evans. The latter also observed far infra red peaks on a Nicolet interferometer at Warwick, and this type of theory explains the data. The peaks are experimentally repeatable on two different instruments and were also observed by a Russian group. On 31st October 1984 I submitted OO185 to Journal of Molecular Liquids on the rotational velocity correlation functions obtained from the far infra red peaks observed by Gareth Evans in chloroform. A series of papers was produced, and considerable effort was expended, on the explanation of these peaks analytically, and computer simulation eventually produced them in late 1984 (OO184 submitted on 17th Jan., 1985). The acknowledgment of OO185 shows that the interferometer was on loan to the EDCL.

Grigolini, Zambon, Leoncini, Ferrario and Marchesoni were brought over to Bangor at one time or another on my first of two Nuffield Foundation grants. During the visit Grigolini became embroiled in a problem and almost disintegrated from anxiety, not for the first time. The others were calmer in nature. During their visit there was a series of earthquakes in Bangor due to the fact that the Menai Strait is a major geological fault. One of these occurred when I was still a Warden at St Mary's College, and woke me up. The solid walls and roof of St. Mary's College were dancing around. The second occurred when I was talking to Zambon in the junk room, and he was alarmed at the swaying Tower. It probably reminded him of Pisa. Zambon was impressed at the fact that I had a copy of the well known biography of Oliver Cromwell by Christopher Hill, Master of Balliol College Oxford. Much later I found that Cromwell was my ancestral cousin, being descended from Tewdwr Mawr the Tudor ancestor. The junk room experience was the most bizarre of my academic life, and often degenerated into farce as foreign academics realized that this was my office, not a brush cupboard. Later, on my second Nuffield Foundation grant, Paolo Grigolini, William Coffey and Elizabeth Hild were hosted in the same junk room. So Boyd's actions were seen as an insult to international science and within two or three years he was gone.

In the late summer and autumn of 1984 the Fellowship treadmill meant that I had to begin to apply once more for another Fellowship in order to be able to stay inside the University of Wales as a fluent Welsh speaker already holding a distinction higher than full professor, the Scientiae Doctor degree. The inherent corruption in the system should be obvious to readers, it was due to corruption in the appointments system and discrimination against talent and Welsh speakers. From a perspective of thirty years no honest scholar should be trapped by such a system, so sweeping reforms are needed. In appealing against the arbitrary decisions and discrimination I went through the theoretical system like a knife through butter. The historical source documents on www.aias.us. record these various appeals in great detail. The entire system was corrupt and ineffective, and in a historical perspective it becomes clear that there was no recourse to real justice. A corrupt administrator such as Boyd could do anything he liked until the Government finally switched off the funding and closed his entire department, rough justice causing the innocent to become redundant. In a historical perspective I discovered new science through my own efforts. The administrative system tried repeatedly to destroy new science and produced nothing itself. The system disappeared but my science did not. A career for a Welsh speaker inside the University of Wales should be available by birthright. I found myself applying for the ninth time for an open competition fellowship, while monoglot English speakers were shadily appointed to tenure all around me. This again is a multiple breach of human rights.

So I applied for a Leverhulme Trust Fellowship, an Alexander von Humboldt Fellowship, an IBM Fellowship and a Pilcher Senior Fellowship of the University of Wales, together with one or two lectureships. These applications had to be done well in advance of the starting date of autumn 1985, when my University of Wales Fellowship would run out. The Fellowship treadmill was an evil imposition but eventually resulted in my world record of sixteen open competition Fellowships. I think that this is the most devastating condemnation of the corruption of that era. These Fellowships are as follows: British Government SRC (1974); Canadian NRC (1974); ICI European (1974); JRF Wolfson College Oxford (1975); British Ramsay Memorial Fellowship (1976); British Government Advanced Fellowship (1978); University of Wales Fellowship Bangor (1983); University of Wales Fellowship Swansea (1983); Leverhulme Trust Fellowship (1985); Alexander von Humboldt Fellowship (1985); IBM Fellowship (1985); University of Wales Pilcher Senior Fellowship (1985); Honorary Fellow University of London (1988); Honorary Fellow University of Lancaster (1988); Leverhulme Trust Fellowship (1990 / 1991); Guest or Fellow of the University of Zurich (1990). Each of these was won fairly in open international competition. So whenever there was fair assessment free of corruption my merit was recognized. but colonial administrators such as Boyd mocked the international assessment system and mocked the British Government. They also regarded the existence of the People of Wales with contempt.

There were all kinds of strange relics at Bangor, mixed with genuine talent from Wales, as usual a small minority of Welsh speakers. These included Noel Owen and Llewelyn Chambers. The historical source documents section on www.aias.us show that the staff were hostile to the idea of lecturing in the Welsh language so the original idea of a People's University had long gone. These days the system has been reformed but the vast majority of the staff of the chopped up University of Wales are hostile to the Welsh language. So it would do no harm if this system were just shut down for a few years until all staff are retrained in Welsh. There were weird attitudes such as those of Otto Stiefvater, who openly admired Adolf Hitler and who knew nothing about Wales at all. After more than a year of junk room occupation even senior staff such as Cunningham and Chambers became openly rebellious against Boyd and I suppose that in the end they managed to get red rid of him and his Ulster bigotry against Welsh speakers. I had come to Bangor with a high reputation, so the entire staff was embarrassed and defensive. I was pressurized into doing some tutoring work without pay, again an illegal act because as University of Wales Fellow I was an independent University researcher. I avoided Boyd like the plague and was fond of talking to the mechanical workshop staff in Welsh, trying to learn some of their most interesting dialects, those of Mo^n and Gwynedd. The Florentine renaissance was to be found among the lathes and workshop paraphenalia, as in Florence itself. They found Boyd and most imported bigots to be infinitely and utterly offensive.

On 17th January 1985 OO184 was submitted to Journal of Molecular Liquids. From the perspective of thirty years this is an obviously important paper. I evaluated correlation functions in the glassy state of dichloromethane out to six picoseconds, and used a window function to get rid of aliasing. So a lot of thought went into this paper. The resulting spectrum shows peaks, thus corroborating the data of Gareth Evans in another way. On 18th January 1985 I submitted OO188 to Faraday II on rotation translation interaction in isotopically substituted chiral molecules using moving frame cross correlation functions and this paper was quickly followed on 4th February 1985 by OO189 submitted to Journal of Molecular Liquids on the numerical integration of the Sturm Liouville equation in the theory of diffusion. As usual after an interval of relative stability, strong and original papers were produced, typified by OO191which I submitted to Physical Review Letters on 5th April 1985 introducing new classes of cross correlation functions both in the moving and laboratory frames of reference. The acknowledgment shows that I had already won the University of Wales

Pilcher Senior Fellowship in open competition, to be taken up at University of Wales Swansea. This is one of my best papers and its methodology was greatly developed in later papers. The development can be followed in all detail on the Omnia Opera. This was followed on 7th June 1985 by OO192 with Gareth Evans to Physical Review Letters reporting the fact that the time autocorrelation functions of the Coriolis and centrifugal forces are different in mirror image molecules. This discovery by simulation was supported by experimental data taken at Aberystwyth by Gareth Evans with samples sent by S. F. Mason, F. R. S. By this time "Molecular Diffusion" (OO161) had been published and was referred to regularly, and I had finished editorial work on volumes 62 and 63 of "Advances in Chemical Physics" (OO177, OO178 and OO179), all produced in the junk room. About this time I was also awarded my second Nuffield Foundation grant, an Alexander von Humbolt Fellowship, a Leverhulme Trust Fellowship, and an IBM Fellowship and was planning a Summer School in Bangor, which also took place in the junk room. This is the most surrealistic happening of twentieth century science. About this time Kerry Pendergast paid me a visit in the same junk room.

In order to win the IBM Fellowship I attended an interview in the University of Newcastle upon Tyne chaired by its Vice Chancellor, David Whiffen, F. R. S. I won the Fellowship but the salary was very low and no one spoke Welsh in Newcastle upon Tyne. During this visit Whiffen indicated that my work in the liquid state was the best since Debye. I also attended an interview for a lecturer in St. Andrew's University in Scotland, but during my visit the head of department announced he was going to resign to take up another post, so that wasted the entire journey. I was also summoned by David Buckingham and John Thomas to go up to an "interview" in the chemistry department at Lensfield Road Cambridge. This was in the early months of 1985, in winter. This turned out to be another of those two to one episodes which took place in John Thomas' lavish, oversized office. The ethnic hostility of David Buckingham towards Wales and the Welsh language was barely concealed and this was the last time I saw either of them. I have a vastly superior post doctoral record to either, and neither understood my work or even read it. As soon as I became a full professor at UNCC in 1992, Buckingham launched a series of hostile personal attacks. I was told that they were trying to help me, and Buckingham very reluctantly offered a fellowship. I did not even bother to refuse and went back to Bangor.

Earlier in the same year of 1985 I had also been summoned to Swansea by the two professors of physics there, Dutton and Grey-Morgan, in order to discuss my newly won Pilcher Senior Fellowship of the University of Wales, a two year Fellowship that followed the two year University of Wales Fellowship, but again in open inter subject competition. I had not wanted to move from the EDCL so the move to Swansea was purely a matter of office space. Dutton and Grey-Morgan were mercenaries interested only in money, not scholarship, and again had never read my work and did not understand it. That requires a minimum level of intelligence and competence wholly lacking in the administrations of Aberystwyth, Bangor and Swansea. They are ranked abysmally by now in the webometrics table of universities. My fiancee Elizabeth wanted me to come back to live near Llanelli or Swansea, so I also interviewed for a wholly unsuitable job in Carmarthen, which meant that I would have had to leave the university system altogether. Conditions at Bangor deteriorated sharply after my tenure of Warden of St Mary's came to an end, and once more I had to occupy slum digs. Back to square one again as in 1968. The constant moving around was caused by the deliberately imposed uncertainty of the Fellowship treadmill. There were also the dangers of walking home to the slum digs at night from work, because of the assorted thugs who staggered out of pubs at that time of night. One night I was assaulted by a thug and violently kicked a number of times until I fought him off and he ran away. Stiefvater saw all this happening but was too frightened (or careful) to do anything. The police, then as now were inert and evaded responsibility. On another occasion I fought off a thug who had been trying to break in to my digs.

There were two types of Bangor, the affluent middle class ticky tacky, and the slummy town itself. St Mary's College was a kind of run down late Victorian building affected by damp. Eventually as the summer of 1985 drew on, I found a room in a student Hall of Residence for the summer, conveniently close to my athletics training field, just in time for the Nuffield Summer School. While safely resident in this Hall, several excellent papers were prepared and submitted. I submitted OO199 on 20th June 1985 to Journal of Molecular Liquids introducing forty four new ways of assessing the interaction of rotation and translation. From the objective perspective of history this is a powerful paper. OO194 was submitted with Gareth Evans on July 2nd 1985 to Physical Review A, following up the two Physical Review Letters of earlier that year. OO194 comes across thirty years later as a strong and very original paper full of new results and ideas, capable of extensive development. On 29th July 1985 I submitted OO198 to The Journal of Molecular Liquids on Coriolis and centrifugal forces, and on July 31st 1985 I submitted OO200 to Faraday II on new patterns of correlation functions in a diffusing asymmetric top. These were all strong and very original papers - I had survived the junk room, Boyd and assorted skinheads.

The main result of the Nuffield Foundation Summer School is OO195, submitted to the Journal of Applied Physics with Elizabeth Hild on 16th September 1985 just before I left Bangor for Swansea. This paper was a new departure for me, and developed reflection spectroscopy of semiconductors making extensive use of the computer. The main theoretical input was from Elizabeth Hild of Budapest, Hungary. In the few weeks prior to the Summer

School it became apparent that conditions at Bangor were intolerable and that no effective remedy was hand. The Bangor administration failed to reprimand Boyd, who could be removed only by closing the department of physics through a University Grants Committee (UGC) assessment which took place in 1986. Boyd's physics department was ranked bottom in Britain, and that came as no surprise. I wrote to the Principal, Eric Sunderland, and talked to him briefly, but there was no offer of tenure and no effective leadership. Shortly thereafter, Noel Owen, a fluent Welsh speaker, resigned to become a Professor of Chemistry and later Chairman of Chemistry at Brigham Young University, Provo, Utah, U. S. A. I informed the head of chemistry at Bangor, Charles Stirling, that I intended to apply for a lectureship in chemistry, but was told that I was overqualified and not to apply. Stirling had advertised the post for an already chosen candidate, and he was not going to be a Welsh speaker. So the hypocrisy and anarchy at Bangor made it clear that my time there was going to be limited. I had driven down to Swansea to meet Dutton and Grey-Morgan, and was promised an office in University of Wales, Swansea. These two seemed intent only on money. I was bringing to them a rarely awarded Pilcher Senior Fellowship of the University of Wales, and an international reputation which went from strength to strength. By that time I had won no less than twelve open competition fellowships, so Bangor was wholly unworthy of my presence. There was seething resentment at Boyd throughout the department. He finally vanished, leaving his department in a shambles. From this perspective in time I was being played around with by a very corrupt system.

I had visited Pisa earlier in the year and discussed the transfer of the Appollo Instruments laser to the physics department in the University of Pisa, where it could be used as intended. Bangor agreed to this readily, because its department of physics was a farce, an embarrassment to the College itself. The laser was crated and shipped to

Prof. Paolo Minguzzi's laboratory in the Physics Institute in the University of Pisa where it could be used for double resonance and other research. Minguzzi was recognized as a leading expert by his colleagues in Pisa. The administrations at Aberystwyth and Bangor had not honoured their contract with the Government to house the laser under stable conditions. So the closures of the EDCL and the physics department at Bangor became inevitable. When the EDCL was finally closed in 1988 I was told that much of the equipment granted to Jeremy Jones had never been used. I would not be surprised at this. At Bangor, the technical staff and others looked on in dismay as the equipment was crated yet again and transferred. This is what colonization did to the University of Wales. Leaders of very low quality were imported, and the Welsh speakers denied tenure. Therefore tenure must be abolished and all staff in the University of Wales must be fluent in Welsh. Until that is done, Welsh speakers are better off educating themselves.

As the summer school began I still occupied my room at the Hall of Residence in Bangor, but had already found a place to live in Swansea and was preparing to leave Bangor. I made the mistake of inviting Paolo Grigolini and William Coffey, who disliked each other intensely and spoiled the atmosphere. Some good work was done on reflectivity with Elizabeth Hild. I used the computer to evaluate her theory, producing some very interesting results as in OO195. On 29th July 1985 I submitted OO198 to Journal of Molecular Liquids, another in a series of elegant papers on the interaction of translational and rotational dynamics. I consider this series to be some of my best work. The use of chiral molecules and their racemic mixture and the use of external fields reveal a wealth of data on dynamics that are inaccessible to any analytical theory. The theory cannot predict the dynamics, the computer simulation can. The final paper from Bangor, OO202, was submitted on 21st Sept . 1985 to Journal of Molecular Liquids. This made an attempt to understand the far infra red work of Gareth Evans at Aberystwyth's EDCL. He was the only member of the group still left there, and still had the interferometer and microwave computer. He had constructed apparatus to investigate the effect of external fields reported in OO179 in "Advances in Chemical Physics" with photographs and complete experimental detail. He had published several papers in Faraday II on these pioneering effects. He was full worthy of tenure, but his career was again blocked illegally by Jeremy Jones, another severe violation of human rights. So the head of department system must be reformed completely to stop this happening to a Government Advanced Fellow, and to Government apparatus. I recall that at one point during the summer school William Coffey and Peter Boyd stood talking to me in the junk room, making no effort to alleviate the conditions and acting as if nothing was wrong. So this was the nut house talked about by Scaife.

In the last few days of September I transferred as much as I could to Swansea, leaving four or five six foot piles of computer output in the junk room as a farewell gift to Boyd. The fluent Welsh speakers of the mechanical workshop wished me all the best, and so did some of the English speaking staff. As I was about to leave I glimpsed a scruffily scribbled note by Boyd still pinned to a notice board, this was the honours results of that year announced in about June but still there in September, blowing in the damp and desolate wind. There were only about four or five names on it, no firsts as far as I can remember now. My room at the Hall of Residence had been adequate but by now the students were returning so I spent the final week in the junk room, using a sleeping bag. The Mini made it over the mountains but on the road past Trawsfynydd nuclear power station overheated, maybe from leaking radioactivity. So I had to stop for a while and look for water to cool the radiator. It was by then an ancient and battered little car that had done very good service. Carrying spare water it made its way through to

Aberystwyth, where I stopped to look in at the EDCL. It was an empty shell and I talked for a while with Dyson Jones of the electronic workshop and with Gareth Evans. They mentioned that the retired head of the chemical storeroom, Colin Thwaites, had just died. He was from Skipton and a good hearted man, Yorkshire blunt on the surface, but kindly. Before he died, he had told Dyson that I was a "good lad" and we were saddened by his passing and by the passing of the EDCL. I must have loaded up the car with some water from the workshop and continued my journey to Swansea, to a nondescript digs in a steep nondescript street in a town that I have always disliked.

The campus at Swansea always looks to me like a concrete dustbin, some of the sixties buildings are black with premature age and I remember it just after it had been built, coming back from trips to Mumbles with my parents and sister. I must have been about ten years old. Its effect on me was one of complete revulsion, a transplant of utterly foreign modernism in an ancient landscape of the Princes of Deheubarth. Only on getting back to "Pant y Bedw" did I feel human again. In the autumn of 1985 it looked that much blacker. This time an office had been found for me, but in the department of Continuing Education. The year at Swansea is well documented in the historical source documents section of www.aias.us. As usual nothing had been prepared, but I must have been shown to my office by the physics secretary. It was next door to the office of a former Principal. My computer programs had been ported to Swansea from Bangor on magnetic tape after having been ported to Bangor from Aberystwyth by magnetic tape. So that summarizes the experience from 1983 to 1986 in one sentence - a pointless transportation. The quality of my scientific work was always acknowledged to be excellent, but the administration was corrupt and destructive of civilization. In the end it destroyed not me, but its own university. For me it was always a matter of survival amid the debris of idealism - the noble ideal of The People's University. At least I had an office, which looked out over Swansea Bay and resonated with foghorns. It was Dylan Thomas' capsized town, and the physics secretary had known Dylan in school. So altarwise by owl light I started my Swansea experience as the terrible cliche goes.

Swansea was indeed the purgatory of the famous sonnet sequence by the young Thomas, known by its opening phrase: "Altarwise by owl light." Dylan always had a half memory of cynghanedd but never learned it properly. These words are a kind of cynghanedd : " L...t, l.... t". Swansea was a stepping stone between two worlds, the old and tired and corrupt world of the meaningless University of Wales, run by grasping foreign mercenaries, and the new world of IBM Kingston, still run by money but with more energy. In the autumn of 1985 however it was back to the same old routine of setting up my programs on the same computer, the UMRCC CDC 7600, but from a different remote locality. Dutton and Grey-Morgan looked to me like two shopkeepers, each with his own till, counting the farthings, and no wonder that Swansea has been described as a glorified grammar school and the graveyard of ambition. Compared with Pontardawe it did not look well, it suffered from blisters and boredom as young Thomas intoned. No one quite knew what they were doing there, and after two minutes the attractions of Mumbles faded with the curtains. As usual, I outproduced the rest of the staff in my year there from Sept. 1985 to Sept. 1986, so there was a tremendous howling about postage costs incurred by the interest in my work, reprint requests, and by the postage costs of submitting scientific papers for publication. All the real money went in to the salaries of imported staff, and there was no complaint about that. For a few brief weeks at Swansea there was again an island of stability after I had managed to restart my simulation work on the CDC 7600. I accessed this through a dusty and ancient terminal set up in dusty and ancient room that no one else ever used. It may have been part of the ventilation system. So no one at

Swansea's physics department had ever heard of computer simulation.

On 8th Nov. 1985 I submitted OO196 to Physical Review A. This is an impressive paper, I am able to judge it with the objectivity of history, as if it has been written by someone else. It uses both analytical and computational methods to investigate the interaction between rotation and translation, the angular velocity of the Coriolis force is also governed in this paper by rotational Langevin equations. The theory was my own, by this time I had essentially given up on both Grigolini and Coffey, whose over complicated formalisms could never address the results of simulation. So by 8th Nov. I was in business at Swansea. On 21st Sept. 1985 I had submitted OO197 as a rapid communication to the Physical Review showing for the first time that linear velocity plays a direct role in rotational diffusion theory. This had been suspected for a long time, ever since the pioneering days of Debye, and on many occasions analytical diffusion theory had tried to address the problem, but here was the first direct evidence. These papers in the autumn of 1985 continued a long series of papers to The Physical Review and other leading journals on these major discoveries of simulation. All these papers were of the highest quality, wherever they were published, the reason being that they were as original as Dylan Thomas in his time and place in literature. Quality was not to the liking of shopkeepers interested in postage stamps and farthings, and who could not distinguish computer simulation from a Friesian in the fields. For a few weeks they did not know I had started, or did not know I was using the computer, so I was let alone to produce outstanding work they knew nothing about. On 5th Dec. 1985 OO215 was submitted to Faraday II with Hennequin, Glorieux and Arimondo of CNRS at the University of Lille on double resonance spectra and pressure broadening in chiral molecules, the results being interpreted with computer simulation. The acknowledgment of this paper thanks the Italian CNR for a travel bursary to the University of Pisa, where Arimondo was working before transfer to Lille. This was the last time I visited the University of Pisa.

I was certainly alone because by then the engagement with Elizabeth Riby had been broken off by her because there was no sign of stability in my life, the University system made sure of that. Who would want to be engaged to a nomad subjected to eccentric rule? It was an amicable parting and I never saw her again but she made a good life for herself, raised a family, and as a good nurse was regularly employed in the usual, decent way. No ordinary person could ever have understood the evil intrigue of a university that was not a university at all. So I started all over again, again, and being still fairly young and idealistic organized a Covenant between Swansea and Prof. Armando Dias-Tavares of a University in Rio de Janeiro in Brazil. Part of my Nuffield Foundation funding was used to bring him over to Swansea, whose inept Principal merrily signed it and just as merrily broke it with a few months. Later he was famously forced to resign, and I forget his name entirely as does everyone else. He was another import from Yorkshire. Politics and ideas never mix, money and ideas never mix. There had been stability for some weeks, and as usual this was a sign of trouble. I was publishing too much again and the burden of postage was sinking the department. I had not quite wriggled free of the dead hand of Jeremy Jones. During the whole of my two years at Bangor he had been complaining bitterly. I had accidentally charged the EDCL for offprints, the only occasion that I had done so. For about two and a half years he had tried to force me to pay for the offprints personally. These terminally sordid events are recorded in the historical source documents section of www.aias.us otherwise no one living today would believe them. Also next door in chemistry was the incredibly corrupt Howard Purnell, who had started the vendetta in the autumn of 1977. Ten years later it was still in full flow. I had caught a glimpse of Purnell from a distance, and he looked like the mafia boss played by Peter Sellers minus the hat and balding. Fortunately I never used the same lift as he did, and never saw him again. He died some years ago.

I had found a new field to do my athletics training, adjacent to the running track in Swansea, and found that the next door office was occupied by Harry Jones, a Tutor in Further Education who was a former coal miner and member of the Council of Wales. As he became aware of my case he made several efforts to help, as recorded in the historical source documents (HSD) section of www.aias.us. Gradually these efforts reverberated around Members of Parliament, senior administration and even the retired principal next door. So it was clear that there was a sense of justice to be found outside the shopkeeping mentality of the heads of department. The head of department system was and is the weakest link in the University of Wales. Far too much power is placed in the hands of one individual, who often has no links with Wales at all and who is often of mediocre ability. Even before Christmas of 1985 it had become clear that Swansea did not honour its contractual agreements. I made strenuous efforts to obtain funding and tenure but from this perspective in time it was a complete waste of idealism. The University of Wales was run by small people, not the People of Wales. This was also the opinion of Harry Jones, and in no uncertain terms as the HSD section records for history. Gareth Evans had helped to make the Covenant with Rio de Janeiro and we were both repelled by the sleazy Swansea administration of that time.

At around Christmas or in to the new year of 1986 the results of the University Grants Committee survey of universities began to appear, grading the chemistry and physics departments at Aberystwyth, Bangor and Swansea all below average. So I may have been unlucky to have chosen these departments in which to work, but historical perspective shows that it was the entire university system that was at fault. My own individual performance was always excellent. No one else in history had won a total of twelve competitive fellowships by 1986, and that world record still stands today, having been increased to sixteen competitive fellowships. On 5th January 1986 another strong paper, OO203, was submitted to Faraday II on the dynamics of liquid methanol using the range of newly discovered cross correlation functions, a method which was to be developed shortly later at IBM Kingston. When the true nature of the Swansea administration became apparent, partly through many harrowing discussions with the despairing Harry Jones, I reluctantly decided to apply for a job at IBM Kingston in New York State in the Clementi environment. I saw jobs being advertized there, and was aware that Mansel Davies had acted as an advisor for the Nobel Prize in chemistry and had mentioned Clementi as a candidate for nomination. So I wrote to Clementi and was offered a full professorship at IBM in his environment. The other professor at the time turned out to be Roothaan. The salary was much higher than anything I had been offered in my various fellowships. So I accepted the offer, and the starting date was set as October 1986.

I was however expecting the usual second year of my Pilcher Senior Fellowship to come around, and was in two minds as to go the United States. Harry Jones, who was in ill health and suffered from coal dust in his lungs, advised me to go to IBM. For me this meant yet another disruption, this time a major one. The historical pattern that emerges is one of good work being constantly disrupted by an administration interested only in themselves, an administration that had lost and betrayed all the ideals of the University of Wales, while I clung on to those ideals with tenacity. The administration often behaved illegally but there were no checks and balances. I am reminded of Beethoven storming out of performances when his aristocratic audience talked over his music. In my case they were completely tone deaf. As the HSD section of www.aias.us shows, I finally fought off the threats and whining by Jeremy Jones about offprints, so there was a short interlude of sanity in the spring of 1986 with one job secured. I told nothing about the IBM offer to the two shopkeepers at Swansea, Dutton and Grey-Morgan, with whom I had nothing in common and never communicated. So good quality papers proliferated once more. I submitted OO203 on January 21st 1986 to Journal of Molecular Liquids, another very original paper on new cross correlation functions in liquid water using a new pair potential of my own devising. On 14th February 1986 OO201 was submitted with J. K. Moscicki and Gareth Evans on the Poley absorption in liquid crystals after Moscicki had been brought over on my Nuffield Foundation grant. I recall that he became very annoyed at the place where I was eating my food at the time, the student refectory. I suppose he expected the lavish treatment, but I was always a Spartan. On 17th March 1986 I submitted OO204 with Gareth Evans on liquid menthol. Spectra were taken by Gareth on the interferometer at the EDCL. The acknowledgment of this paper mentions the award of the Leverhulme Trust Fellowship and bursary and the offer of the IBM professorship by Clementi. OO204 is one of the most elegant papers of my pioneering and uniquely original work on computer simulation, the finding that the dynamical difference between an enantiomer (or optically active molecule) and the fifty fifty mixture of left and right handed molecules is due to the interaction between rotation and translation.

The flow of excellent papers had begun again, so I suppose that it was time for the axe to be applied once more in that evil farce of a system. I was Pilcher Senior Fellow and a Scientiae Doctor but still treated as a graduate student. No Principal would do anything about it. So the little notes began again, this time from Dutton. The first sign of trouble was a summons to another of those two to one "interviews", this time with Dutton and Grey-Morgan as the official interrogators. I think that this was the first time I had seen Dutton's lavish office space. If possible, this interview was even more offensive than the

Jones / Williams double act of 1983, or the Boyd / Coffey double act of 1985. I was told that I was going to “run out” of fellowships and then I would be on the dole for the rest of my life. They had not won a prestigious fellowship between them and would be comfortably tenured on high salaries, followed by an inflation linked pension. Life to them was engraved on pound notes. I had written to a Member of Parliament on departmental notepaper so my postage and mailing would be curtailed. If I replied to too many reprint requests my envelopes would be placed back on my desk unopened, because Dutton was an honourable man who would never open my mail to see what was inside. If I consumed too much postage the departmental future would be endangered, having just been graded well below average. In any case they had no idea what the hell I was doing. I was not going to get my second year of the Pilcher Senior Fellowship because they did not feel like having me around. They were going to write to the Principal and Registrar to revoke the Covenant unilaterally.

They were going to try to make me pay for the use of the UMRCC 7600 computer, even though the department was not charged for these costs. A fierce battle ensued in which I refused to pay for the use of the computer and continued to produce work of the highest quality. This entire episode is again a multiple breach of human rights, especially as the two “professors” were aggressively hostile, edging on outright verbal abuse and verbal common assault. A donation of about fifty thousand pounds worth of equipment from British Telecom was going to be refused, because the donation was going to be made to me. Even though this was what they craved for, money, it was politically inconvenient. My work was of no significance at all, and I was a nuisance who won too many fellowships that incurred unreasonable departmental postage expenditure. Above all, I could speak Welsh. There were two of them so they could deny everything. After an hour or so of this drivel I told them that I was now a full professor and therefore a half god come to join them in Valhalla. Suddenly the entire tone of the conversation changed, and Grey-Morgan broke into a forced and crooked smile. He seemed to have yellowing false teeth. I was going to IBM in the United States, and how well that reflected on their department. I threw up in the bathroom and once more began to publish too much.

By this time I had found a better flat for myself in the old Penclun School in Craig Cefn Parc, with a Welsh speaking family. My grandmother had attended that school and was under threat of having a block of wood hung around her neck with the words "Welsh not" engraved on them. No one could speak English so the blocks were used for lighting steam coal fires. Penclun was infinitely preferable to suburban Swansea, whose atmosphere always oppresses me in to the ground. In that flat I wrote some poetry in both languages, back in the familiar atmosphere of Craig Cefn Parc. Now that I knew I had to remove myself trans atlantically I was able to concentrate my mind. I had no wish whatsoever to go to IBM in New York State, but at least there were going to be computers there. On 8th April 1986 OO210 was submitted to Proceedings of the Royal Society with Coffey and Corcoran on the role of dipole dipole coupling in dielectric and far infra red spectroscopy. This was a typical run of the mill paper with the Coffey type itinerant oscillator theory, the fact that it was submitted to the Royal Society has no particular merit to it. This was my final visit to Trinity College Dublin except for one unofficial trip from the States in 1987. I was appointed a Visiting Academic of Trinity College, but unpaid, so that meant very little to me, it was just an after thought. Of far more scientific importance is OO206, which I submitted on 30th April 1986 to the Physical Review A on the interaction of rotation and translation in a spherical top molecule, thus showing that this type of interaction occurs for all symmetries, and that there can never be purely rotational diffusion as in the Debye theory, or purely translational diffusion as in the Langevin theory.

Analytical theory is still unable to match the peak of knowledge achieved in that paper.

On 29th May 1986 I submitted OO209 with Gareth Evans to Journal of Molecular Liquids on reflectivity from surface liquid films. This comes across now as a brilliantly original paper because spectra of many different types were generated, especially in pi polarization near the Brewster angle. If there had really been a university at Swansea all of these ideas would have been turned into new technology, bringing in kudos and above all, money, the only thing they understood. They certainly did not understand correlation functions.

This paper was followed by OO207, which I submitted to Chemical Physics Letters on 2nd June 1986, and on 5th June 1986 OO208 was submitted to Il Nuovo Cimento with Coffey, Vij, Marchesoni, Colin Reid and Gareth Evans on far infra red absorption, a long delayed paper that records Colin Reid's address as Mile Stone Cottage, Sennybridge. Shortly later he would be married to Jennifer Davies at Brecon Castle and I would help find him a job at the Mass Spectroscopy Unit in Swansea shortly before I was kicked out of Swansea in October 1986. On 14th July 1986 I submitted OO224 to Journal of Molecular Liquids on non inertial accelerations in molecular dynamics simulation and the theory of molecular dynamics, revealing many more types of statistical cross correlation that analytical theory still cannot address today (June 2013). The acknowledgment shows that I had visited Trinity College Dublin, and I recall that on returning to a damp, dreary digs I found the new accommodation in Craig Cefn Parc. On 24th July 1986 I submitted OO227 to Journal of Molecular Liquids on a very original theory of power reflectivity in thin surface films, using my Mori theory of the early seventies to give what is essentially a new subject area. On 31st July 1986 was submitted to Molecular Physics with Coffey and Corcoran on the existence of far infra red absorption peaks detected by Gareth Evans, who had come under criticism by Birch and

Yarwood. Our unpublished reply to this criticism is OO211B, undated. OO212 was submitted with Coffey and Corcoran to Molecular Physics, also on 31st July 1986, on a routine application of the itinerant oscillator theory.

My productivity during the year of my Pilcher Senior Fellowship was therefore outstanding, and outstandingly original and well received with many reprint requests. The staff of the physics department at Swansea never communicated, and I was never invited to give a lecture, so I worked in the Department of Continuing Education and communicated with Harry Jones. During this time he developed into a fine poet in his own right. Probably, I outproduced the entire physics staff combined, and also did so from 1983 to 1985 at Bangor and from 1978 to 1983 at the EDCL. I worked steadily and with great dedication for as long as I possibly could in the University of Wales, and in the autumn of 1986 began to prepare for the move to IBM Kingston, in the Hudson Valley of New York State. This meant loading my programs yet again on to magnetic tape, and arranging for them to be sent to the Clementi environment, Department 48B / 428, IBM, Neighborhood Road, NY 12449, U. S. A. On 20th August 1986, I submitted OO226 on the power reflectivity of low dimensional surface materials to Journal of Molecular Liquids, again using my Mori formalism to produce spectra of great originality. This paper was followed on 8th September 1986 by OO221, with Elizabeth Hild and Gareth Evans to Journal of Molecular Liquids on a new practical method for determining the spectral properties of monolayers by power reflectivity, giving a variety of fascinating results. All these papers are just as relevant today in June 2013 and could be developed. This work was supported both by the Nuffield Foundation and by the Leverhulme Trust and Elizabeth Hild worked in Hungarian Telecom in Gabor Aron 65, Budapest, Hungary.

Transportation time was nearing for publishing too much again, so I began to be told to clear out my office, as if I needed a reminder. There was time however to attend

Colin's wedding to Jennifer in Brecon Castle so I was let out of jail for the occasion. Colin had first met Jennifer during our time at the EDCL, and they were living at the time in Mile End Cottage near Senny Bridge, or Pont Senni. I drove Vij down to see him at the cottage when I was still at the EDCL. On that occasion I did my eight or ten mile road run in the morning and drove the sixty miles or so down to see Colin. In the autumn of 1986 I drove across the mountains from Swansea past Craig y Nos Castle to Brecon Castle, which I knew vaguely from childhood visits. It was a pleasant occasion but overshadowed with the thought of transportation. In the eighteenth century, people from Ystrad Gynlais in the Swansea valley would be transported for coining half a crown, I was transported for a new category of capital crime - original thought - and in history such punishment is hardly unknown. At the end of the wedding I drove back over Crai, and suddenly in the moonlight the magical landscape of Glyn Tawe appeared, as if bidding farewell. As usual when being forced to leave your homeland, it never seems so beautiful and endearing, and Glyn Tawe is beautiful even in a rainstorm. The alternative to IBM Kingston would have been not quite the coal mine, but dreary boredom. So I prepared to leave for Kingston, leaving some books behind for safekeeping, and leaving the battered Mini with my parents.

On 22nd Sept 1986, a few days before leaving, two papers were submitted, OO222 and OO223 to Journal of Molecular Liquids. I submitted the former in single authorship applying the full range of my newly discovered computer simulation techniques to liquid water with a potential that I developed myself. OO223 was submitted with Gareth Evans, Minguzzi, Salvetti, Reid and Vij on the simulation and submillimetre spectroscopy of liquid water. I had been awarded a travel grant by the University of Pisa and this was used to allow Colin Reid to work on the Appollo laser in the Institute of Physics. Guiseppe Salvetti worked in the Italian CNR's Institute of Atomic and

Molecular Physics in Via Giardino, Pisa. The laser had been put to good use and was set up in the physics institute of the University of Pisa. On 30th September 1986, the day I was due to leave the physics department, I submitted OO233 as "a gesture of defiance" to Journal of Molecular Liquids on the implications of rotation / translation interaction in fine and hyperfine structure in quantum mechanics. This made sure that the department incurred postage costs. My key was dutifully returned to the secretary who had known Dylan Thomas. I said goodbye only to Harry Jones, who was very depressed at the whole scene, but bid me all the best in the new world. I visited him once in Pontneathvaughan (Pont Nedd Fechan) about 1992 with my first wife Laura, and he died shortly later, leaving his poetry to me in another gesture of defiance against injustice and the dusty fate of coal miners in general.

There are a few papers that were produced in Swansea but which were submitted from IBM Kingston. I submitted OO237 on 12th Nov. 1986 to Journal of Molecular Liquids on the computer simulation of correlation functions of irrotational and vortex fields, ideas taken from hydrodynamics. This was followed on 20th. Nov. 1986 by OO218 to Physical Review A on laboratory frame cross correlation functions in spherical tops, producing a range of new results that were eventually to be developed at IBM Kingston with supercomputers and array processors of that pioneering era. Another paper completed at Swansea is OO216 on the simulation of carbon tetrachloride water mixtures, which I submitted to Journal of Chemical Physics from IBM Kingston on 20th November 1986. This was the first time that I had adapted my code to deal with liquid mixtures. On 22nd Dec. 1986, with my first Christmas at Kingston approaching, OO217 was submitted to Journal of Chemical Physics on a set of new correlation functions and fundamental dynamical processes generated by use of a frame of reference that rotates with respect to the laboratory frame. In retrospect this stands out as a brilliantly original paper which must have been prepared again in chaotic conditions at the physics department in Swansea. The administration was not even aware that these papers were being produced, and of course, never read any of them. They produced no papers of interest of their own, but tenure meant that they were highly paid whatever they did. At Swansea I produced two highly original papers with C. A. Chatzidimitriou-Dreismann of the Technical University in Berlin. These were OO234 and OO235 submitted respectively on 30th March 1987 and 9th April 1987, as Spring was already present in the Hudson Valley. The former was on the non-stationary character of correlation functions in microcanonical ensembles, and the latter in non-equilibrium ensembles. On 14th April 1987 OO228 was submitted with Gareth Evans, a long delayed paper finally submitted to Journal of Molecular Liquids from IBM on the interaction of rotation and translation, a rich new subject area entirely of my own devising and on 11th May 1987, with the heat of summer approaching in New York State, OO246 was submitted from IBM with Gareth Evans on the correlation between rotation and translation in a dilute gas. By that time I had already met my first wife Laura, a multi award winner of IBM, a Princeton Ph. D. and concert pianist, so my world had brightened up considerably despite the fact that my contract at IBM was due to end in October 1987. Finally the last links with the so called "University of Wales" were severed in OO247, submitted to Journal of Molecular Liquids on 4th Dec. 1987 with Abas and Rangel-Mondragon on Quasi Crystals and Penrose tiles in the Orville-Thomas special issue that I had been asked to edit. This was a long delayed submission when the snow already lay deep outside our little house on RD4 near Port Ewen, and I had almost forgotten completely about Swansea.

As September drew to a close in 1986 I had found a place to live in Kingston, Lake Katrine Apartments situated as I was shortly to discover between two gigantic

IBM buildings, but at the time I did not know it from hell or the garden of Eden. I was not even aware that Kingston was one hundred miles north of New York City. For three or four days between 30th September and about 5th October I was without an office in Swansea but had my flat in Penclun, Craig Cefn Parc, a corner of the old Victorian school there. Out of habit I still trained on the field adjacent to the athletics track in Swansea and was in excellent condition. My travel expenses were paid by IBM, which had a policy of respect for the individual as is well known, and I was due to fly out from Heathrow to New York City, probably Kennedy Airport on Long Island. I took a long time taking my leave of the old familiar surroundings, and finally took my leave of my parents, by now grey haired and immersed in looking after their grandchildren. My father was about to retire after a miserable time working as a labourer. He had been forced to do this by the collier's unwanted companion, dust in the lungs. I tried to assure them that I would be away for only a year, and that they could keep in touch by telephone, but I was not sure what was awaiting me in the new world. I travelled up to a hotel in London near a tube station and spent the night there before beginning the journey to Heathrow. The pattern of small green fields and suburban sprawl slowly disappeared under cloud cover, and the University of Wales was already a distant past.

CHAPTER NINE

In this last chapter of volume two I wish to draw some lessons from history to see if the university system can ever be made to work, or whether the freedom of thought of AIAS is going to become necessary inevitably for any intellectual capable of original thought. When I first arrived at Aberystwyth I found a place that was infinitely remote from the ideals that had founded it and I was driven onwards by habit, the system of scholarship that I had devised at the Grammar School. In comparison with the scholarly ideal, the trappings of university life were irrelevant from the very beginning. It was less scholarly than my own village of Craig Cefn Parc. In order to participate in university life it was necessary to lose the language, because very few at the EDCL could speak the language. The place had a split personality. It was supposed to be the People's University founded on the pennies of the poor to give their sons and daughters an education, but what I found were a few adolescents jumping off the bridge in rag week. So there was nothing there of interest and it tended to look down on coal miners. Scholarship was the only way to rescue myself from this self imposed trap. The people who inhabited this university did not know the Welsh language and refused to learn a word of it. So I automatically withdrew from them into scholarship. The first lesson of history is that the People's University was a myth, it was a deception imposed on the unwary scholar and a piece of self imposed hypocrisy. Therefore from the very beginning I was at odds with this hypocrisy because I had a clear mind and a clear idea of what a Nation should be and this was not it.

A Nation cannot be based on shallow hypocrisy, but human society is to a large degree just that, a murky compromise between savagery and order. In the early renaissance in Florence the culture and language were those of the Tuscan People. In Aberystwyth when I arrived there in the late sixties approximately seventy percent of the student population could not speak the language and many were hostile to it. Even though I was studying a science tripos I could not turn a blind eye to this invasion and destruction of culture. So most of my time off as first year undergraduate was spent in fighting prejudice. The lesson to be learnt from history is that hypocrisy of this deep seated nature is a kind of illness, or iron in the soul. From the very beginning the scholar is at odds with the university, and this system of hypocrisy has indeed destroyed itself by corruption. History teaches that an honest scholar cannot be embroiled in bureaucracy. The lectures in the university system were sometimes incomprehensible, and that is a metaphor for the chaos brought about by this hypocrisy. The People's University was an ideal of the late nineteenth century, a noble ideal, but the system I found in the late sixties mocked that great idea with mediocrity and hostility towards the foundational ideas. So the system could not stand, it had undermined itself and was bound to fall. If a scholar relied on hypocrisy no learning would ever have evolved.

It was evident from the very beginning that there was no real interest in the scholar, there was interest in student numbers, careerism, and in bureaucracy itself. The bureaucratic system craved bureaucracy. The destiny of the University was in the hands of others from afar. If for example I tried to speak my own language I would be met by hostility, so far had the ideal of the People's University been corrupted. The People which founded the University spoke their own noble language, but their University knew nothing of it. If the ideas that were handed down to the scholar were challenged, the scholar would fail examinations. So I had to go through the process of doing well at examinations in order to survive. No University or system can teach original thought, because that would mean teaching the unknown. The latter emerges from the mind in a mysterious way. The lectures consisted of material taught by a machine, there were lecturers and students but no scholars. The first thing that I learned that imagination could not be taught. There were many facts, and many of these were half known by the teachers, who taught sometimes in contempt of what they had to recite. The machine controlled all. The student numbers caught in this machine loathed its cranking and creaking of facts upon the overladen mind.

The students did not want to be scholars, the basic aim was to get a degree, so that they could get a job. In so doing all hope of creativity was almost always lost. The scholar in infinite contrast wanted to learn, but society could tolerate him only if he went through the cranking and creaking, and he had to do this with enthusiasm. Imagination had always to be held at bay and let loose at last when the machine had run out its time. So I struggled on as if through a blizzard. It all came down in the end to memory, so right at the end of the three years of my first degree I memorized five hundred pages of notes which I had more or less written myself. The system demanded that there be an initial and second degree, but for the scholar, it would have been much easier to launch straight into the imaginative. A prime example of this is the poet Dylan Thomas, who produced most of his poetry before he was twenty years old, and gradually learned how to be a mature mind. He did all of this himself, so a scholar is such a poet, but he machine destroyed him before he was forty. The university produced nothing but self seeking geriatrics who honoured each other for forgetting and destroying the language, the greatest poet of all, the distilled wisdom of thousands of generations. The university was saturated with self awarded honour of the most shallow kind, a hypocritical play upon an empty stage, played before a deaf auditorium.

The students were often threatened by the machine, at examination time. Very often this was their only contact with reality, many drifted off into alcoholic oblivion, or into childish games such as jumping off a bridge at rag time. So the People's University was distilled down into a room full of nervous despair and scribbling. The scholar had to lurk behind the curtains and bide his time, when he could be free to imagine. The worship of hypocrisy was honed into a money making mechanism, within which only the sons and daughters of the very rich could thrive. Now it is worse than ever, the sons and daughters and the pennies of the poor are unwanted. The scholar is more than ever shunned by society because scholarship is the antithesis of hypocrisy, and loathes the shallow trappings of the university. A scholar is one who delves deeper into received wisdom, and in so doing rejects what he is taught. The scholar is the most undogmatic of beings and is the most innocent mind. The student is a cog caught in a money making machine, and must recite facts that are hardly learned. The harshest and truest lesson of history is that the poet must stand away from society, the scholar must stand away from the university.

When I was still a child I found the rough edge of society in Aberystwyth itself, on holiday in the damp little town - the evident class hypocrisy, the hostility to coal miners. In this savage landscape the people who worked in most danger were the most contemptible to be found. This landscape could be found on holiday amid sun, sea and scenery, commodities that the coal miner lacked. A poet stands away from a society rotten with such hypocrisy. The scholar stands away from a university that is saturated with dogma, and it can be argued that physics is the most hypocritical subject of all. It devised the atomic bomb while declaring itself enlightened. If there really were a People's University all the lecturers would be coal miners and would be eager to work underground. None would produce an atomic bomb or irradiate an innocent population, or work for murderous dictators. The lesson of history is that civilization exists among forces that always seek to destroy it, civilization is nurtured by the coal miner and ground into dust by the degree mill. A degree mill is not civilization, it produces students who are as prejudiced against knowledge as ever, and worship the pieces of silver as never before. Neither a worthy poet nor a worthy scholar is interested in pieces of silver. Hordes of students were imported into Wales, and none would learn the language. I had to contend with these hordes and survive. Why this should be so is answered in these pages, it was one of history's accidents and I never had anything in common with the degree mill.

The scholar is the innocent child of harsh, lurid, hypocritical society, and exists among savagery, and history is a hard task master. If the scholar is not worthy his work will be forgotten by history as surely as the snows melt away in spring. If he is dogmatic he will be caricatured as the truth. Lecturers and professors were elevated by the workings of the machine to the status of half gods among products of the working classes, who had been let out at last to learn in the sixties. Before then, and again in our present time (the early twenty first century) only the rich were allowed to learn. Hypocrisy gambled for gain with tiny grants awarded to the working classes, scraps from the high table. Hypocrisy allowed a pitiful sum to each emerging scholar at whom the half gods looked askance and in alarm. It was an invasion of Parnassus by a long haired virus, and hypocrisy was the Landlord of Parnassus, the Lord of the cardboard digs dug out of sun, sea and scenery. Only the rich had been allowed to become professors, so the working class virus listened to the sound of silence, silver pieces mouthed by the machine in the guise of unheard wisdom. These pages show that the wisdom was as lead. Often the words of the half god fell upon ears already laden and leaden with incomprehension. The scholar had to contend with this and make lead into gold - the five hundred pages of notes, hear the faintest of golden echoes buried in a blasted noise like lead. The harsh lesson of history is that the half gods resented the invasion by a row of damp viruses in the rebellious and turbulent sixties. The half god often talked rubbish in a very large lecture theatre, which reverberated with that leaden echo. The scholar's ears strained for the golden echo of imagination, and was determined to hear it.

In the very large lecture theatre the sounds of dogma were heard for the first time by working class innocence used to death by dust and manual labour. Hear this or fail the examinations. In order to obtain money, more pieces of silver that weighed like lead, the cold, damp theatre echoed to the sound of leaden dogma, which in the ensuing fifty years grew into monstrous proportions and consumed billions of the money of poor and ordinary people not rich enough to be allowed to learn or understand their way past the noisy propaganda. The poor are heavily burdened now by dogmatic lead and told to pay for it. They obey very meekly, they supplicate to the leaden half god whose wisdom was once that of Parnassus, but that is now the most commonplace of rants. A student of the long haired sixties who was discovered to be thinking too originally, and offending the half gods, would be exterminated by examination, a dalek in disguise. The scholar closed his ears and created from within him the golden echo, heard the golden echo from within. The outward appearance of the ragged scholar was that of the ragged student, the half god was ablaze in golden finery, a suit and tie, inwardly, the scholar was secretively clothed in the finery of original thought. The degree mill ground on amid the threat of nuclear war, the threat of weapons created by enlightened physicists amid an earlier, terrible war. The shreds and shards of civilization were scattered all over the very large lecture theatre, and the task of the scholar was to piece them back again, create a phoenix of new thought. The student stepped over the shards and shreds of history, learning nothing.

Time looked back and the scholar returned from afar and these shards of learning were scattered in a ruined machine - glass from windows smashed by vandals. The hypocrite still saw nothing but success. There were ghosts of lecturers and students and the harsh lessons of history blew the wind through ruined windows into the very large lecture theatre, echoing like lead from whispers of the past. The machine had stopped, the mill no longer ground, and only the golden echoes from within had travelled with time. The half god had returned to Parnassus and the wind had blown his leaden echoes away. History the taskmaster lectured now, and taught that ideas from afar lead only to an eerie silence. In the People's University golden imagination would be let loose upon the world without fear of this terrible ruin. Time looked back and all my past was scattered over the floor of the very large lecture theatre, an intricate device of humankind, a laser, was torn apart and discarded as if it were rubbish. The hypocrite, the bureaucrat, the corrupted half god, had destroyed civilization from within, and put an iron in the heart of nascent civilization. If there were a People's University, Parnassus would come alive again, and language, poetry, learning and art would flourish. The hypocrite lectured to an empty row of old, decaying seats, some torn apart by vandals who had invaded the garden of the half gods and turned it into salted, poisoned ground. The hypocrite had sown the garden of learning with salt, and the People had died of famine.

The scholar fought for the favour of the corrupted half gods, supplicated without to their leaden wisdom, struggled within to keep the golden echo alive. The half gods and lecturers saw the scholar as student, and were pleased. The student was their work, and could be used to bring in more money in order to keep themselves alive. The student was the product of a machine, and was happy to be a tiny cog that always turned smoothly. The student never offended the gods, every golden echo was kept out of their hearing and he built up a perfect academic record. Even so the scholar within was not content. The slightest challenge to the machine would be met with castigation, any original thought would be pushed aside. Every problem solved in the manner not prescribed would be grit that would be oiled off the cog. Grit on a small cog would slowly ruin all the clockwork of the machine, and grind it to a halt. Original thought is always a dangerous thing. The student never questioned this outwardly, because he wanted with his whole being to keep the golden echo alive. One day he would be allowed to think freely. So the lesson of history is always to allow freedom of thought in a worthy mind. Universities must recognize and nurture scholarship.

Inwardly the scholar yearned for the freedom of original thought, so the golden echo might be heard in the outer world, and burst free of the leaden machine. In so doing he believed that the world was ready for his ideas, and would be honest enough to listen. So in the interval between my first and second degrees a metamorphosis took place in that tiny room of "Pant y Bedw" as these pages record. I was not entirely aware of this change from student to scholar. Since then I have stood outside the university. The golden echo is heard clearly on these pages and the music of Parnassus took the form of original science, or original knowledge which cannot be taught. The lesson of history is to allow the scholar freedom of thought. The lesson for society is to allow the worthy poet to sing, and not to keep him in abject poverty. The lesson for the university is to allow the worthy scholar to think without fear of retribution and starvation. None of these lessons have ever been learned down the ages, yet the true poet and the true scholar still mesmerize history. Encased in the sixties concrete of Room 262 the golden echo burst into song. It had to do so, and the half gods of the time allowed the golden echo to be heard. The world outside Parnassus heard the song.

The student turned scholar was enchanted with its beauty, and discarded the outside world, the half gods too. The scholar fought for this golden echo, this inner beauty, for truth and for the annihilation of hypocrisy and leaden dogma, the scholar fought therefore for science, or knowledge as the word really means. Science for the scholar is the Land of the Eternally Young, and such was the beauty of the Book of Kells to its scribes, or the beauty and serenity of art and letters and architecture to the early renaissance. Out of the harsh, money ridden, world of hard headed Florence flowered a golden beauty that has mesmerized the best minds to this day. Out of wild Iona flowered the wonderful intricacy of the insular scribes. Encased in sixties concrete flowered the beauty of knowledge. To the Greeks, knowledge was beauty which resided on Mount Parnassus, and beauty in human guise was to them geometry. There is also an essay on Yeats entitled "He too was in Parnassus", and he too was a worthy poet too poor to buy a postage stamp. A terrible beauty was born out of abject poverty, the golden echo burst in poetry upon the world. The lesson of history is that society and the university must recognize the beginnings of civilization, and protect it with all their strength from the decay brought on by hypocrisy the vandal, he who scatters shards of shattered glass in the fields of knowledge.

That terrible beauty of Yeats was born out of savagery, and history teaches us that civilization is a very faint golden echo that exists among the roar of gunfire, and amid the chaos of the human condition, the small cog in the infinite universal machine. The lesson of history is not to reject that which is not understood, to listen to golden song amid the rubble of a moneyed and frenzied world without ideas. The lesson of history is that hypocrisy becomes the destroyer of worlds, along with the first atomic bomb, the hawk on fire of the poet Dylan Thomas hanging still over the estuary and Sir John's Hill, the innocent birds, humankind below, oblivious to their destiny. A People's University that cannot speak the language is hypocrisy and the destroyer of ancient values, leaving nothing but shards of smashed glass in a roaring wind. The lesson of history is that the People's University has yet to be founded, and it must nurture the language and ideals of the People above all, because these are the gifts of a Nation to its children and the outside world. Each Nation has these gifts to bear like the three wise men.

Hypocrisy is the thief of hope, and obliterates the golden echo with the freezing, blasting noise of dogma. These are the twin enemies of knowledge in our times, and in any time known to humankind.

So as I worked in Room 262 in the early seventies I forgot all about the machine and its merciless wheels and cogs, its merciless driving of that which created it, humankind. I yearned for the world to hear my golden song. This is what every worthy poet, worthy artist and worthy scientist always wants. These three are the same in disguise, and that was me in the early seventies. This much is very clear from these pages, I wished to gift to the world my inner, golden song and the golden echo of the poet Gerard Manley Hopkins. In so doing the leaden machine tried to force upon me its exigencies, as the poet R. S. Thomas memorably wrote. The machine would allow me only brief interludes to create the golden echoes untarnished by exigency. Otherwise as these pages show I led a driven and chaotic existence because my fellow human beings of the time had the power not to help. They had the power only of accumulating money for themselves. They tried to force the scholar to become once more the student or lecturer or post doctoral, or any kind of slave. The scholar fought back with all his being, and so it has continued to this day, in June 2013.

Hypocrisy looked on. The scholar was claimed to be the long lost child of a university that had no knowledge of its People. The golden echo was heard and thought to be a money making commodity, a business opportunity. It could be used to make money, to enhance the reputation of the department in the language and land of the bureaucrat. The song could be heard, but the half gods were corrupt, and deaf to its meaning. They had not taught this song yet it was heard by all but themselves. The meaningless words of the lecturers had been transfigured into golden echo. Surely the department must be credited. The scholar could be left to starve. Time looked back and all the bureaucrats sang in unison. Neither the scholar nor the department ever existed. The wind blown ruin of the very large lecture theatre could not have endangered the perennial success of the university. Parnassus must always be graded 5*. There had never been lecturers and students in that desolate ruin of the very large lecture theatre. The scholar had never existed, and to the bureaucrats his song had never been heard. All the world is bathed now in golden echo, but the bureaucrats hear nothing. So the university destroyed itself in the early twenty first century and nothing is left of it but wind blown shards.

In room 262 may be found now a piece of pottery that looks like a bone, a civilization that never existed. On the bone is written hypocrisy. Time will hear the golden echo and transport it into the future, but the leaden echo is discarded. A university that has no meaning will be a slight disturbance of landscape, a bone in Room 262. Only the worthiest of ideas survive the wandering of time. Very shortly nothing will be left of any of those who inhabited the EDCL in the sixties and seventies.

Craig Cefn Parc, 17th June, 2013.

www.ingramcontent.com/pod-product-compliance
Ingram Content Group UK Ltd.
Pitfield, Milton Keynes, MK11 3LW, UK
UKHW041953190726
13854UKWH00005B/1948

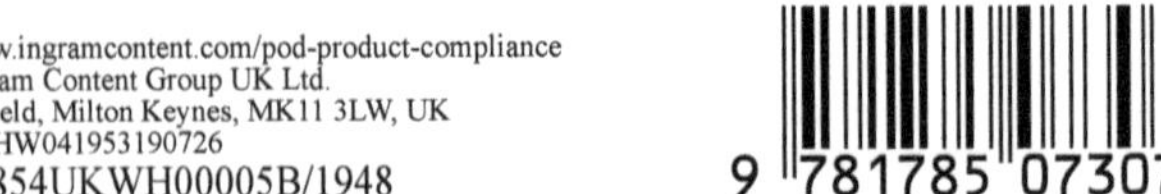

9 781785 073076